D1359940

Deconstructing Heterosexism in the Counseling Professions

MULTICULTURAL ASPECTS OF COUNSELING SERIES

SERIES EDITOR

Paul B. Pedersen, PhD
Professor Emeritus, Syracuse University
Visiting Professor, Department of Psychology, University of Hawaii

EDITORIAL BOARD

VOLUMES IN THIS SERIES

Deconstructing Heterosexism in the Counseling Professions

A Narrative Approach

James M. Croteau
Western Michigan University

Julianne S. Lark
Independent Practice

Melissa A. Lidderdale
Western Michigan University

Y. Barry Chung
Georgia State University

Editors

Multicultural Aspects of Counseling Series 20

SAGE Publications
Thousand Oaks ▪ London ▪ New Delhi

For information:

Sage Publications, Inc.
2455 Teller Road
Thousand Oaks, California 91320
E-mail: order@sagepub.com

Sage Publications Ltd.
1 Oliver's Yard
55 City Road
London EC1Y 1SP
United Kingdom

Sage Publications India Pvt. Ltd.
B-42, Panchsheel Enclave
Post Box 4109
New Delhi 110 017 India

Printed in the United States of America

Library of Congress Cataloging-in-Publication Data

Deconstructing heterosexism in the counseling professions: A narrative approach / James M. Croteau . . . [et al.].
    p. cm.
—(Multicultural aspects of counseling series; v. 20)
Includes bibliographical references and index.
ISBN 0-7619-2981-9 (cloth)—ISBN 0-7619-2982-7 (pbk.)
    1. Counseling. 2. Heterosexism. 3. Gay counselors. I. Croteau, James M.
II. Series.
BF637.C6D39 2005
158.'3'0866—dc22

                                    2004008076

04   05   06   07   10   9   8   7   6   5   4   3   2   1

Acquisitions Editor:	Art Pomponio
Editorial Assistant:	Veronica Novak
Production Editor:	Melanie Birdsall
Copy Editor:	Carla Freeman
Typesetter:	C&M Digitals (P) Ltd.
Proofreader:	Mary Meagher
Indexer:	Sylvia Coates

Contents

Foreword

These 36 authors are asking us, the readers, a question regarding the principle of inclusiveness in the practice of counseling. The book is intensely personal, and each author took a considerable risk in the degree of self-disclosure in his or her narrative story. This is a book not only about lesbian, gay, and bisexual (LGB) issues but, more important, also about the deeper issues of being inclusive with regard to the thousands of differences, including demographic, status, and affiliation as well as ethnographic characteristics, which combine to define our individual identities. This book is a test of the legitimacy of counseling, and if the field of counseling fails this test, then it has lost a great deal of its professional legitimacy. There is a great deal at stake here, not just for the authors but for the readers as well.

The *Multicultural Aspect of Counseling (MAC)* series is honored to include this book among the several dozen books that address culture-centered issues of the counseling profession. It is interesting to note in the introduction to Section II that the decision to publish this book in the *MAC* series was carefully made, both to address LGB as a culture and to address at the same time how LGB is addressed differently in each cultural context. The editors decided to follow the principle of cultural inclusiveness and publish this book in the context of other multicultural books of the *MAC* series to emphasize the interactivity of LGB issues with other aspects of our cultural identities.

This is a book of stories told by professionals that will transform the reader as well as educate, connect, and empower the generic competencies of counselors. It is not only a book about a special LGB population. It is a book about liberation over oppression and the "core alignment" of counseling on achieving human potential. Many of the stories led LGB readers to exclaim, "It was just like that for me!" We hope many of our other readers will be able to see how these stories are "just like them" as well. In the editors' own words, "We contend that the telling, listening, and reflecting on stories about navigating sexual orientation within the counseling professions comprise the missing 'map' or 'key' in the journey to bring LGB affirmation more fully into the heart of what it is to be a counseling professional" (Croteau, Lark, & Lance, Ch. 1, this volume).

This is a book about change in how counseling is provided and received so that the change can be positive with regard to inclusiveness. This comprehensive text seeks to move LGB-affirmative practice, training, and research from the edge to the center of counseling professional discourse. The first section of 18 chapters provides the "narrative voices" of the authors speaking out about their own personal and private journeys as they take risks about how you, the reader, will interpret their choices. The second section of two longer chapters focuses on the special issues and contexts for the narrative perspectives. The concluding chapters of the book link the narratives and special issues in "deconstructing, envisioning, and making practice suggestions" to the reader. The book does not limit itself to identifying what is wrong but also makes concrete and practical suggestions for making things right.

Many of the authors talk about the risks they were taking in writing these chapters and how vulnerable they felt having disclosed such personal information to the relative strangers who will read this book. Many of the stories demonstrate the extent and power of inappropriate exclusivity that remains strong in the profession of counseling. The profession of counseling has a long way to go, but progress is being made.

—Paul B. Pedersen
Senior Editor
Multicultural Aspects of Counseling Series

Preface

At its heart, this is a book of stories about the lives of lesbian, gay, bisexual, and heterosexual counseling professionals as they confront sexual orientation issues in their personal and professional lives. All four of us who are editors of this book have dedicated significant energy in our careers to lesbian, gay, and bisexual (LGB) issues. All of us have lived our professional lives openly lesbian or gay. The book is "about us" in a profound way that has been unique in our professional writing experiences.

LGB lives have historically been rendered invisible in the wider society and popular culture. Even with today's increasing public visibility, LGB lives too often remain invisible, with any representation remaining an exception or exotic event. Amidst significant developments in LGB-affirmative practice and scholarship in the counseling professions, our lives as LGB counseling professionals continue to feel marginal. We continue to be "the only one" in most of our professional contexts, and our daily work occurs most often in institutional and social structures steeped in heterosexism. Our own stories of struggles and successes as LGB professionals seem genuinely honored only in LGB-focused professional groups (e.g., the Association for Gay, Lesbian, and Bisexual Issues in Counseling, the Society of Counseling Psychology's Section on Lesbian, Gay, and Bisexual Awareness).

The promise of professional visibility and validation that this book brings to our own lives as LGB professionals has made our editing and writing work a deeply emotional experience. We feel honored and empowered by the opportunity to make this book a reality. We acknowledge that we would not have had this opportunity if not for the LGB and heterosexual ally counseling professionals who pioneered the LGB-affirmative counseling movement. We also acknowledge that we would not have been able to take advantage of the opportunity to do this book without the many people in our lives right now who provide us with personal and professional support and nurture.

We placed a strong value on inclusiveness in putting this book together. We wanted this book to be more inclusive than is the norm in sexual orientation literature in our field. While it is rewarding to take account of our progress toward greater inclusion, it is also painful to take account of how such progress has been only modest or marginal. We do think this book is stronger than prior literature in being a deeper and more honest inclusion of issues around both race and bisexuality. We have done some justice to inclusion in other ways, too. The voices of professionals who manage their minority sexual orientations in less public and "out" ways are present in the book. Gender weaves through the writing and is there to be considered by readers. There are stories and commentary related to issues around professional and economic status. Included is the often-ignored disability voice. On the other hand, despite our efforts, we had little success in finding a way to give voice to the transgender experience among counseling professionals; transgender issues are only briefly mentioned in a few places in the book. The absence of transgender in the book title, thus, is meant to represent the lack of genuine inclusion and to avoid the false impressions that can be created by nominal inclusion. We do acknowledge and support the historical and cultural movement toward the inclusion of transgender people and issues in the LGB-affirmative counseling movement. We encourage work toward a transformation in the counseling professional that will be inclusive of both sexual and gender diversities.

Sharing coming-out stories is an LGB cultural phenomenon that holds great transformative power. We share our coming-out stories to educate and challenge others in formal situations such as LGB speakers' panels. We share our coming-out stories to increase connectedness in intensely personal contexts, such as disclosing our sexual orientations to our families of origin. We share our coming-out stories with other LGB people to gain the mutual empowerment that comes from discovering commonality in the struggle to overcome heterosexism. Though the stories in this book are not coming-out stories per se, the stories do render professional experiences with sexual orientation issues more visible or more "out." We hope that this book of professional storytelling can be transformative: serving to educate, increase connectedness, and empower lesbian, gay, bisexual, and heterosexual counseling professionals in their work on sexual orientation issues.

Years after coming out, having lost two lovers to AIDS and living and dying with the disease himself, Paul Monette wrote a memoir about his own coming-out experience. In that powerful book, he described the emotional significance that such stories still held in his life:

> I still shiver with a kind of astonished delight when a gay brother or sister tells of that narrow escape from the coffin world of the closet. "Yes, yes, yes," goes a voice in my head, "it was just like that for me" . . . we laugh together then and dance in the giddy circle of freedom. (Monette, 1992, p. 2)

The transformative power of coming-out stories may lie in how such stories "align at the core" but not necessarily in the details (Monette, 1992, p. 2). Perhaps that core alignment is really about the human potential for liberation over oppression. We hope that this book can touch some part of that core of human experience and be a transformative force for liberation within the counseling-related professions. We hope that at times the readers of this book will react to the stories and commentary herein with a sense of "astonished delight" and hear an internal voice that says, "It was just like that for me." Our greatest hope for this book is that it be one more step toward a day when sexual orientation equity is a genuine reality in our disciplines, and all counseling professionals can truly "laugh together then and dance in the giddy circle of freedom. . . ."

Reference

Monette, P. (1992). *Becoming a man: Half a life story.* San Francisco: Harper.

Acknowledgments

In the preface, we acknowledged the pioneers of the LGB-affirmative counseling movement and the people in our lives who support us personally and professionally, and here we want to make special acknowledgement of the book's contributing authors, who have told their stories with extraordinary clarity, courage, and passion.

In addition, we acknowledge Julie Meredith Davis and Victoria E. Cane, doctoral students at Western Michigan University, for their editorial and clerical assistance. The following reviewers are also gratefully acknowledged: Mary Andres, University of Southern California; Jason Platt, Alliant International University; and Shoshana D. Kerewsky, University of Oregon. Finally, our appreciation goes to the editorial staff at Sage: Art Pomponio, Veronica Novak, Melanie Birdsall, and Carla Freeman. We especially thank Art and Carla for their wise guidance, very competent copyediting, and warm support.

1

Our Stories Will Be Told

Deconstructing the Heterosexist Discourse in the Counseling Professions

James M. Croteau

Western Michigan University

Julianne S. Lark

Independent Practice, Kalamazoo, MI

Teresa S. Lance

Western Michigan University

It has now been 25 years since homosexuality has been removed from a diagnostic category of mental illness. How much longer will it take to explore LGB issues as natural forms of human diversity worthy of study and professional support?

—Douce, 1998, p. 777

But every memoir now is a kind of manifesto, as we piece together the tale of the tribe. Our stories have died with us long enough. We mean to leave behind some map, some key, for the

*gay and lesbian people who follow—that they may not drown in
the lies, in the hate that pools and foams like pus on the carcass
of America.*

—Monette, 1992, p. 2

Taken together, these two quotations embody the purpose and method of
this book. The first quotation is from Louise Douce, self-described as the
first president of the Society for Counseling Psychology who has had the
opportunity to be openly lesbian, gay, or bisexual (LGB) at the time of her
presidency (Douce, 2004). In her commentary regarding a major contribution to *The Counseling Psychologist* on training related to LGB issues, she
noted the clear progress that has been made on LGB-affirmative perspectives in counseling, and then explained how emotional it was for her to
review material that shows the extent to which LGB issues and people
continue to be ignored and/or overtly and covertly devalued within professional circles (Douce, 1998). The quotation is a plaintive reference to the
frustrations that many LGB-affirmative counseling professionals feel:
"How much longer" are LGB issues to be "kept at the edge" of the profession? The second quotation is from Paul Monette, one of the most passion-
ate voices of the contemporary gay American experience. It is part of his
award-winning memoir about coming out, written as he battled the HIV
disease that took his life in 1995. His words speak to the power in the
telling of stories that break through a history of hate-enabling silence about
sexual orientation and how such storytelling can be a guide in overcoming
social oppression. Inspired by the words of both these LGB community
leaders, we contend that the telling, listening, and reflecting on stories
about navigating sexual orientation within the counseling professions comprise the missing "map" or "key" in the journey to bring LGB affirmation
more fully into the heart of what it is to be a counseling professional.

Indeed, we have designed this book to be an avenue for listening to
and making meaning from the voices of lesbian, bisexual, gay, and heterosexual counseling professionals, who narrate their personal experiences
with sexual orientation issues within the counseling professions. A special
issue in the *Journal of Counseling and Development (JCD)* (Robinson &
Ginter, 1999) addressed racism from a narrative perspective and serves in
some sense as a model for this book. In that *JCD* issue, 17 diverse professionals wrote moving narratives about their own experiences with racism,
and three authors presented commentary on the themes contained in those
narratives. The commentators noted that "the experience of racism is difficult to define without the use of storytelling" (Watt, 1999, p. 54) and that
the narratives gave "personal, intimate glimpses of the authors' struggles

with racism . . . creat[ing] horizons from which to view racism and understand at a deeper level some of the legacies of racism" (Glauser, 1999, p. 62). In a similar vein, we think that the experience of heterosexist oppression within the counseling professions is difficult to understand without using the medium of storytelling. Only with the "personal, intimate glimpses" that the authors in this book so bravely provide is it possible for counseling professionals to get a deeper understanding of the status of the discourse on LGB issues in the counseling professions; that is, a deeper understanding of the quality and extent of both the progress toward LGB affirmation and the continuing enmeshment in heterosexism.

This book contains chapters that are the personal narratives of counseling professionals' own experiences. There are also chapters that use the personal narratives to "piece together the tale" of sexual orientation in ways that address particular purposes; that is, creating positive change in the professional discourse, shaping training programs, and guiding individual counseling professionals. Each chapter in the book, and especially the book as a whole, serves as a means for individual and collective self-examination that we hope will help transform the culture and norms of the counseling professions toward greater equity in regard to sexual orientation.

The various authors in this book are all professionals in counseling or counseling psychology who are writing primarily to graduate students, practitioners, and academicians across the many subspecialties of counseling. The authors' primary purpose is to provide perspectives to their readers concerning navigating and working for positive change on sexual orientation issues in the counseling professions. We expect, however, that the book will also have much to say to other helping and allied health professionals (e.g., social workers, clinical and school psychologists, health educators, etc.), as those individuals and their professions also journey toward more genuine and complete LGB affirmation. We find that the narrative method employed in this book is an engaging medium that is uniquely suited to both inspire and inform the kind of individual and systemic change that is needed to move these professions toward greater sexual orientation equity. Essentially, we hope that this book will help to move LGB-affirmative practice, training, and research from "the edge to the center" of the counseling and other helping professions, so that LGB issues and people can come to genuinely and fully "belong" in those professions (Douce, 1998, p. 784).

The purpose of this introductory chapter is to present a more detailed rationale for the book and its approach, as well as to introduce the structure and specific aims of the various sections within the book. In the first part of this chapter, we argue that while there has been much progress on sexual orientation issues, these issues often continue to be neglected, approached with bias, and rendered marginal within counseling. Furthermore, we argue that a key to changing this marginalization is to critically examine the discourse of heterosexist dominance within the counseling professions. Second, we explain the necessity for the conscious articulation of multicultural contexts in the stories and analyses contained in this book. In the third part of this chapter, we discuss the particular power of narrative storytelling for deconstructing dominant discourses and its suitability as the primary method employed in this book. In the next part, we provide a guide for the reader in understanding the development and structure of this book. We explain the content and specific purposes of each section and how the three sections of the book were developed to build upon one another to accomplish a critical examination that can drive positive change on sexual orientation issues within the counseling professions. Finally, we conclude with our own personal reflections on the work and aim of this book.

The Discourse of Heterosexist Dominance and the Continued Marginalization of LGB Issues

Robinson (1999) and Robinson and Howard-Hamilton (2000) employed the concept of "discourse" in providing a social constructivist viewpoint regarding racism, sexism, heterosexism, and other forms of social oppression. A discourse is a set of ideas and assumptions that underlie the social interchanges from which people construct meaning and take action (Robinson, 1999; Winslade, Monk, & Drewery, 1997). According to Robinson (1999), the "isms" are socially constructed through an interlocking system of discourses that rank social identities (i.e., valuing White people over people of color, those who are able-bodied over those with disabilities, and men over women, etc.) These discourses are referred to as "dominant" discourses to emphasize that the key principle within these discourses is one of dominance, or the valuing of one group over another. The discourse of dominance with regard to sexual orientation recognizes and values a heterosexual orientation while excluding and devaluing LGB orientations. This book of professional self-examination centers on the analysis of how the dominant discourse on sexual orientation is manifested and/or contradicted *within* the counseling professions and what this discourse analysis means for individual and collective action to bring about LGB-affirmative change within the counseling professions.

Great progress has been made in promoting LGB-affirmative perspectives in counseling and in moving the counseling field beyond pioneering on LGB issues (Brown, 2000; Croteau & Bieschke, 1996; Croteau, Bieschke, Phillips, & Lark, 1998; Douce, 1998; Mobley, 1998; Morrow, 1998; Perez, DeBord, & Bieschke, 2000; Rothblum, 2000). Nevertheless, research and the assessment of leading scholars indicate that LGB issues continue to be ignored, approached with bias, and rendered marginal in professional practice, research, and training (Bahr, Brish, & Croteau, 2000;

Bieschke, Eberz, Bard, & Croteau, 1998; Bieschke, McClanahan, Tozer, Grzegorek, & Park, 2000; Douce, 1998; Haldeman, 1994; Lark & Croteau, 1998; Mobley, 1998; Morrow, 1998; Phillips, 2000; Phillips & Fischer, 1998; Tozer & McClanahan, 1999).

Several authors have recently assessed the current status of LGB issues in counseling and related fields (Brown, 2000; Croteau, Bieschke, Phillips, & Lark, 1998; Douce, 1998; Mobley, 1998; Morrow, 1998). Brown (2000) wrote that the "enormous growth in theory and scholarship . . . in the last 3 decades now provides guidance" in work with LGB clients (p. xii). She declared that the "era of discovery" is over and that skilled work with LGB clients no longer requires "self-invention and discovery" (p. xii). Similarly, Croteau, Bieschke, Phillips, and Lark (1998), in a major contribution to *The Counseling Psychologist* on LGB professional training, used the term "beyond pioneering" to describe the current status of LGB-affirmative scholarship. Phillips, Ingram, Grant Smith, and Mindes (2003) provided a concrete representation of such progress in their content review of LGB literature in counseling journals in the 1990s. They claimed a threefold increase in the "sheer quantity" of LGB articles in counseling journals in the 1990s, compared with the previous 12-year period analyzed in an earlier content analysis (Buhrke, Ben-Ezra, Hurley, & Ruprecht, 1992). Phillips and her colleagues (2003) also noted increases in "free-standing" journal articles addressing LGB topics published outside of special issues or sections on LGB issues and concluded "that LGB issues have been increasingly integrated" into the counseling literature (p. 44).

While great progress has been made, the description of being at a point of readiness to move beyond pioneering implies that there is a long way to go before LGB-affirmative perspectives become established in the counseling professions. Mobley (1998) stated that recent productivity in LGB scholarship "in no way meets the urgent needs of this unique cultural group" (p. 794). While acknowledging the progress on LGB issues within counseling psychology, Morrow (1998) noted that LGB issues continue to be relegated to "special topic" status, off to the margins of the profession (p. 797). Research on professional training and practice has indicated that LGB-affirmative perspectives are far from being well rooted in the counseling professions, with frequent biases and inattention in practice, training, and research/scholarship (e.g., Bahr et al., 2000; Bieschke et al., 2000; Bowman, 2003; Phillips, 2000; Phillips & Fischer, 1998; Phillip et al., 2003; Rodolfa & Davis, 2003).

A specific sign of the persistence of nonaffirmative perspectives is the recent upsurge in professional writing advocating conversion or reparative therapies to change LGB orientations and the relative lack of unqualified condemnation of such practices in mainstream professional circles (see discussions by Bieschke et al., 2000; Haldeman, 1994; and Tozer & McClanahan, 1999). Furthermore, while the recent LGB counseling literature content analysis discussed earlier (Phillips et al., 2003) showed substantial increases in counseling scholarship that addresses LGB or sexual orientation issues, the overall percentage of articles addressing LGB issues in the counseling journals reviewed was about 2%. The authors noted that LGB issues continue to be "underrepresented in counseling journals given that issues related to gender attraction and sexual orientation likely affect a much higher percentage of the population" (Phillips et al., 2003, p. 44). In fact, in commentating on the content analysis, Bowman (2003) noted that 2% is "barely a blip on the radar" (p. 64) and is indicative of a lack of inclusion, and Rodolfa and Davis (2003) labeled the small quantity of literature found as "haunting and abysmal" (p. 78).

What has led to this continuing relegation of sexual orientation issues to the margins of the counseling professions? What is needed to more fully integrate affirmative perspectives on sexual orientation issues into the counseling professions? Elsewhere, we have noted that advances in LGB-affirmative counseling have been the result of the work of a small but growing community of counseling professionals who are focusing on LGB issues in their training, scholarship, and practice (Croteau, Bieschke, Phillips, Lark, Fischer, & Eberz, 1998). While these efforts have had some significant success, as discussed previously, we believe that an additional perspective is needed if LGB-affirmative perspectives are to become more central and pervasive in the counseling professions.

From a social constructivist viewpoint, the discourses of the counseling professions are what shape the way individual counseling professionals approach research, training, and practice. We believe that the failure of the wider profession to examine the professional discourse concerning sexual orientation is what keeps LGB-affirmative approaches on the margins of the profession. In a recent model of multicultural competence, Sue (2001) emphasized that efforts aimed at increasing multicultural counseling competence must be focused not only at the level of individual counseling professionals but also at organizational and systemic levels within the counseling professions. Consistent with Sue's emphasis, we agree with Robinson (1999) that there must be an identification of "how oppressive dominant discourses are perpetuated in the counseling profession" (p. 73). An examination of individual, interpersonal, and institutional norms and practices concerning sexual orientation within the counseling professions—an examination of the professional discourse—is needed. This book is designed for that purpose.

Making Central the Multicultural Context

We contend that the discourse of heterosexist dominance exists in a multicultural context and "interlocks" (Robinson, 1999) with the other discourses of dominance (e.g., racism, sexism, classism). Numerous authors have noted that the greatest deficiencies in current counseling perspectives on LGB issues have to do with the lack of attention to racism and multi-cultural issues (e.g., Bowman, 2003; Croteau, Bieschke, Phillips, Lark, Fischer, & Eberz, 1998; Fukuyama & Ferguson; 2000; Greene, 2000; Lowe & Mascher, 2001; Morrow, 2003; Phillips et al., 2003; Smith, 1997). Too often, LGB-affirmative counseling has assumed a culture-less, race-less, economic class-less guise. LGB research has included predominantly White economically and educationally privileged research participants, and LGB scholarship has mostly been grounded in the cultural assumptions of the dominant social groups in this society. Greene (2000) provided what is probably the single most comprehensive and complex examination of how deeply the experience of sexual orientation is shaped by the cultural assumptions and the issues of privilege and oppression that surround age, race, ethnicity, economic class, disability, and gender. Indeed, there is growing literature in the counseling professions that outlines the limitations of considering only one social identity and that begins to construct more multidimensional perspectives (e.g., Arrendondo et al., 1996; Bingham, Porche-Burke, James, Sue, & Vasquez, 2002; Boden, 1992; Chan, 1992; Constantine, 2002; Croteau, Talbot, Lance, & Evans, 2002; D'Andrea & Daniels, 2001; Fassinger & Ritchie, 1997; Gutiérrez & Dworkin, 1992; Jones & McEwen, 2000; Morales, 1992; Pope-Davis & Coleman, 2001; Ridley, Baker, & Hill, 2001; Ridley, Hill, Thompson, & Ormerod, 2001; Robinson & Howard-Hamilton, 2000). Greene (2000) advocates strongly that ignoring multicultural contexts and other social identities in LGB-affirmative study and practice is "an oppressive act . . . [that] does not ulti-mately undermine heterosexism because heterosexism has an interlocking relationship to other forms of oppression" (p. 39).

Thus, an examination of the professional discourse on sexual orienta-tion, void of an explicit multicultural context, would be inevitably oppres-sive, limited, and distorted. An inclusive multicultural perspective is needed to "authentically achieve . . . a transformation of the discourse" (Greene, 2000, p. 40). The chapters in this book were written with the intent of rendering explicit the powerful influence of cultural contexts and of the convergences and intersections of multiple social and cultural identities.

The Power of Storytelling to Deconstruct the Heterosexist Dominant Discourse

The aims of this book are the deconstruction of the heterosexist dominant discourse on sexual orientation in the counseling professions, the envisioning of a discourse of greater equity, and the provision of practical guidance to counseling professionals in navigating and changing that heterosexist professional discourse. The means to accomplish these aims center on the use of narrative storytelling concerning the experiences of counseling professionals. Narrative has been defined as one of the means by which persons, individually and collectively, attempt to find and make meaning from the chaotic collection of experiences in their lives (Chase, 1995; Gonclaves & Machado, 1999; Monk, Winslade, Crocket, & Epston, 1997; Wilbur, 1999). Stories are "how people make sense of their experiences" and are used "to cope with the present and make decisions about the future" (Wilbur, 1999, p. 49). In essence, storytelling illustrates and shapes social discourse. Thus, to deconstruct the heterosexist dominant discourse in the counseling professions, there must be an avenue for listening to the stories, or "meaning makings," of counseling professionals concerning their own experiences with sexual orientation within the profession. This book serves as that avenue.

After reviewing a number of authors' perspectives on the power and purposes of storytelling (Chase, 1995; Glauser, 1999; Gluck, 1979; Mintz & Rothblum, 1997; Monk et al., 1997; Reinharz, 1992; Robinson & Ginter, 1999; Watt, 1999; Wilbur, 1999), we have come to believe that the telling of stories, and the critical examination of such stories, is a particularly potent means of challenging the heterosexist dominant discourse in the counseling professionals, for three primary reasons. The first reason has to do with the potency of storytelling in breaking through minimization, denial, and apathy in ways that other forms of education and/or training do not. In commenting on the personal narratives on racism in the aforementioned *JCD* special issue, Glauser (1999) said that the narrative structure allows for the myths that "perpetuate racism and other forms of prejudice" to be taken apart and examined anew (deconstructed) (p. 67). The narratives about racism show the reader the "how" of racism in a way that does not allow the reader to "underestimate or deny" racism, its impact, and its perpetuation (p. 62). Thus, the personal narratives in this book are aimed at exposing the norms of the heterosexist dominant discourse with an indisputable clarity that abstract explanation could never provide.

Second, the particular power of narratives to confront and challenge oppression may also be related to the narrative's ability to "access emotionality" (Schreier & Werden, 2000, p. 367). Put simply, it may be a moving experience to read the firsthand accounts of the human pain that is wrought by heterosexism in the lives of the narrative authors. For the reader of the narratives, the process of personal internal change is then moved to the affective domain, where beliefs and attitudes are often rooted. Stories of discrimination may create motivation for change far beyond any mere quantitative documentation of oppression (Croteau & Talbot, 2000). In other words, some stories about oppression have "an uprooting effect because they do not settle peacefully in our ears, our hearts and our minds" (Robinson & Ginter, 1999, p. 3).

The third reason for the potency of a narrative approach is that the telling and reading of stories is a process that can empower those invested in changing the prevailing discourse of heterosexist dominance. Storytelling leads to empowerment and community building for the story-teller *and* for those persons who see their own experiences reflected in the story. From a perspective central in the feminist tradition, hearing one another and oneself to voice has been a means of making women's experience visible and audible where it had been denied, obscured, or ignored (Gluck, 1979). Because members of oppressed groups have often been deprived of their own experiences being reflected in the meta-narratives of the popular culture, there is incredible power in just hearing another speak or write about an experience that is similar to one's own (Gross, 1991). The impact often brings a sense of feeling validated and no longer alone with one's experience and perspective; in turn, leading to the formation and/or strengthening of community. The collective telling of stories of oppressed peoples carries the powerful message "We are here, we exist."

Only a few isolated essays have given voice to counseling profes-sionals' experiences with the heterosexist dominant discourse and provided the consequent opportunity for community empowerment (e.g., Croteau, 1999; Dworkin, 1997; Fygetakis, 1997; Gerber, 1997; Morrow, 1997; Reynolds & Pope, 1997). We believe that the systematic telling of such stories in the public professional forum of this book is particularly timely at this point in the history of the counseling professions, a point where, for the first time, there is a "diverse multigenerational commu-nity of lesbian, gay, and bisexual affirmative" counseling professionals (Croteau, Bieschke, Phillips, Lark, Fischer, Eberz, 1998, p. 810). For the last two-and-a-half decades, there have been increasing numbers of coun-seling professionals who have had the opportunity and courage to explic-itly integrate sexual orientation issues into their professional lives. So now, for the first time in the history of the counseling professions, there are graduate students as well as new, midlevel, and senior professionals who openly identify themselves as invested in LGB-affirmative perspec-tives. There are now generations of lesbian, gay, bisexual, and heterosex-ual voices in the counseling professions who need to speak their stories about sexual orientation, and generations of ears that need to hear those stories. This community of LGB-affirmative counseling professionals must grow in number and strength to provide strong opposition to the het-erosexist dominant discourse and to create a widespread and viable model for an alternative discourse of equity. The telling of these stories in the wider professional forum of this book will help further strengthen this community of LGB-affirmative counseling professionals in their work to change the discourse of heterosexist dominance that still pervades the counseling professions.

A Short Guide to the Development, Content, and Structure of the Book

The first section of the book, titled "Narrative Voices" (Chs. 2–19), contains narratives by counseling professionals who describe their own personal experiences with the discourse on sexual orientation in the counseling professions. We selected these narrative authors by compiling a longer list of potential authors whom we believed had compelling and informative stories to tell about their experiences. Then, we invited authors from that list based on the criterion of having a group of authors who would capture a diversity of experiences. Thus, the narrative chapter authors are lesbian, gay, bisexual, and heterosexual counseling professionals of different racial, ethnic, cultural, gender, economic, ability/disability, and religious contexts and backgrounds. The authors work in academic as well as private, agency, and university counseling center practice settings. Furthermore, they represent a balance of graduate students, new professionals, midlevel professionals, and senior professionals.

We asked each author to write a personal narrative focusing on a significant experience, or set of experiences, concerning sexual orientation issues in their professional lives. We told them they could draw material from their professional or personal lives, past or present, but to focus their narratives in ways that directly relate to the discourse on sexual orientation within the profession. We asked them to focus on simply narrating their experiences and sharing how they reacted and made sense of such experiences. We also asked the authors to explicitly consider how their cultural contexts and multiple social and cultural identities affected their experiences and perspectives. Finally, we asked them to briefly comment about the implications of their experiences for the counseling professions.

The narrative chapters (Chs. 2–19) appear in alphabetical order by author last name. To allow the reader to be selective as to which narrative chapters to read at any given time, we have classified information from each chapter that indicates the authors' race, ethnicity, gender, sexual orientation, economic background, disability/ability status, and religious heritage, as well as their work roles and settings. This classification information appears in the introduction to the first section of the book, following this chapter. To facilitate individual and group exploration of the narratives, we also provide reflection questions in the introduction that can be used in professional education and training.

The second section of the book (Chs. 20 and 21), titled "Narrative Perspectives on Special Issues," provides narrative perspectives on two issues that we believe need particular attention in order to fully understand the discourse on sexual orientation in the counseling professions. Chapter 20 responds to a limitation of the approach to narratives taken in the first section of the book. The narratives in the first section are by authors who were willing and able to name themselves as LGB (or as a heterosexual ally) in the public forum of this book. In contrast, Chapter 20 attempts to illuminate the often-untold stories of counseling professionals for whom that type of public self-disclosure is too risky given their personal/professional contexts or for whom such public disclosure is incompatible with their cultural or personal constructions of sexual identity.

Chapter 21 provides narrative perspectives on a second often-unvoiced issue: the professional discord that can exist over the inclusion of sexual orientation alongside race in multicultural counseling. Approaching this sensitive issue with some depth, Chapter 21 includes discussion of the minimizing or obscuring of race and racism that can occur when sexual orientation is included in multicultural counseling, as well as the neglect of sexual orientation that can occur when multicultural counseling focuses primarily on race.

The purpose of the final section of the book, titled "Deconstructing, Envisioning, and Making Practice Suggestions," is to employ the preceding narrative-oriented chapters in the first two sections of the book to explicitly deconstruct the professional discourse on sexual orientation, to envision a discourse of greater equity, and to make practical suggestions for counseling professionals in navigating sexual orientation and challenging the heterosexist dominant discourse. Chapter 22 focuses its analysis at the level of discourse and illuminates the current heterosexist discourse in the counseling professions, the current LGB-affirmative counterdiscourse, and how that affirmative counterdiscourse can be strengthened. Chapter 23 focuses on the implications of the narrative information in this book for academic and clinical training. Last, Chapter 24 focuses on how attention to affect, relationships, and power can help guide individual counseling professionals as they cope with and act to change the heterosexist discourse in the counseling professions.

Reflections on Storytelling Toward Equity

Inspired and challenged by the many authors in this book who have written so powerfully about their personal stories, we wanted to conclude this introductory chapter by grounding the work of this book in a point of view that is based in our own perspectives and experiences as lesbian (Lark and Lance) or gay (Croteau) counseling professionals. For LGB people like ourselves, there is often a time in our lives when we internalize the heterosexist dominant discourse and live in shame, even self-hatred, about our sexuality and capacity to love. This has certainly been true in one form or another for all three of us who authored this chapter. The painful isolation and desperate emptiness of that experience are difficult to describe to those whose sexual orientations are privileged rather than stigmatized. Paul Monette (1992) spoke eloquently about this painful time and at one point described it as a time in his life in which "I was the only man I knew who had no story at all" (p. 1).

The history of the oppression of LGB people in the larger society is intimately tied to enforced silence, rendering LGB people both psychologically and socially "story-less." The counseling professions have shared in that history of enforced silence. The silence in the larger society is beginning to be broken, and the silence in the counseling professions has certainly been broken in the last decade. Those of us who are LGB-affirmative counseling professionals of any sexual orientation are no longer without voice or story in professional circles. Yet our stories of navigating sexual orientation as counseling professionals have neither been told nor heard in any systematic or extensive way. Our stories have certainly never been explored for the key they can provide to building a professional counseling community that is truly committed to sexual orientation equity.

We conclude this introduction by returning to the notions contained in the Monette and Douce quotations that began this chapter. Speaking on behalf of the more than 30 counseling professionals who have contributed to this book, we declare: We are here. Our stories will now be told! In the telling, we hope to leave a map that can empower and guide counseling professionals toward actions that will move LGB-affirmative practice, training, and scholarship from the margins to the center of what it means to be a counseling professional.

References

Arrendondo, P., Toporek, R., Brown, S. P., Jones, J., Locke, D. C., Sanchez, J., et al. (1996). Operationalization of the multicultural counseling competencies. *Journal of Multicultural Counseling and Development, 24,* 42–78.

Bahr, M. W., Brish, B., & Croteau, J. M. (2000). Addressing sexual orientation and professional ethics in the training of school psychologists in school and university settings. *School Psychology Review, 29,* 217–230.

Bieschke, K. J., Eberz, A. B., Bard, C. C., & Croteau, J. M. (1998). Using social cognitive theory to create lesbian, gay, and bisexual affirmative research training environments. *The Counseling Psychologist, 26,* 735–753.

Bieschke, K. J., McClanahan, M., Tozer, E., Grzegorek, J. L., & Park, J. (2000). Programmatic research on the treatment of lesbian, gay, and bisexual clients: The past, the present, and the course of the future. In R. M. Perez, K. A. DeBord, & K. J. Bieschke (Eds.), *Handbook of counseling and psychotherapy with lesbian, gay, and bisexual clients* (pp. 309–335). Washington, DC: American Psychological Association.

Bingham, R. P., Porche-Burke, L., James, S., Sue, D. W., & Vasquez, M. J. T. (2002). Introduction: A report on the National Multicultural Conference and Summit II. *Cultural Diversity and Ethnic Minority Psychology, 8*(2), 75–87.

Boden, R. (1992). Psychotherapy with physically disabled lesbians. In S. H. Dworkin & F. J. Gutiérrez (Eds.), *Counseling gay men & lesbians: Journey to the end of the rainbow* (pp. 157–174). Alexandria, VA: American Association for Counseling and Development.

Bowman, S. (2003). A call to action in lesbian, gay, and bisexual theory building and research. *The Counseling Psychologist, 31*(1), 63–69.

Brown, L. S. (2000). Foreword. In R. M. Perez, K. A. DeBord, & K. J. Bieschke (Eds.), *Handbook of counseling and psychotherapy with lesbian, gay, and bisexual clients* (pp. xi-xiii). Washington, DC: American Psychological Association.

Buhrke, R. A., Ben-Ezra, L. A., Hurley, M. E., & Ruprecht, L. J. (1992). Content analysis and methodological critique of articles concerning lesbian and gay male issues in counseling journals. *Journal of Counseling Psychology, 39,* 91-99.

Chan, C. S. (1992). Cultural considerations in counseling Asian American lesbians and gay men. In S. H. Dworkin & F. J. Gutiérrez (Eds.), *Counseling gay men & lesbians: Journey to the end of the rainbow* (pp. 115-124). Alexandria, VA: American Association for Counseling and Development.

Chase, S. (1995). Taking narratives seriously: Consequences for method and theory in interview studies. In R. Josselson & A. Lieblich (Eds.), *Interpreting experience: The narrative study of lives* (pp. 1-26). Thousand Oaks, CA: Sage.

Constantine, M. G. (2002). The intersections of race, ethnicity, gender, and social class in counseling: Examining selves in cultural contexts. *Journal of Multicultural Counseling and Development, 30,* 210-215.

Croteau, J. M. (1999). One struggle through individualism: Toward an antiracist White racial identity. *Journal of Counseling & Development, 77,* 30-31.

Croteau, J. M., & Bieschke, K. J. (1996). Beyond pioneering: An introduction to the special issue on the vocational issues of lesbian women and gay men. *Journal of Vocational Behavior, 48,* 119-127.

Croteau, J. M., Bieschke, K. J., Phillips, J. C., & Lark, J. S. (1998). Moving beyond pioneering: Empirical and theoretical perspectives on lesbian, gay, and bisexual affirmative training. *The Counseling Psychologist, 26,* 707-711.

Croteau, J. M., Bieschke, K. J., Phillips, J. C., Lark, J. S., Fischer, A. R., & Eberz, A. B. (1998). Toward a more inclusive and diverse multigenerational community of lesbian, gay, and bisexual affirmative counseling psychologists. *The Counseling Psychologist, 26,* 809-816.

Croteau, J. M., & Talbot, D. M. (2000). Understanding the landscape: An empirical view of lesbian, gay, and bisexual issues in the student affairs profession. In N. Evans & V. Wall (Eds.), *Toward acceptance: Sexual orientation and today's college campus.* Washington, DC: American College Personnel Association.

Croteau J. M., Talbot, D. M., Lance, T. S., & Evans, N. J. (2002). A qualitative study of the interplay between privilege and oppression. *Journal of Multicultural Counseling and Development, 30,* 239-258.

D'Andrea, M. D., & Daniels, J. (2001). RESPECTFUL counseling: An integrative multidimensional model for counselors. In D. B. Pope-Davis & H. L. K. Coleman (Eds.), *The intersection of race, class, and gender in multicultural counseling* (pp. 417-466). Thousand Oaks, CA: Sage.

Douce, L. A. (1998). Can a cutting edge last twenty-five years? *The Counseling Psychologist, 26,* 777-785.

Douce, L. A. (2004). Society of Counseling Psychology Division 17 of APA Presidential Address 2003: Globalization of counseling psychology. *The Counseling Psychologist, 32,* 142-152.

Dworkin, S. H. (1997). Female, lesbian, and Jewish: Complex and invisible. In B. Greene (Ed.), *Psychological perspectives on lesbian and gay issues: Vol. 3. Ethnic and cultural diversity among lesbians and gay men* (pp. 63-87). Thousand Oaks, CA: Sage.

Fassinger, R. E., & Ritchie, B. S. (1997). Sex matters: Gender and sexual orientation in training for multicultural counseling competencies. In D. B. Pope-Davis & H. Coleman (Eds.), *Multicultural counseling competencies: Assessment, education, and training and supervision* (pp. 83-110). Thousand Oaks, CA: Sage.

Fukuyama, M. A., & Ferguson, A. D. (2000). Lesbian, gay, and bisexual people of color: Understanding cultural complexity and managing multiple oppressions. In R. Perez, K. DeBord, & K. Bieschke (Eds.), *Handbook of counseling and psychotherapy with lesbian, gay, and bisexual clients* (pp. 81–106). Washington, DC: American Psychological Association.

Fygetakis, L. M. (1997). Greek American lesbians: Identity odysseys of honorable good girls. In B. Greene (Ed.), *Psychological perspectives on lesbian and gay issues: Vol. 3. Ethnic and cultural diversity among lesbians and gay men* (pp. 152–190). Thousand Oaks, CA: Sage.

Gerber, B. W. (1997). Becoming a lesbian in academia. In B. Mintz & E. Rothblum (Eds.), *Lesbians in academia: Degrees of freedom* (pp. 69–73). New York: Routledge.

Glauser, A. S. (1999). Legacies of racism. *Journal of Counseling and Development, 77,* 62–67.

Gluck, S. (1979). What's so special about women? Women's oral history. *Frontiers, 2*(2), 5.

Gonclaves, O., & Machado, P. (1999). Cognitive narrative psychotherapy: Research foundations. *Journal of Clinical Psychology, 55,* 1179–1191.

Greene, B. (2000). Beyond heterosexism and across the cultural divide: Developing an inclusive lesbian, gay, and bisexual psychology: A look to the future. In B. Greene (Ed.), *Education, research, and practice in lesbian, gay, bisexual, and transgendered psychology* (pp. 1–45). Thousand Oaks: Sage.

Gross, L. (1991). Out of the mainstream: Sexual minority and the mass media. *Journal of Homosexuality, 21,* 19–46.

Gutiérrez, F. J., & Dworkin, S. H. (1992). Gay, lesbian, and African American: Managing the integration of identities. In S. H. Dworkin & F. J. Gutiérrez (Eds.), *Counseling gay men & lesbians: Journey to the end of the rainbow* (pp. 141–156). Alexandria, VA: American Association for Counseling and Development.

Haldeman, D. C. (1994). The practice and ethics of sexual orientation and conversion therapy. Special section: Mental health of lesbians and gay men. *Journal of Consulting and Clinical Psychology, 62,* 221–227.

Jones, S. R., & McEwen, M. K. (2000). A conceptual model of multiple dimensions of identity. *Journal of College Student Development, 41*(4), 405–414.

Lark, J. S., & Croteau, J. M. (1998). Lesbian, gay, and bisexual students' mentoring relationships with faculty in counseling psychology: A qualitative study. *The Counseling Psychologist, 26,* 754–776.

Lowe S. M., & Mascher, J. (2001). The role of sexual orientation in multicultural counseling: Integrating bodies of knowledge. In J. A. Ponterotto, J. M. Casas, L. A. Suzuki, & C. M. Alexander (Eds.), *Handbook of multicultural counseling* (pp. 755–778). Thousand Oaks, CA: Sage.

Mintz, B., & Rothblum, E. D. (1997). *Lesbians in academia: Degree of freedom.* New York: Routledge.

Mobley, M. (1998). Lesbian, gay, and bisexual issues in counseling psychology training: Acceptance in millennium. *The Counseling Psychologist, 26,* 786–796.

Monette, P. (1992). *Becoming a man: Half a life story.* San Francisco: Harper.

Monk, G., Winslade, J., Crocket, K., & Epston, D. (1997). *Narrative therapy in practice: The archaeology of hope.* San Francisco: Jossey-Bass.

Morales, E. S. (1992). Counseling Latino gays and Latina lesbians. In S. H. Dworkin & F. J. Gutiérrez (Eds.), *Counseling gay men & lesbians: Journey to the end of the rainbow* (pp. 125–140). Alexandria, VA: American Association for Counseling and Development.

Morrow, S. L. (1997). This is the place. In B. Mintz & E. Rothblum (Eds.), *Lesbians in academia: Degree of freedom* (pp. 141–146). New York: Routledge.

Morrow, S. L. (1998). Toward a new paradigm in counseling psychology training and education. *The Counseling Psychologist, 26,* 797–808.

Morrow, S. L. (2003). Can the master's tools ever dismantle the master's house? Answering silences with alternative paradigms and silences. *The Counseling Psychologist, 31*(1), 70–77.

Perez, R. M., DeBord, K. A., & Bieschke, K. J. (Eds.). (2000). *Handbook of counseling and psychotherapy with lesbian, gay, and bisexual clients.* Washington, DC: American Psychological Association.

Phillips, J. C. (2000). Training issues and considerations. In R. M. Perez, K. A. DeBord, & K. J. Bieschke (Eds.), *Handbook of counseling and psychotherapy with lesbian, gay, and bisexual clients* (pp. 337–358). Washington, DC: American Psychological Association.

Phillips, J. C., & Fischer, A. R. (1998). Graduate student's training experiences with lesbian, gay, and bisexual issues. *The Counseling Psychologist, 26,* 712–734.

Phillips, J. C., Ingram, K. M., Grant Smith, N., & Mindes, E. (2003). Methodological and content review of lesbian-, gay-, and bisexual-related articles in counseling journals: 1990–1999. *The Counseling Psychologist, 31*(1), 25–62.

Pope-Davis, D. B., & Coleman, H. L. K. (Eds.). (2001). *The intersection of race, class, and gender in multicultural counseling.* Thousand Oaks, CA: Sage.

Reinharz, S. (1992). *Feminist methods in social research.* New York: Oxford.

Reynolds, A. L., & Pope, R. L. (1997). Beyond silence: Life as academics and a lesbian couple. In B. Mintz & E. Rothblum (Eds.), *Lesbians in academia: Degree of freedom* (pp. 165–170). New York: Routledge.

Ridley, C. R., Baker, D. M., & Hill, C. L. (2001). Critical issues concerning cultural competence. *Counseling Psychologist Special Issue: Multidimensional Facets of Cultural Competence, 29*(6), 822–832.

Ridley, C. R., Hill, C. L., Thompson, C. E., & Ormerod, A. J. (2001). Clinical practice guidelines in assessment: Toward an idiographic perspective. In D. B. Pope-Davis & H. L. K. Coleman (Eds.), *The intersection of race, class, and gender in multicultural counseling* (pp. 191–211). Thousand Oaks, CA: Sage.

Robinson, T. L. (1999). The intersections of dominant discourses across race, gender, and other identities. *Journal of Counseling and Development, 77,* 73–79.

Robinson, T. L., & Ginter, E. L. (1999). Introduction to the *Journal of Counseling and Development* special issue on racism. *Journal of Counseling and Development, 77,* 3.

Robinson, T. L., & Howard-Hamilton, M. F. (2000). *The convergence of race, ethnicity, and gender: Multiple identities in counseling.* Upper Saddle River, NJ: Prentice Hall.

Rodolfa, E., & Davis, D. (2003). A comment on a haunting number and a challenge for psychology. *The Counseling Psychologist, 31*(1), 78–84.

Rothblum, E. D. (2000). Somewhere in Des Moines or San Antonio: Historical perspectives on lesbian, gay, and bisexual mental health. In R. M. Perez, K. A. DeBord, & K. J. Bieschke (Eds.), *Handbook of counseling and psychotherapy with lesbian, gay, and bisexual clients* (pp. 57–79). Washington, DC: American Psychological Association.

Schreier, B. A., & Werden, D. L. (2000). Psychoeducational programming: Creating a context of mental health for people who are lesbian, gay, or bisexual. In R. M. Perez, K. A. DeBord, & K. J. Bieschke (Eds.), *Handbook of counseling and psychotherapy with lesbian, gay, and bisexual clients* (pp. 359–382). Washington, DC: American Psychological Association.

Smith, A. (1997). Cultural diversity and the coming out process: Implications for clinical practice. In Beverly Greene (Ed.), *Ethnic and cultural diversity among lesbians and gay men* (pp. 279–300). Thousand Oaks, CA: Sage.

Sue, D. W. (2001). Multidimensional facets of cultural competence. *The Counseling Psychologist, 29*(6), 790–821.

Tozer, E. E., & McClanahan, M. K. (1999). Treating the purple menace: Ethical considerations of conversion therapy and affirmative alternatives. *The Counseling Psychologist, 27,* 722–742.

Watt, S. K. (1999). The story between the lines: A thematic discussion of the experience of racism. *Journal of Counseling and Development, 77,* 54–61.

Wilbur, M. P. (1999). The rivers of a wounded heart. *Journal of Counseling and Development, 77,* 47–50.

Winslade, J., Monk, G., & Drewery, W. (1997). Sharpening the critical edge: A social constructionist approach in counselor education. In T. L. Sexton & B. L. Griffin (Eds.), *Constructivist thinking in counseling practice, research, and training* (pp. 228–245). New York: Teachers College Press.

Section I

Narrative Voices

The first section of this book contains narratives by counseling professionals who describe their own personal experiences with the discourse on sexual orientation in the counseling professions. We, the editors of this book, hope that the counseling and other helping professionals who read the following narratives will find them as compelling, challenging, and inspiring as we did. The storytelling that is contained in these narratives and the two narrative-based chapters in the second section on special issues are the heart of this book. These narratives are the basis upon which the three integrative chapters in the final section of the book are written. We expect that the stories of lived experiences in these narrative chapters will inspire counseling professionals toward the kinds of self-reflection and actions suggested in the final chapters.

There are 18 narratives in this section of the book, and some readers may wish to be selective about which narratives to read at any one given time. The authors of the narratives are diverse in terms of select socio-demographic characteristics, as well as professional roles, settings, and levels of experience. Table 2.1 summarizes some of the diversity that each narrative represents. Thus, readers can use this table as a tool in selecting to read about the experiences of professionals who are similar and/or different from themselves in race, ethnicity, gender, sexual orientation, disability status, socioeconomic background, and religious or spiritual affiliation. Readers can also use the table to select readings based on what professional settings or roles are discussed in the narrative.

While we provide commentary and reflection on these narratives in the final three chapters of the book, we think the narratives also stand on their own as avenues for readers to use in personal and professional self-reflection. To help with such reflection, we also provide a series of questions that may

Table 2.1   Sociodemographic Identifications Made, and Professional Roles Discussed, in the Narrative Chapters

Author(s) & Chapter Number	Race and/or Ethnicity	Gender	Sexual Orientation	Disability Status	Socioeconomic Background (of Origin)	Religious or Spiritual Affiliation or Heritage	Professional Roles Discussed in the Chapter
Adams, 2	White, Anglo-Saxon	Female	Lesbian	Able-bodied	Upper middle class	Protestant	Graduate student, faculty
Berkowitz, 3	White, Jewish	Male	Heterosexual	NS	NS	Jewish	Practitioner
Bowman, 4	African American	Female	Heterosexual	NS	NS	Nonreligious	Graduate student, faculty
Carrubba, 5	Italian American	Female	Bisexual	NS	NS	NS	Graduate student, practitioner
Chan, 6	Chinese, from Hong Kong	Male	Gay	NS	NS	NS, Discusses religious experiences	Graduate student, practitioner
Chen-Hayes, 7	White	Gender-variant	Bisexual, gay	NS	Upper middle class	NS	Graduate student, practitioner, faculty
Douce, 8	White	Female	Lesbian	NS	Middle class	Christian	Graduate student, practitioner, POL
Dworkin, 9	Jewish	Female	Lesbian, bisexual	NS	NS	Jewish	Faculty, POL
Gallor, 10	Hispanic	Female	Lesbian	NS	NS	NS	Graduate student, POL

Author(s) & Chapter Number	Race and/or Ethnicity	Gender	Sexual Orientation	Disability Status	Socioeconomic Background (of Origin)	Religious or Spiritual Affiliation or Heritage	Professional Roles Discussed in the Chapter
Goodman, 11	Jewish, White, Eastern European	Female	Heterosexual	NS	Middle class	Jewish	Faculty, practitioner, POL
Johnson, 12	African American	Male	Heterosexual	NS	NS	NS	Graduate student, practitioner, faculty.
Mobley & Pearson, 13	African American	Male & female	Gay & heterosexual	NS	NS	Christian	Graduate student
O'Brien, 14	Irish Catholic	Male	Gay	NS	Middle class	Catholic	Graduate student
O'Halloran, 15	Irish Catholic, White	Female	Heterosexual	NS	Middle class	NS	Faculty
Perez, 16	Filipino	Male	Heterosexual	NS	NS	NS	Graduate student, practitioner, POL
Phillips, 17	White, English descent	Female	Bisexual	NS	Middle class	NS	Graduate student, practitioner
Pope, 18	Native American, Cherokee	Male	Gay, two-spirited	With a disability	Economically poor	NS	POL, faculty, practitioner
Wiebold, 19	European descent	Female	Lesbian	With a disability	NS	NS	Practitioner, faculty

NOTE: The above chart is based on the identifications made by the authors in their chapter, as well as the professional roles discussed in their chapter (not necessarily their current positions or roles).

NS: Not specified; POL: Professional Organization Leader.

assist the readers in focusing their reactions and reflections. While the questions that follow will be useful for professionals and students who are reading this book on their own, the questions may be particularly helpful for establishing common areas of reflection that can be discussed as a group in classroom, clinical training, or staff development situations.

1. Identify one or more incidents, experiences, or perspectives in the narrative that you found compelling or interesting. How do these incidents, experiences, or perspectives compare with your own? What sense do you make of any similarities or contrasts?

2. How has the narrative changed or added to your understanding of the discourse on sexual orientation in the counseling professions?

3. How do other social and cultural identities and contexts (e.g., race, ethnicity, culture, gender, socioeconomic status, disability/ability status, etc.) help shape the author's experiences around sexual orientation or heterosexism? How does the author's experience compare with, and inform, your own experience of how your multiple social and cultural group identities interact and influence one another?

4. What are the implications of the narratives for your own development concerning sexual orientation/heterosexism? What are the implications for your own future actions to promote sexual orientation equity?

2

Moving From Random Acts of Inclusion Toward LGB-Affirmative Institutions

Eve M. Adams

New Mexico State University

I believe I've been pretty lucky regarding how much my sexual orientation was accepted throughout my training and professional experiences as a counseling psychologist. As a lesbian living in a heterosexist society, I think I have managed to survive and thrive in this environment due to a number of factors, such as having a supportive network of family, friends, and colleagues who validate and appreciate my existence. Also, I have the benefits that come from being White, able-bodied, and raised in an upper-middle-class family. In particular, as a WASP, I was raised by parents who highly valued achievement, so career aspirations were nurtured both emotionally and financially. I learned early how to argue my point of view, and, being able-bodied, I learned the advantages of being competitive in the athletic as well as academic realms. I also unconsciously learned not to believe in victims.

From this socialization process, I am now aware that I have the ability to deny the level of oppression that does exist and, at times, to even collude with those who are oppressive, including collusion with my own oppression (I still don't like to use the word *victimization*). Writing this narrative has been uncomfortable at times because I am forced to examine my marginalized existence more closely. Specifically, I am more aware of how much I have minimized the myriad ways in which the heterosexist discourse is enforced, while I have attempted to view the random acts of inclusion as a sign that equality has been achieved.

Looking back on my training, I believe I have had some very nurturing experiences that illustrated how, particularly in the early 1980s, some of the heterosexist discourse was being challenged (Douce, 1998). As an undergraduate, I was awarded a departmental research award for my senior thesis, which examined differences in feminist and nonfeminist lesbians. In my graduate training, there were out gay and lesbian graduate students, instructors, and supervisors. Both my pre- and postdoctoral internship experiences were very lesbian-, gay-, and bisexual (LGB)-affirmative.

As a professional, I have a number of LGB individuals or heterosexual allies as role models and mentors. All of the professional associations I belong to have LGB divisions or committees. There is a feeling of inclusiveness on a number of different levels. In many ways, I feel much more optimistic and less marginalized within counseling psychology, compared with the psychology or counseling professions as a whole, and compared with the various institutions at which I have worked. Within Division 17 of the American Psychological Association (APA), there seems to be a critical mass of relatively like-minded professionals.

As I write this, I find myself thinking, "Shouldn't that be enough to feel fully on the center of the page, not relegated to the margin?" But I have to remind myself that my experiences have not always been positive, and, compared with other LGB counseling professionals, my experiences are more the exception than the rule. There is an allure to random acts of inclusion because, without changing the system, these acts can be held up as examples of how equity exists. It is essential that counseling professionals be clear about what levels of inclusiveness we have for various groups at a systemic level, and where we still need to grow. In the following pages, I will attempt to make this distinction.

Part of what makes it difficult to discern the level of inclusion is that I have experienced a confusing variety of situations within one institution. For example, at one university, I had the experience of sitting at a baby shower, thrown by the college where I worked, for my partner, myself, and our newly adopted son. At that moment, I felt acceptance and validation on a very fundamental level. At the same institution, I sat and listened to a staff member in the benefits office say that she'd have to "check with her supervisor" to determine whether both my partner and myself were eligible for family leave. I also watched a university regent turn down a proposal for domestic partner benefits based on nothing more than his own opinion that homosexuality was wrong and shouldn't be rewarded or legitimized in such a way.

As I reflect back on these situations, I am somewhat amazed at my reactions to the negative events. I remember feeling not surprised, but instead disappointed, and rather resigned. It was to be expected from a conservative administration in a rural area, where there is a relatively small identifiable population of gays and lesbians. Feeling outraged is particularly exhausting when your numbers are so few, so complacency is an understandable alternative. Therefore, I often choose to focus more on the random acts of inclusion rather than the systemic heterosexism.

There is a bumper sticker that says, "If you're not outraged, you're not paying attention." It usually takes more than one person's outrage to increase others' awareness. I believe that counseling professionals need to become less complacent and pay more attention to institutional heterosexism if we are truly going to interrupt the heterosexist discourse. I have seen individual acts of heterosexism confronted by counseling professionals when they have written letters to editors denouncing homophobic acts, provided LGB-affirmative workshops for student leader groups, and lectured on the issues of the LGB community for counseling classes. However, as a profession, we still have much to do. I have been at four universities where domestic partner benefits and affirmative action did not exist for LGB individuals, and I never saw any organized effort by counseling professionals to confront this institutional discrimination.

Not only are counseling programs not actively confronting the larger institutional heterosexism, I have yet to experience a department that has modeled a systemic inclusion of LGB issues throughout the curriculum. In the training programs with which I have been affiliated, counseling gays, lesbians, and bisexuals is a topic that is usually relegated to one day in a multicultural counseling class or a counseling women class. At one institution, I was never asked by my colleagues to speak in the sole class period where LGB issues were addressed, even though I was an out lesbian and an identified expert in this topic. I'm not sure whether this was a function of a desire to not make me the "token" or due to a lack of concern on their part in really making sure that the students had some competency in this area. We never had an open discussion about it.

For me, a clear example of a first step toward systemic inclusion is a strong statement that an organization actively recruits people who have previously been excluded. Yet I feel particularly marginalized by the lack of affirmative action policies for LGB individuals. On accreditation organizations' yearly reports, we are asked about the gender, disability, and race/ethnicity of the students we are recruiting. What about the sexual orientation of our students? Doesn't that add to the diversity of our student body? No one seems offended by this omission. When I had this discussion with faculty, the concern seemed to be about invading the students' privacy and not wanting a student being "outed." I think that the very fact that faculty worry that students don't feel safe being out is perhaps the clearest message that we have some work to do in our departments. Another sign of concern for safety that I have witnessed is that students, gay or straight, still wonder whether conducting research on gay topics will hurt their chances for obtaining internships or jobs. I wonder how tenure and promotion committees will view my research on lesbian and gay issues. Claims of objectivity within the counseling profession and by individual faculty members do not assuage my fears when I have witnessed the power of unconscious biases.

In my experience, the profession does not embrace LGB individuals as part of a "desired minority" when conducting job-searches. It is a rare occasion that I see in a job announcement, "LGB individuals are encouraged to apply." While I don't feel I have been discriminated against when applying for jobs, I certainly haven't felt that a faculty or staff member who was LGB was an important addition to the group. Again, the importance of such diversity has not been institutionalized by either the university or by accreditation standards.

The last example of marginalization I would like to share has been the most painful. I have had numerous discussions with several African-centered psychologists about issues of oppression and how homosexuality is viewed within an Africentric context. While the vast majority of my interactions with Africentrists have been rewarding and validating, three Africentrists have stated that because homosexual acts did not result in procreation, such acts were not normal and therefore homosexuality was disordered. These experiences were particularly disappointing because these are people whom I admire. They aren't part of the unenlightened "them." If I expect discrimination, I'm more likely to assume it will come from White heterosexual males. I expect support and empathy, not bigotry, from others who have been oppressed. But those who are marginalized can also marginalize others.

Conversely, I feel disloyal and uncomfortable criticizing members of another oppressed group because I think we should support each other. My understanding of oppression as a lesbian has grown exponentially as a result of my relationships with those who have experienced other forms of oppression. I treasure my connection to others who have reflected on, and continue to examine, the impact that oppression has on the psyche.

I'm aware that this heterosexist viewpoint isn't shared by most Africentrists, so is it really worth bringing up? Yet this is an example that shows that a hierarchy of oppressions exists and the intricacies involved when organizations (such as the counseling profession) are concerned with making multiple groups feel included. When a few well-known theorists of Africentric psychology are also heterosexist, this creates a values clarification dilemma for the counseling professions. How can counseling embrace these individuals without causing others to feel marginalized? I feel outraged when openly heterosexist individuals are honored within the counseling professions; when religious anti-LGB beliefs go unchallenged in the face of empirical findings, the lived experiences of well-functioning LGB individuals, and professional standards; and when multicultural competence does not include competence with LGB individuals. At this point, I am not just experiencing an individual act of heterosexism; now it has grown to an institutional level. And I have experienced this institutional heterosexism because the counseling organizations' concerns for religious tolerance and not perpetuating racism are greater than its concern for reducing heterosexism. Perhaps my interpretation of these events is a function of my worldview and of my social identity development stage (Myers et al., 1991), but it still shines a light on some level of conscious or unconscious institutional heterosexism.

Implications and Recommendations

My training was richer as a result of having classmates and fellow interns who were racially and ethnically diverse. I believe having LGB individuals as classmates, professors, and supervisors also enriches training. When diversity in sexual orientation is not present, we need to realize that we are doing a disservice to our students. It's not enough to say, "We accept LGB individuals in our discipline." We need to encourage and inspire LGB individuals to enter the profession in order to create, "an inclusive, diverse, and multigenerational community of LGB-affirmative" counseling professionals (Croteau et al., 1998, p. 809).

We must make sure that curriculum and training opportunities require more exposure to LGB issues (Phillips & Fischer, 1998). Given that LGB individuals are disproportionately represented as clients (Liddle, 1997), such a deficit in training is a serious one. It is just as likely that our graduates will provide services to LGB individuals as it is that they will address clients' career needs. Our curriculum needs to reflect a commensurate amount of training. It's not enough to have one class period addressing LGB issues. One class period only allows students the opportunity, at best, to develop well-meaning stereotypes about this "other" group.

Part of those training opportunities should include outreach efforts. If our professional role includes being a social change agent and we are called to prevention as much as we are to remediative treatment (Romano & Hage, 2000), we should be troubled if the programs with which we are affiliated aren't engaged in some sort of prevention efforts to confront heterosexism. Because heterosexism remains a socially sanctioned form of prejudice, there are so many opportunities to disrupt this dominant discourse and to be role models to our students as we engage in this social justice work.

We also need to encourage and reward more research on LGB issues (Bieschke, Eberz, Bard, & Croteau, 1998). An institutional barrier that may curtail how much LGB research will be conducted is the lack of external funds supporting research in this area (Douce, 1998). Where are the training grants for LGB students and curriculum development, as well external funds for LGB research? Could counseling psychology be in the forefront of those in dialogue with the National Institute of Mental Health (NIMH) and other funding agencies? The lack of LGB funding priorities is another example of how LGB individuals and issues are not viewed as "desirable" or "valued" minority groups.

From a scientist-practitioner perspective, if a program does not have faculty or students engaged in LGB research at least occasionally, then such a program is not adequately preparing their students to meet the needs of LGB clients. I say this because research is a reflection of scientific thinking about an issue. If research isn't happening, then adequate training and curriculum development probably aren't either.

Finally, while counseling professionals call many places home, counseling is particularly well represented in institutions of higher education. I believe that we need to take more ownership in these colleges and universities, whether we are academics, counseling center staff, or alumni, and interrupt the heterosexist discourse that is reflected at the institutional level. We should be no more tolerant of a lack of domestic partner benefits or other heterosexist institutional policies than if they were happening in our own counseling departments or agencies. As Lark and Croteau (1998) found when they interviewed graduate students, perceptions of safety include the university in which the training program resides.

Interrupting any dominant discourse takes a great deal of energy, and there are so many biases and institutionalized "isms" to address. It is easy to feel overwhelmed by all that has to be accomplished in order to develop a discourse of equity. While random acts of inclusion can be steps toward this goal, they can also be a detour when we think such acts are enough to interrupt the heterosexist discourse that still runs deep and is still very much legitimized. I hope that counseling professionals become the trailblazers who can help move society from the detours to a path of systemic inclusion.

References

Bieschke, K. J., Eberz, A. B., Bard, C. C., & Croteau, J. M. (1998). Using social cognitive career theory to create affirmative lesbian, gay, and bisexual research training environments. *The Counseling Psychologist, 26,* 735–753.

Croteau, J. M., Bieschke, K. J., Phillips, J. C., Lark, J. S., Fischer, A. R., & Eberz, A. B. (1998). Toward a more inclusive and diverse multigenerational community of lesbian, gay, and bisexual affirmative counseling psychologists. *The Counseling Psychologist, 26,* 809–816.

Douce, L. A. (1998). Can a cutting edge last twenty-five years? *The Counseling Psychologist, 26,* 777–785.

Lark, J. S., & Croteau, J. M. (1998). Lesbian, gay, and bisexual doctoral students' mentoring relationships with faculty in Counseling Psychology. *The Counseling Psychologist, 26,* 754–776.

Liddle, B. J. (1997). Gay and lesbian clients' selection of therapists and utilization of therapy. *Psychotherapy, 34,* 11–18.

Myers, L. J., Speight, S. L., Highlen, P. S., Cox, C. I., Reynolds, A. L., Adams, E. M., & Hanley, C. P. (1991). Identity development and worldview: Toward an optimal conceptualization. *Journal of Counseling & Development, 70*(1), 54–63.

Phillips, J. C., & Fischer, A. R. (1998). Graduate students' training experiences with lesbian, gay, and bisexual issues. *The Counseling Psychologist, 26,* 712–734.

Romano, J. L., & Hage, S. M. (2000). Prevention and counseling psychology: Revitalizing commitments for the 21st century. *The Counseling Psychologist, 28,* 733–766.

3

Coming Out to My Homophobia and Heterosexism

Lessons Learned in the Journey of an Ally

Alan D. Berkowitz

Independent Consultant, Trumansburg, NY

The alarm had been ringing for 10 minutes. It was clear that my daughter was not waking up for school. I bounded up the stairs to try and rouse her. As she smiled in her sleep, I said, "Maybe one day you will have a girl-friend or boyfriend who wakes you up in the morning when you need help getting up." She smiled again and rolled over.

I noticed the comfortableness of this remark. It didn't matter to me whether her lover was male or female. How did this come about? My personal commitment to address homophobia and heterosexism in myself, others, and society has evolved as a result of specific lessons learned and reinforced over time in my personal and professional life. This narrative reviews eight of these lessons and draws implications from them for the counseling profession.

The first and most important learning is that I am guilty of engaging in homophobic thoughts and actions even when I may not be aware of them or their effects. I have often been an unintentional perpetrator by expressing misinformation and stereotypes about other groups without understanding their significance or potential to hurt. Accepting that I am unintentionally homophobic has allowed me to be more compassionate with myself when I make mistakes or express prejudices and to also be more open to feedback that will help me correct them. I have benefited tremendously by having friends and allies from other groups who can point these out. A recent family event provided a reminder when a neighbor and childhood friend related that her first exposure as a young girl to derogatory language about lesbians came from me. When I am open to stories like this one, I hear more of my own mistakes from family, friends, and colleagues. I have thus accepted that I am unintentionally homophobic and hetero-sexist and learned to welcome these revelations as an important part of my journey.

As a child, I don't remember hearing overt prejudices toward gay and lesbian people. My memories of gay men are limited to stories about child molesters in the newspapers and quiet gossip among adults who wondered about the sexual orientation of the only male teacher in my elementary school. Added to this were the normal adolescent put-downs of teenage boys, who kept each other in line with homophobic remarks that kept me silent despite my discomfort. And although I was never comfortable with the many of the roles I was assigned as a male, I never really thought about issues of sexual orientation and didn't know any gay or lesbian individuals.

My second lesson relates to how I manage my personal discomfort with lesbian, gay, and bisexual (LGB) issues, both inside myself and in situations around me. For example, I love to dance, and in college I sought opportunities to go out dancing. The campus "Gay and Lesbian Liberation Front" hosted the best parties, but I was nervous about attending. I eventually found the courage to go by bringing a female date. Having a heterosexual woman with me was a form of protection that allowed me to feel safe and have fun. Now, much later in life, I often ask male friends to dance and am more comfortable accepting and receiving affection from men. Thus, I have learned to use situations that feel uncomfortable as growth opportunities and actively seek ways to resolve my discomfort by not avoiding them.

Another example of transformed discomfort came later in college, when I was visiting a girlfriend in the city. When I walked outside on the street, I occasionally received smiles and looks from men who were checking me out. At first, I was uncomfortable, but then I realized that I was being complimented. Eventually, I decided that a compliment about my appearance was a compliment independent of the sex of the person making it, and I became comfortable accepting them.

Another way I often experience discomfort is with the homophobic words and actions of others. My awareness of my own homophobia has allowed me to be more open and observant of the prejudices I encounter in others. I can be more compassionate of others' mistakes because I have made them myself. This allows me to be thoughtful and intentional in developing strategies to intervene in the behavior of others.

A third lesson is that my own growth and liberation as a straight man is tied to the liberation and growth of gay men. Recently, a gay friend asked me to explain my commitment to being an ally. I normally answer this question by affirming my desire for justice and fair treatment for all. But somehow his question pushed me deeper, and I realized that I was doing it for myself. To be fully human and healthy as a man, I have to be able to love other men and express my feelings toward them freely. I need to hug men, hold hands with my close friends, and be emotionally connected, and yet I still consider myself to be straight. When my friend made this comment, I saw how the homophobia that he experienced as a gay man was also limiting for me as a straight man and that our liberations were intertwined as men. In a unique sense, confronting homophobia is a form of being an ally to myself.

My first job was as a counseling psychologist at a college where I provided therapy and supervised resident advisor (RA) hiring and training. At that time in my life, I saw myself as completely accepting of gays and lesbians. One of my first clients was a gay man who was struggling with the process of coming out on campus. I thought I was very tolerant and understanding of his dilemmas and pain, in the neutral and nonjudgmental way I had been taught. Thus, I was very surprised to receive feedback from a colleague who knew that this young man had doubts about my support and acceptance of his sexual orientation. I was counseled to be more open and clear about my acceptance and more outspoken as a therapist about myself as an ally. I realized that my clinical tolerance and neutrality left this client confused about my feelings and triggered his internalized homophobia. If I wanted to be a good therapist and provide a healing environment, I had to be active and clear about my position and commitment to being an ally. This experience led to my fourth lesson: that being an ally is an active and conscious process in which I must take responsibility for demonstrating and acting on my convictions, in the therapy hour, with friends and family, and in professional circles.

A fifth way in which I have learned to be an ally is to create opportunities for LGB individuals to tell their own stories. For example, during RA training I brought members of the local LGB Alliance to speak to RAs. Hearing the stories and experiences of others has been another important lesson in my journey. As an ally, it is my responsibility to use my privilege and access to resources to create these opportunities. In doing so, I also acquire new information that allows me to further my own growth.

A sixth lesson has been to understand my privilege as a straight White person. For example, when I am outspoken in meetings and at conferences, colleagues from oppressed groups often make comments such as, "I'm glad that you said that, because when I say that, no one listens." As a result of these comments, I became aware that I had a voice as a straight White male that others did not have. Similarly, as I learn from others about their experiences of oppression, it has been clear to me that I am not subject to the same mistreatment. I have struggled with how to act on this awareness. These realizations have helped me be more conscious of my personal power, earned and unearned, and how I use it in personal and professional situations. Knowledge of my everyday unearned privilege has enabled me to be a more forceful and active agent of change, and I try to act on this understanding in a number of ways. First, I continually remind myself that I may not understand or be able to speak for the experiences of others, and I actively try to listen and see myself as a learner. I have also learned to use the opportunities provided by my privilege to undermine it. For example, when conducting trainings and giving lectures, I strive to be very inclusive and create opportunities for comments and input from groups that are traditionally denied voice.

Recently, I became aware of my privilege as a heterosexual and of my unconscious heterosexism. I felt that I was actively affirmative of LGB issues. But I noticed that I made many assumptions that were based on unacknowledged heterosexual privilege. For example, I didn't ask LGB friends whether they planned to have families. Now that I do, I hear many beautiful stories about friends' desires to share their lives with children. This has generated a new awareness of my privilege and increased my commitment to using more inclusive language and actions.

My activism on behalf of others led me to notice a contradiction. While I was outspoken on behalf of other groups, I was closeted as a Jewish person. Rather than claiming my identity, I was leaving it as unspoken and unacknowledged. I could affirm and embrace the traditions of others but did not disclose or share my own. Through some powerful experiential workshop experiences, I discovered previously unconscious fears of being out as a Jew. One of the personal directions that I have taken as a result is to present and affirm my Jewishness. This encounter with my own fears and internalized oppression has been crucial in allowing me to become a stronger ally and advocate around issues of oppression because it has helped me to understand how internalized oppression works. Thus, the need for personal healing and awareness of the hurts we have experienced within our individual identities is my seventh important lesson.

My final lesson is the understanding that the experience of oppression can foster psychological and spiritual strength. A lesbian colleague I knew and her partner had adopted many difficult-to-place children. I was very accepting and supportive of their family and considered them to be perfectly suitable parents. Much later, I realized that as lesbians who had learned healthy ways of coping with a marginal identity, they were actually better as parents of hard-to-adopt, marginalized children than I would have been as a straight person with dominant identities. This realization took me beyond tolerance and acceptance to appreciate the unique gifts and wisdom that come from living on the margin. I now actively strive in my personal and clinical relationships to identify and affirm the skills and resiliencies that can come from living with mistreatment, as a way of supporting my clients' growth and also a way of learning for myself.

These eight lessons share a common theme: that being an ally is a life issue and not just a professional issue. The important experiences that empower us professionally are often life experiences outside of our professional identities. We must seek out these life-changing experiences and provide the same for our students and clients. We can create friendships, therapy, and learning environments where others can give us feedback about our unconscious prejudices, where personal discomfort can be used as a growth edge, and where LGB individuals can speak about their own experiences. To be an active ally requires a commitment to using inclusive language, learning, and teaching skills to interrupt homophobic behavior and taking personal responsibility for contradicting heterosexual privilege. Finally, we must create opportunities to do our own work and healing in the identities where we have been hurt; in my case, growing up with less resources than my peers, as Jewish, and as a man uncomfortable with how I was taught to be male.

Internalizing the commitment to be an ally is thus a lifelong learning and healing process that must be actualized in word, thought, and deed. As counseling professionals, we can accept this challenge with the understanding that our personal fate and well-being is intertwined with the fate and well-being of others. The opportunity to contribute to this book has helped me to deepen my understanding and awareness of these issues.

4

Over the Rainbow

My Experiences as an Ally

Sharon L. Bowman
Ball State University

I am not a lesbian or bisexual woman, nor do I play one on TV. I am, however, a lesbian, gay, and bisexual (LGB) ally in both my personal and professional life. I live in this world as an African American, heterosexual, married woman, mother of none, nonreligious, a counseling psychologist and college professor, born, raised, and currently living in the Midwest. I have other identities, of course, but those are the ones most salient at this stage in my life. Some of the aforementioned aspects of my identity have been particularly relevant in my development as an LGB ally. My journey over the rainbow to becoming an ally, then, requires that I also discuss my personal identity development.

When I discuss identity development in my undergraduate and graduate classes, I usually make two things clear. First, we cannot "know" anyone else until we know ourselves, so we must spend time understanding our own backgrounds, values, and beliefs before we can seriously examine someone else's. Second, we do not confront and examine our own core beliefs until we are forced to do so, generally as a result of a significant interaction with someone who is different from us. In other words, I cannot begin to comprehend what the world is like for a lesbian woman until I understand what the world is like for me as a heterosexual woman. And I will not begin to think about and examine my core beliefs about sexual identity if all of my significant interactions are with other heterosexuals. I need to see the reflection of the other side of the rainbow to show me that not everyone lives in and experiences the world the way I do. Only then can I begin to grasp another person's world. To further understand this concept of awareness, see Sue and Sue's (1999) discussion of racial identity development.

My path as an LGB ally began when I was in college. While doing my requisite fast-food stint, I learned that one of my coworkers was gay. I can truthfully say that I was clueless about what that really meant. I had no preconceived notions about homosexuality, having never heard it discussed in my home, and so I naively did not view him any differently than anyone else with whom I worked or interacted. Eventually, I realized that other workers viewed him as "different," but the best support I could offer him was mild protest when he was unfairly mistreated at work. People around me assumed that as a budding psychologist I was being trained to "cure" him. I had no idea what to do with this information overload, so I did what seemed best at that time: I mentally retreated from the situation.

As an ally in the making, I had the opportunity, advantage, option (you choose the word) to be able to melt back into the heterosexual community whenever I wished. After all, I was not one of "those" people, and I could easily choose not to be around them. For several years, I continued to move on the fringe, able to casually mention having a gay friend but not taking things any further. Clearly, I was more comfortable on that very superficial level, but in retrospect, my energies were also focused on defining myself, first as an African American, then as a woman. My ability to be an effective LGB ally was blocked while I came to a better understanding of myself as an African American woman moving in a predominantly Caucasian world.

During my graduate years, there were several events that reflect the complexity of my development as an ally. I earned my doctoral degree in a very rural community with few African American professionals in evidence. One of my African American colleagues spent a significant amount of money (for a graduate student) having her hair elaborately braided. Imagine my astonishment a few days later when she complained that the rural community mental health center where she worked found her hairstyle to be too ethnic and insisted that she remove it. At another point, a gay male classmate was told that one of his proposed internship sites would not accept a gay intern. Another classmate was interrogated during an internship interview about her ability to work with male clients, implying that a lesbian could not work with men. The first event touched me personally, forcing me to question how my HAIR, my Blackness, was a threat. The other two events I initially protested from a superficial standpoint, but over time I understood them from a more personal level. Who would dare ask me whether I could work well with Caucasians or hint that ethnic minority candidates would not receive offers? It was painful to recognize the privilege I had as a Black woman in comparison to my friends, a privilege I had not previously addressed.

I entered a new phase of my life as an ally in my last year or so of graduate school. As I began to crystallize who I was as an African American woman, I was better able to understand my friends' and clients' struggles with sexual identity issues. I was able to relate to the feelings of being alone, somehow separate from those around me. I identified with the hypersensitivity or initial aloofness with new situations and people, never knowing when the next negative experience will materialize. That hypersensitivity for me is usually based on anticipated reaction to my skin color, but that is nothing compared with making the decision whether (and to whom) to reveal one's sexual identity. The potential for a vocal, negative reaction is incredible, not to mention the potential for physical harm in a few select cases.

As a faculty member, I have been privileged to meet numerous students over the years. I have served as an advisor, mentor, or just a sounding board for students trying to wend their way through an environment that some find null and others find quite hostile. My interactions with LGB graduate students tend to fall into three groups: students who are early in the self-identification process; students who are comfortable with themselves, but private; and students who want to be open about their identities. With all three groups, my overall goal is to help them have as positive an experience in graduate school as is possible. The first group includes students in the early stages of identifying themselves as gay, lesbian, or bisexual. I sometimes walk a fine line between advisor/mentor and therapist with these students. It is not appropriate for me to counsel them through their coming-out process. I can, however, provide answers related to the interaction of their academic careers and personal development, and sometimes I help them find someone to provide the counseling they may seek.

The second group of LGB graduate students are secure in their identities but choose to be open with and seek mentoring and support from only a few select people. Spending significant amounts of time in a biased atmosphere (whether racist or heterosexist) is emotionally draining. At least once each year, a student comes to me to express disillusionment that the profession is not as open and accepting about oppressed group issues as he or she imagined it would be. LGB students sometimes seek a sympathetic ear in an ally, someone to validate the difficulty of their experiences. As an ally, I am also in a unique position to verbalize concerns that LGB and other oppressed students do not believe that they could safely express to the larger department. The fear of repercussions often paralyzes students but should not be equally paralyzing to faculty and professional staff.

The third group of LGB students are interested in publicly merging their personal and professional identities. Some of their questions may include: Will public acknowledgment of one's sexual identity affect the student's ability to secure a predoctoral internship? To complete one's degree? To find a job postdegree? Tales of past mistreatment by faculty and other professionals toward students can take on "urban legend" status. My role as ally with these students is to help them separate the rumors from the realities of the profession. While I can honestly say that the reports of heterosexist or homophobic behavior toward students have lessened over the last decade, I would not want someone to naively believe that there are no problems left.

I know that LGB graduate students will be presumed heterosexual unless they state otherwise. Some may fear being penalized, mistreated, or denied opportunities as a result of their sexual identities, and perceive little recourse to challenge such actions in this fairly antihomosexual society (Savin-Williams & Cohen, 1996). LGB students have legitimate worries about the academic and professional repercussions to challenging heterosexist and homophobic comments from peers and faculty members. As an ally, I sometimes must be reminded that the world, or even my university, is not as safe as I might like to believe. I know it is sometimes threatening for even faculty to challenge biased statements, but I cannot expect my students, LGB or otherwise, to put themselves on the line if I am not willing to do it myself. At this point in my career, I have much more power to be heard than they do, and it is much more likely that I can facilitate changes than they can. Faculty and professional staff, degrees in hand, usually do not face the same career repercussions that students fear. Ideally, they also recognize that they have more power than do their students, and thus their voices will carry farther in demanding that changes be made.

Expressing interest in conducting LGB research is a study in how one's personal and professional development can collide. How many students have been discouraged from doing LGB research because "someone" might have a negative reaction, or told it would be impossible to publish in the "right" journals? There is still a stigma or fear to doing such research, sometimes in the eye of the budding researcher—but more often in the eye of other professionals (Pilkington & Cantor, 1996). Over the past decade, my advisees who have worked on LGB research have consistently been questioned about their own sexual identities and told that they might want to consider the impact of such research on their careers. In actuality, a student's sexual identity is not a factor in his or her ability to do good research. It is so disheartening to me to witness the continued existence of a heterosexist agenda in the counseling professions because the implication is not only that conducting LGB research is unacceptable or problematic, but that being a gay man, lesbian woman, or bisexual person is also unacceptable.

Finally, I must remember that I am an ALLY, not a full-fledged member of this group. One of my students gave me an "honorary lesbian" button, which hangs in my office and evokes interesting looks from visitors. Being an ally, however, means that I sometimes am exposed to the unflattering side of heterosexism. For example, two of my LGB students were sharing amusing examples of heterosexist experiences. Initially, I laughed along, but I soon began to question aloud whether I should really be part of this discussion or whether they might be more comfortable without me around. They replied that they were not talking about me, and they knew I would understand, so of course I could stay. How many times has that same statement been made to the sole man in a group of women, or the sole Caucasian in a group of African Americans? As an ally, I know that I can be WITH my LGB students and friends, I can SUPPORT them, I can SHARE in their joys, pains, and glories, but I remain quite aware that my status is at best honorary. Allies who forget this may be challenged about their motives, either directly or indirectly, by members of the LGB community.

What are the implications for a faculty member who is also an LGB ally? Well, that varies depending on one's focus. For my LGB students, having a faculty ally (I hope!) is a help as they move through the generally grueling process of graduate school. Spending significant time in an environment that does not feel welcoming is emotionally draining. For those of us who are minorities in a majority world, finding someone to be an active supporter in such an environment can mean the difference between "finishing" and "surviving" the program.

It may seem that my non-LGB students would not need a faculty ally. Not true: The nature of being an ally means being available to ALL students interested in LGB issues, regardless of the students' sexual identities. Some of my student researchers involved in LGB issues have been heterosexual; they have been subjected to the same biased, negative reactions as their LGB colleagues. Allies also have plenty of opportunities to challenge misperceptions and misinformation in classes and other arenas. Just as Caucasians speaking against racism are important models for other Caucasians, LGB allies speaking against heterosexism can be equally powerful for other heterosexuals. I learned long ago that my students (undergraduate and graduate) will openly discuss anything related to race and ethnicity in my multicultural classes. When I move to LGB issues, however, suddenly most people become very, very quiet. Allies can encourage the dialogue necessary for people with disparate views to listen to and understand each other.

Finally, allies can be supportive to their colleagues in the profession, both in the workplace and nationally. Heterosexist (and homophobic) comments are made every day, sometimes inadvertently and sometimes quite on purpose. Some LGB counseling professionals and students are perfectly comfortable challenging the status quo that exists in our field, with relatively little regard for the safety of their careers. Others do not believe that they are safe from repercussions from colleagues or clients, and so speaking out is not an option. LGB counseling professionals and students need allies to speak out and be true to their consciences, not a "silent majority" standing behind them in the shadows. Perhaps what non-LGB counseling professionals have forgotten is that their LGB colleagues and students have more than their careers on the line: They have their very identities on the line.

References

Pilkington, N. W., & Cantor, J. M. (1996). Perceptions of heterosexual bias in professional psychology programs: A survey of graduate students. *Professional Psychology: Research and Practice, 27,* 604–612.

Savin-Williams, R. C., & Cohen, K. M. (Eds.). (1996). *The lives of lesbians, gays, and bisexuals: Children to adults.* Fort Worth, TX: Harcourt Brace.

Sue, D. W., & Sue, D. (1999). *Counseling the culturally different: Theory and practice* (3rd ed.). New York: John Wiley.

5

Invisibility, Alienation, and Misperceptions

The Experience of Being Bisexual

Maria D. Carrubba

Miami University

I realized that I was attracted to women during my master's program. I was at a gay bar, which I had been to numerous times before, and had an intense attraction to a female bartender. I was in my mid-20s, had a long history of dating men, and had never questioned my sexual orientation. Until that time, my understanding of sexual orientation was the two-box explanation: a person was either straight or gay, and, since I was attracted to men, I had to be straight. Once I realized that I was definitely attracted to this woman, and I was also still attracted to men, it changed my whole world dramatically. Ten years later, I am a 35-year-old, Italian American, bisexual, counseling psychologist working full-time in a university counseling center. I have a much different level of understanding about sexual orientation, and much of that has to do with my own personal journey as it relates to being in the counseling profession.

I entered the world of counseling psychology as a doctoral student. When I applied to doctoral programs in counseling, I wasn't "out," and I never considered the implications of attending a program that wasn't affirming of lesbian, gay, and bisexual (LGB) persons. I hadn't reached any conclusions about my sexual orientation, and I still had no concept of how or whether being attracted to both men and women would fit into my professional life.

I was still just starting to become comfortable acknowledging to myself, and several close friends, that I was attracted to women as well as men. Luckily, I was admitted to an LGB-affirmative program with a relatively large number of gay and lesbian students, and I think eventually one other bisexual. Although my doctoral program didn't overtly recruit gay and lesbian applicants, they were supportive once they realized that we were there.

The dominant discourse in the counseling profession still favors Caucasian, male, heterosexual, socially advantaged, able-bodied persons. Within that overriding force, when I think about what made my program a supportive place to be, a number of factors come to mind. The most important factor is the social environment and the presence of a critical mass of diverse people, and not just with regard to sexual orientation. "Isms" are "isms," and someone accepting of racial/ethnic diversity has a much greater chance of being accepting of diverse sexual orientations. When I hear someone say anything prejudicial of any group, it makes me think twice about being open about my sexual orientation with them. Just the presence of a diverse group of people brings different awareness to the conversation, and that's how we really learn about the nuances of difference. A close friend of mine was out and partnered when he was admitted to the program, and just the constant presence of him and his partner made a huge impact. When I think about training programs that support LGB persons, I consider the following questions. When you chat with the secretaries or professors about your life, can you mention your same-sex partner? Can you bring your same-sex partner to departmental social events? When people ask about whom you are dating, do they assume the person will be of the opposite sex? When you are going through your "gay pride" period, can you wear your freedom rings around the department? Do people look uncomfortable about the details of your life, or do they just take it in stride? If you come out during your training, are there people there to direct you to LGB-affirmative therapists? Does your advisor notice that you are struggling and help you figure out how to handle coming out while you continue to progress in school? I am always looking to see whether people flinch or look uncomfortable when I talk about LGB-related topics. When I do see it, it greatly decreases the chance that I'll bring it up again, especially if it's someone who has power over me, like faculty.

Outside of my doctoral program, I became active in the lesbian community on campus, and this aided me in changing my perceptions of gay men and lesbians overall. I found that lesbians are a lot like straight women, and they sometimes share many of the same phobias and prejudices. In addition, I confronted my idealization of lesbian and gay cultures and began to understand the complex relationship between gay men and lesbians. Finally, I began to seek specific information about being bisexual and to learn about the difficulty that bisexuals face in belonging to the lesbian or gay community. Being in a critical mass of gay men and lesbians allowed me to have personal conversations about my struggles; this was exactly what I needed. Another way that training programs can really help LGB persons is to know how to connect LGB persons with the LGB community outside the department.

Within the academic curriculum, professors addressed diversity issues to some degree in the majority of my classes. Students and graduate programs seem to co-create each other, and having a critical mass of LGB students ensured that sexual orientation would be addressed in our coursework and discussions to some degree. But LGB students are always wondering where the line is. Can LGB students expect that every class will address LGB issues? Can we ask about applicability to LGB persons as often as we want? My program was tolerant of a fair amount of questions, and, in addition, one professor was receptive to a request for a specific seminar course on LGB issues in psychology. That was amazing for me to have an entire course just on LGB issues.

In addition, it was common during this time for LGB graduate students to present panel discussions to undergraduate and graduate classes, giving them a chance to interact with gay, bisexual, and lesbian persons. This type of learning experience seems particularly effective with students in challenging personal stereotypes. I believe it is also beneficial for panel participants in helping them to better understand their identities and develop strength and pride in being LGB. It was sometimes difficult for me because I was constantly confronted with the stereotypes about bisexuals. For instance, common questions I received were as follows: Aren't you attracted to everyone you see, so how do you focus on your life? If you can choose a straight relationship, why wouldn't you? Don't your partners worry that you're unfaithful? Do you think you'll eventually decide that you're lesbian (or straight)?

On another level of discourse within the field of psychology, the mid-1990s were a time when the research literature began to address bisexuality in its own right and not just as an add-on to gay and lesbian studies. This is another very important level of academia because what's being published greatly affects what we are taught as trainees. A number of important books about bisexuality came out at this time, and the Internet became an amazing tool in disseminating information to LGB persons.

Ironically, just as I was coming to terms with the idea of possibly being partnered with a woman, I fell in love with a man. Prior to meeting him, my concern had been how lesbians would deal with me being bisexual in identity but dating women. I hadn't thought that my next long-term relationship would be with a man, and I didn't really want it to be. It felt like backsliding. But when I looked inside myself, I realized that I was in love with him, and that that is what being bisexual is; sometimes I'll fall in love with a woman and sometimes with a man. This gave me my first long-term experience of what it was like to negotiate my bisexual identity with a man, the fears it raised both in him and in me. I wondered if I could ever be satisfied dating just one sex. Although gay and lesbian friends were primarily happy that I had found someone I loved, they couldn't completely hide their disappointment that that person was a man. Conversely, straight friends seemed a little too happy that that person was a man.

Professionally, I felt trapped. Could I be a bisexual psychologist if my partner was a man? I was developing an identity as a specialist in LGB issues, but is a bisexual woman in a long-term relationship with a man credible? In addition, during this time period, "lesbian chic" emerged in some circles, and experimenting with same-sex relationships became fashionable. Is that what I had done? I now felt pressure to inform people that although I was bisexual, my partner was a man. It not only felt like a betrayal to the LGB community, but I began to question myself. Had I really been attracted to women? One of the major struggles with being bisexual is that you are defined by the sex of your partner. Other people felt this, and I felt this too.

An important area in which LGB persons need mentoring is in the professional application process. This became relevant for me as a bisexual woman when I applied for internship. Because I knew that I was ready to be out and because diversity issues were my specialty area, I applied to programs that emphasized diversity. During this time, a group of internship sites were open to gay and lesbian applicants. Since internship spots are so highly coveted, some people "caringly" suggested that I not say that I was bisexual. This was a direct experience with biphobia. It was okay to be gay or lesbian, but being bisexual was not. Which would be worse, not getting a placement, or being accepted somewhere that was biphobic? Was I "gay" enough for sites that wanted gay candidates? Would they be disappointed when they found out my partner was a man? In addition, others said that being gay or lesbian would "help" ensure a spot, so would internships think that I said that I was bisexual to appear gay? As it turned out, my internship was also LGB affirming and offered me new opportunities to understand my bisexuality at a deeper level. At a time when I was transitioning from student to psychologist, I was able to see how other LGB psychologists managed their identities within the profession.

Bisexuality can be expressed in a number of ways. I found that I am monogamous, and what bisexuality means to me is that partner sex is like eye color—it's not a trait that I preference on. It may sound absurd to compare someone's physical sex to something so menial, but that is how it is for me. The person that I partner with has a similar personality regardless of gender. Although my relationship with that particular man ended with internship, it helped me realize that I am the same person professionally and personally regardless of whom and whether I am dating. I fit into the LGB community whether or not I appear to be gay by anyone else's standard. There are some events in the lesbian community that a male partner couldn't be part of but I could. In addition, I can always find a segment of the gay and lesbian community that is inclusive and accepts my partner choice, just as I can in the straight community. As do most things, a lot of it for me came down to personal security. Once my identity made sense to me, I was able to help others understand it, too.

I thought that I had reached an identity plateau after internship, but applying for jobs brought new challenges. Again, was I ready to be out and proud and take a chance that I wouldn't get a job? Or should I not say anything about my sexual orientation and get hired someplace homophobic? I really struggled with myself personally, politically, and practically. I decided to let my vita speak for itself. Since my specialty was diversity issues, I hoped that places that were really homophobic wouldn't want me anyway, and I hoped that others who were more sensitive might consider that I was not necessarily heterosexual. I was really lucky and found a job in a university counseling center that I love, and I am now partnered with a woman. My colleagues are very LGB affirming, and I couldn't be happier. My colleagues are not only comfortable hearing about my professional and personal life and struggles as a bisexual woman, but I can also bring my female partner to all of our social events. When I was first hired, there was a large bulletin board in the hallway dedicated to the achievements of LGB people. It was amazing how good it made me feel to walk down the hall every day.

I had been at my job less than a year when I was asked to write this narrative. This raised new challenges for me. It was clear to me that the counseling center and the broader division were affirming, but what about the wider institution? Being a student and an intern are transitory roles, but managing a gay identity in a place you plan to stay is different. I know now that being a bisexual counseling professional raises continuous questions that will have answers over time. Perhaps that is what I have learned the most—patience and tolerance for the unknown and the importance of security in myself. People really do take my lead. When I am okay with myself and my choices, for the most part others respond in kind. What do LGB persons need? As students and professionals, LGB persons need to feel a sense of belonging and acceptance. In our own ways, each of us can feel invisible, alienated, and misperceived, and it doesn't feel good for anyone. Counseling professionals need to move beyond tolerance to understand at a core level that our differences are what make us interesting and unique—and at the same time, they do present real challenges. For the most part, the dominant discourse in the counseling professions still favors White, socially advantaged, able-bodied, male heterosexuals, but, as sheer numbers force everyone to accept greater diversity, this has begun to change. I was really fortunate to find the part of the counseling professions that embraces me at its best moments and tolerates me at its worst.

6

Transforming Heterosexism

Starting From Myself

Kin-Ming Chan

Western Michigan University

The first "person" to whom I came out was God. I was then 14 years old and was secretly in love with a male classmate. Around the same time, I first learned from a sermon in church that homosexuality was sinful. Subsequently, for a couple years, when I prayed at night, I asked God in tears to take back my life as soon as possible because He must have made a mistake in creating my "wrong existence." I felt ashamed, guilty, and was in pain to think of my gay orientation. Nevertheless, I could neither deny my feeling of love toward that classmate nor understand the intrinsic sinfulness of genuinely loving another person. Now, at the age of 39, I come out to you here, embracing my identity as a gay man. Unlike my earlier years, I now look forward to continuing my life—happy and gay. It has been a long and difficult journey for me to evolve to this stage of my personal and professional life as I choose to come out in this public forum. In this narrative, I first describe what it meant for me to be a gay person living in a conservative Chinese culture. Then, I narrate my experiences as a gay professional in the counseling field within that culture and what it meant for me to come out in my profession. Afterward, I share my current experience as a student in a doctoral program in counseling psychology in the United States. Finally, deriving from my own personal experience, I share my insights into transforming heterosexism in the counseling profession.

My Background

I am Chinese, from an ex-colony of Britain, Hong Kong. It is a place, similar to most parts of the United States, where gay and lesbian people are deprived of equal opportunities in society and can be fired from work without legal protection. In addition, it is a place, more conservative than the United States, where gay people kissing in a public place may run the risk of getting caught by police for their "indecent behavior"; where there are no gay pride parades; where almost no Chinese celebrities claim an openly gay identity; where there are no lesbian, gay or bisexual (LGB) student associations at schools or in most universities; where getting married and continuing one's family lineage is extremely valued; where I had not known of any LGB classmates, teachers, friends, and colleagues until I started revealing my sexual orientation; and from where I have chosen to escape in order to live with a more open gay identity.

I had not received any formal education about sexual diversity at school nor known of any LGB-affirmative messages in Hong Kong before my master's program. My first coming-out experience to humankind happened during my undergraduate years when I decided to come out to four friends individually. One of these so-called friends shunned me after my revelation, telling me that he did not know how to deal with this piece of information. Another "friend" responded by wishing me to become a normal man and stating that he felt like vomiting to think of homosexual men. Our friendship ended. I felt severely hurt and devastated. On the other hand, the other two friends loved me and respected me more after my disclosure. One even told me that because of my coming out to her, she later openly defended gay people's rights in front of colleagues in her conservative field of education. Being accepted by these two friends was important in affirming how I felt about my worth as a person. These positive experiences also encouraged me to take further risks to come out to other people later in my professional life.

My Experience as a Gay Professional in the Counseling Field in Hong Kong

I received training as a counseling professional from a master's program in Hong Kong. I subsequently worked as a counseling professional for 10 years in different settings. Prior to entering into the counseling field, I was ignorant and innocent enough to think that the counseling profession must be an open and understanding field where all professionals were LGB affirmative. I gradually came to know, as I entered into the profession, that this belief was only an ideal, if not a complete illusion. I experienced that many counseling professionals were very ignorant of LGB issues, homophobic, and very heterosexist in essence.

Only one professor, among all my classes, taught us to respect and to accept people with minority sexual orientations. Even so, it was crucial for me to hear someone with his academic authority telling me that I had every right to be respected as a gay person. This learning was instrumental in establishing my self-esteem; being gay should not be associated with shame and guilt. However, in a predominantly Chinese society and program, the professor's viewpoint was outrageous to many students and some faculty at that time. Many students made jokes of his teaching. Although some students agreed conceptually with what he said, they still continued to make gay jokes, as if believing that they would not encounter LGB people in real life.

My experience at work in the counseling field was even worse than in the academic setting, where "radicals" could still be tolerated within the romance of academic ideological pursuit. In Hong Kong, being gay was considered to be undesirable in general, and many counseling professionals were uncomfortable with LGB people. I experienced anti-gay jokes as not uncommon among these professionals. I actually heard some colleagues making jokes about gay clients. A former employer even turned down a gay association's application for a meeting venue because there was a nursery in the agency. The agency was unwilling to allow the gay association to use the building because of their stereotype of gay people as being somehow associated with child molestation. The agency did not want to be connected with a gay association and have a negative image in the community. I felt angry that they treated the gay association so unjustly. Through this experience, I became even more aware that it was unsafe for me to expose my identity openly at work and risk being stigmatized.

From the beginning of my training to the end of my work as a counseling professional in Hong Kong, I struggled to come out to classmates and colleagues within the field for various reasons. I did not feel comfortable enough to openly disclose my gay identity because I did not feel safe enough to do so and also did not want to risk my professional career by exposing myself in that way. Yet during this time, I still chose to come out to 25 people in the counseling field. Most of them previously had held negative stereotypes of LGB people and had no prior personal experience with LGB people or issues. In the beginning, my reason for coming out to them stemmed from my own personal desire to be connected with and accepted by a few colleagues with whom I could establish meaningful friendships. I was therefore more careful in choosing the people to whom I wanted to come out, wanting to avoid being hurt. But I gradually realized that my coming out to these people could actually change their views toward and influence their practice with LGB people. Then, I became more willing to come out to colleagues whom I believed might have the capacity to understand my experience as a gay person. Beyond my desire to be able to connect meaningfulness with these colleagues, I also wanted to be able to dispel their negative biases against LGB people. My experiences coming out to some colleagues were not pleasant, as they had difficulty accepting my gay identity due to their religious faith in fundamentalist Christianity. Fortunately, most of the colleagues to whom I disclosed my sexual orientation were thankful for my disclosure. They expressed that they even respected and loved me more because of my revelation.

One of the most gratifying parts of my coming-out experiences within my professional world was the change I could see in colleagues afterward. For example, I did not hear any gay jokes from them anymore, and one even cared enough to apologize for having made anti-gay jokes. One indicated that my disclosure challenged her stereotypes associated with gay men as having casual sex, AIDS, and feminine personalities. She shared with me how she now understood that I was just a normal, sensitive, and genuine person who was seeking love. As a result of my coming out to her, she said that her acceptance of diversity had increased and her counseling practice had become LGB affirmative.

Current Experience as a Student
in the Counseling Professions

More than 3 years ago, I came to the United States to begin work on my doctorate in the counseling field, in a training program that is very LGB affirmative. Within this environment, I have experienced significant changes regarding my sexual orientation identity management and personal development. Rather than needing to calculate the risks of coming out as in my previous training and work settings, I feel free to openly disclose my sexual orientation to my professors and fellow students. This sense of freedom stems from a professional culture that has been developed within the department in which LGB people are respected and valued. In this affirmative professional culture, I have experienced that LGB professors and students are safe to disclose their identities without risking many of the negative consequences I feared in my past. Also, partners of LGB faculty and students are included in social functions of the program, just like those of heterosexual faculty and students. Moreover, the message of embracing diversity including the LGB population has been assimilated into most of the courses and training experiences. Furthermore, I have been empowered by the experience of taking a course specially tailored for students' learning on LGB issues in counseling and development. This course offered a safe environment in which students had oppor-tunities to share their own sexual identity development and to examine heterosexist biases and internalized homophobia. In addition to my openly disclosing my gay orientation in the program, I have also experienced myself coming out to more people outside of the program. Hence, because of the liberating environment and affirmative experiences within my training program, I have further developed my inner strength to openly affirm my identity both inside and outside of the professional circle.

Personal Insights and Implications
for the Counseling Professions

Looking back on my own journey, I have gleaned some personal insights in relation to transforming heterosexism, especially in the counseling profession. First, I have learned that my coming-out stories can make changes that generate a ripple effect of further changes for others and myself. Because of my coming out, some of my professional colleagues engaged in more self-reflection regarding their heterosexist biases and became more LGB affirmative in their professional practice. In return, their transformations empowered me and affirmed my self-identity. In light of this mutually influential process, I encourage LGB counseling professionals to take time and calculated risks to come out to some colleagues or classmates for both the benefits of enhancing personal growth through deeper connections with people and transforming the profession. From my experience, there are still professionals who are less informed of LGB issues but who are capable of understanding LGB issues when given the chance. Experiencing coming-out stories in real life, they may become less heterosexist and more LGB affirmative.

Second, my experience of the existing heterosexism within counseling professionals points to the need for effective training to discourage heterosexism and for LGB affirmation in counseling training programs. From the contrasting experience of my previous training and my current training, I consider it essential for a training program to cultivate an LGB-inclusive and -affirmative learning environment in which people not only talk about embracing diversity but also model this goal consistently throughout training and integrate it into all courses. Another way to achieve this affirmative environment is offering a regular course on LGB development and issues in counseling to promote students' understanding of LGB issues. Such a training environment could then create a growth-enhancing context for student and faculty, LGB and heterosexual.

Third, my experiences of the existing homophobia and heterosexism within practice settings also suggest that agencies and professionals need to seriously self-examine their policies and practices so that LGB clients are not discriminated against or stigmatized. I strongly relate to the fact that my positive self-identity has evolved as a result of the acceptance and affirmation I have received from other people. Hence, it is imperative for counseling professionals and agencies to be supportive and affirmative of LGB clients in any setting. Professional agencies and counseling professionals actively working toward advocating for LGB rights could greatly affect the affirmation of LGB individuals' experience.

Conclusion

Arriving at this point of my personal and professional journey, I take pride in my gay identity as it makes my life more meaningful and beautiful. I am also happy that I have come out to more and more counseling professionals and other people. I am well aware that there are limitations to my ability to change people's attitudes about LGB issues and that there are some people who will remain unwilling to change their heterosexist viewpoints. Yet I have learned from my coming-out experience that creating change is possible, though it may seem to be on a small scale, and that this change can occur even within a conservative culture. Over the years, gradually learning to accept that I live in an imperfect world where discrimination is tied to sexual orientation, I have gained a bit of wisdom about my role in changing the impact of this oppression. Instead of allowing helplessness to eat away my self-esteem, I rather choose to use myself to create a more safe and affirming environment for myself and others; that is, taking responsibility to transform the heterosexism around me.

7

Challenging Multiple Oppressions in Counselor Education

Stuart F. Chen-Hayes

Lehman College of the City University of New York

Being "out" as a gay, gender-variant counselor educator in a multiracial/ multilingual family has led me to witness numerous instances of oppression. *Oppression* is defined as prejudice multiplied by power used by members of the dominant group to keep nondominant group members from accessing resources and opportunities. For example, persons from nondominant family structures, sexual orientations, gender identities and expressions, languages, and racial and social class identities are denied access to resources individually, culturally, and systemically via heterosexism, transgenderism, linguicism, racism, and classism. I conclude with implications for overcoming multiple oppressions in counselor education.

My noticing and naming oppressions began in the 1980s as a graduate student in a Counseling MEd program whose student body and faculty were almost exclusively White and monolingual, with an occasional multilingual international student of color. As a master's student, I presented at my first American Counseling Association conference and quickly found the Association for Gay, Lesbian, and Bisexual Issues in Counseling (AGLBIC). Most members were lesbian or gay, White, monolingual, and none identified as transgendered or gender-variant. Their strength was affirming nondominant sexual orientation from a middle-class perspective.

After working in college student development and family and school counseling, I returned to counselor education for a PhD at a different school, where two faculty members were gay-affirming, heterosexual women of color. Based on discussions with them and other graduate students, I came out in their classes and began a graduate student lesbian, gay, bisexual, and transgender (LGBT) campus group. One of the faculty allies invited me to do guest LGBT lectures in her multicultural counseling classes, and we eventually codeveloped a sexuality counseling course. The other faculty ally taught unlearning oppression workshops and eventually asked me to be a copresenter. A White female faculty member in a related area, when told that a group of us planned to submit an article to an LGBT journal, said, "You'll want to publish that in a real journal; an LGBT journal is perceived as easy to publish in." The implicit message was that LGBT journals weren't seen as scholarly or important. So we wrote an LGBT-themed article, submitted it, and were accepted in a non-LGBT journal.

The faculty had several LGBT-affirming folks, and large numbers of White, monolingual LGBT students entered this program (and came out, too!). Having allies on the faculty (or out LGBT faculty) clearly made more LGBT students feel safe in applying, being accepted, and feeling affirmed as counselor education doctoral students. But as the two women of color on the faculty were informally providing mentoring and support to many more students of nondominant cultural identities than were their own advisees, they received no tenure or promotion rewards for their "double duty"; that is, supporting and affirming graduate students of multiple nondominant cultural identities.

As I job-searched, I applied for counselor education jobs in major metro areas due to the likelihood of finding less heterosexism and transgenderism and more LGBT affirmation, visibility, and social support in cities. I received one offer in a major urban area. I interviewed out-of-the-closet on paper; my vita contained LGBT presentations, affiliations, and scholarship interests, but I did not divulge LGBT specifics in the spoken interviews. Once hired, I came out as bisexual to individual faculty members and to students. Over the time that I spent at that institution, I shifted my identity to gay. Living in the heart of the LGBT community in the city counterbalanced my work on a religiously and politically conservative campus in the suburbs. I had chosen to become a counselor educator in part to be an ally, mentor, and role model for LGBT students. I had some powerful challenges along the way.

My students were mostly heterosexual, traditionally gendered, White, monolingual, and from middle class to wealthy. Of the LGBT students, one was a gay White man, and there were a few Black lesbians. My colleagues were exclusively heterosexual (or closeted), traditionally gendered, monolingual, middle class or wealthy, and mostly White or Jewish.

When I arrived, I decorated my office with artwork that affirmed my multiple cultural identities and the identities of other nondominant groups. For example, I had an ACT-UP poster displayed that a few years before had been banned by the city's transit system after appearing on buses and other mass transit vehicles. So many identities and so much ruckus on the poster: three interracial couples of various ethnicities and races kissing—two men, two women, and one man and one woman. The AIDS/HIV activist message at the bottom read, "Kissing doesn't kill, ignorance and indifference do." The poster made people think, and it had people on campus talking. Occasionally, I would learn that some staff or students were uncomfortable seeing it in my office. Were they uncomfortable because it was about HIV/AIDS? Or were they fearful because the poster displayed three multiracial couples or that two of the couples were of the same gender?

I also discovered White persons of conservative religious identities who wished to use religious scriptures as scholarly references, usually to challenge gay people's existence. Other than discussing issues of religion or spirituality, I explained that using religion in place of scientific journals or texts was usually not an acceptable scholarly reference in counseling. In most cases, I was able to assist religiously conservative students balance a worldview that honored their religious identities and that affirmed persons who didn't fit their religious beliefs, using empathy and being non-judgmental. However, some students with whom I was not successful wrote teaching evaluation comments about how I talked too much about gay rights or that I had "issues." For many students, I was the first out gay person they had ever met (as far as they knew). My presence was enough to create drama simply by being in the classroom or on campus.

However, I had less influence over the staff, who at times created a hostile work environment. One incident occurred when a gay-video mailing list obtained my name and periodically sent a list of titles (and pictures, which were anything but G-rated) to my campus mailbox. The faculty mailboxes were in a public hallway where anyone could access them, and one nosy staff member with a conservative religious belief system apparently examined my mail regularly, found the video guide (not the first time), and complained to the administrator of my department. That administrator handled the situation by explaining to her that she was engaging in a federal crime by stealing other people's mail and that if she didn't desist, she could face arrest, firing, and a lawsuit. Although I never received an apology, the administrator took effective action when confronted with the problem. I did have to seek out the administrator, however, to find out how the situation was handled. However, I was more disappointed with a faculty colleague's classic victim-blaming reaction that I "shouldn't be having that type of mail sent to my work address in the first place." I responded that it was junk mail and it would be unfair to assume that I had ordered it for my own use but that even if I had, legally, I had the right to do so.

Another issue at this school was resistance to using my new multiracial surname after I had a sacred commitment ceremony with my partner. While some colleagues said they would not use the new name "until it was legal," even after it legally changed, I had to continually prompt people to use it. If I had "married" a monolingual White woman, would it have been remembered easily? After 5 years on the job, it was time to get out.

Job-searching had its own set of oppressions. In one search, I interviewed for a position and presented some LGBT scholarship. I later learned that two of the faculty were closeted. One even asked me personal questions about the scholarship I presented; and, some time later, in a phone call, after I had been turned down for a position. I assumed being out was part of why I didn't receive an offer, as no one gave any other feedback about why I wasn't chosen. Another school offered me a job, and while the faculty were gay affirming, we decided that living in a tiny cow (no offense, cows!) town (read "White, monolingual residents," except for international students and a few faculty of color) 1.5 hours from the nearest city was not ideal for a multilingual, multiracial gay couple. In yet another search in a gay-friendly city, I came out in an interview "off the record" as a drag queen. I never received an offer. Was gay okay but not gender-variance?

I eventually accepted an offer at my current institution, which has usually been LGBT affirming. I interviewed "out" and discussed the heterosexism that I had encountered elsewhere. The response of one faculty member was outstanding in her clear advocacy for LGBT colleagues and her clarity that if anything like that ever occurred, she would want to know and would "raise hell." It also helped that there were many tenured, out LGBT faculty on campus and elsewhere in the system, including an internationally recognized LGBT studies center.

Another area that made this school attractive was that it had domestic partner benefits, unlike my prior employer. I came out to selective colleagues and students as gay and gender-variant prior to tenure and found most students affirming. Some faculty colleagues were a bit wary and used a "control-the-deviance" theme with me: "Just don't do drag on campus or dye your hair purple until you've got tenure." So I did not, but there were plenty of hair colors with which to resist in the meantime.

I also found that LGBT students on campus often have to deal with racism, linguicism, classism, and cultural constraints at the same time. The student body at this school is 85% people of color, primarily Dominican, Puerto Rican, African American, and African immigrants, most of whom are bilingual and poor or working class. LGBT students of color vary in their comfort at being out, whereas White and Jewish LGBT students are usually out. Some students of color choose to be out to me but not others. Well-meaning activists have incorrectly assumed that being out is universally good, but this is a cultural bias. I've also been advising a campus progressive student group with a number of students just beginning to unlock the closet door. They have appreciated my advising them to go at their pace, honoring multiple ethnic, racial, linguistic, social class, and sexual orientation/gender identities.

The implications of my work to challenge multiple oppressions, and the work of others in the field, are many for counselor education. We need to recruit and retain culturally and linguistically diverse LGBT students, staff, and faculty; collect data on out LGBT students/staff/faculty in graduation and tenure and promotion rates; implement student/faculty development workshops on creating affirming climates for diverse students/faculty; and create more role models for overcoming the barriers of multiple oppressions. In addition, we need to advocate for domestic partner benefits in all schools; create more counselor education PhD programs in major urban centers in the Northeast and on the West Coast with large multilingual, multiethnic, and LGBT populations; discuss multiple oppressions in counselor education job-searches for candidates and faculty; hold professional associations accountable for supporting and nurturing LGBT students and faculty of multiple cultural identities; and present in classes and workshops about the research, publishing, graduation, hiring, tenure, retention, and promotion process for LGBT persons of multiple nondominant cultural identities.

In sum, on my counselor education journey I have bonded with students, faculty, and colleagues across similarities and differences. As a gay, gender-variant, antiracist White, antilinguistic monolingual, anticlassist upper-middle-class ally, I have worked with heterosexual and LGBT students and faculty of color from poor, working-class, and multilingual backgrounds to collaboratively and creatively confront heterosexism, transgenderism, racism, linguisticism, and classism. We have a powerful partnership perplexing multiple oppressions. However, counselor education, as a profession, still struggles with implementing and affirming equity for all. Only when we have large contingents of nondominant group members in positions of power in counseling associations, journals, faculties, and administrations will there be systemic shifts.

8

Coming Out on the Wave of Feminism, Coming to Age on the Ocean of Multiculturalism

Louise A. Douce

The Ohio State University

The most effective way to keep a group out of any discourse is to keep them invisible. The struggle to be visible and validated is a common theme in contemporary lesbian, gay, bisexual, and transgender (LGBT) cultures. Prior to 1973, the experience of LGB counseling professionals was complete invisibility. It was only in 1973 that homosexuality was removed from the *Diagnostic and Statistical Manual of Mental Disorders* (American Psychiatric Association) as an illness. Prior to the 70s, anyone known to be homosexual or "LGB" was at great risk to lose his or her job, home, and family. Students were suspended and expelled from most colleges and universities for being known to be homosexual. The operative phrase here was "known to be," an early form of "Don't ask, don't tell." The price of being out to yourself was the deep closet. That closet took many forms: (a) the professional closet, with a healthy personal life, closed support network, and careful efforts to protect one another; (b) the painful closet of nearly complete secrecy and fear; or (c) the closet of internalized self-hatred or complete denial to self and others.

I was an undergraduate in the late 60s and started graduate school in 1971. As we know, the late 60s were a period of great social change that fostered several paradigm shifts. The most important for me was a social analysis of the roles of women and the birth of the feminist movement.

I had the privilege of being the national president of the Intercollegiate Association of Women Students, which was very involved in the life of women in higher education. As president, I was invited to represent "the youth" at a number of incredible events and was exposed to some incredibly brilliant and powerful women of the times. My own aspirations soared. I am sure that there were straight and lesbian women among those strong and healthy role models. However, sexual orientation was silent, and it was crystal clear that the way to do this lifestyle was from a professional closet.

I was taught directly by one mentor to look and act as expected, but think and speak radically. She was a tough lady. She is the only person I ever saw smoke and brush her teeth at the same time. At the time she mentored me, I was still closeted to myself. I do remember wondering about her; but whatever her self-definition, it was invisible. Though sexual orientation could not be visible at that time, she had a very visible presence. She established one of the first women's centers and mentored hundreds of young women to believe in themselves and fulfill their dreams. She encouraged me to think way outside of the box—25 years before that concept was articulated. She showed me that women could be involved in the politics of life, could negotiate with men to establish things those men did not really understand, and could truly make a difference.

In graduate school, I moved far enough away from my small-town Christian family, with missionaries and ministers on both sides, to begin to address my true attractions. The 1970s on college campuses were the age of feminism. We examined institutions, relationships, policies, books, and movies in terms of *Sexual Politics* (Millet, 1967). It was a thrilling time to be a young woman, to discover truth and ourselves. We rejected the patriarchy of traditional marriage as "ownership." We really thought we discovered women. We acknowledged our older sisters in the first feminist movement, but we knew that we really could be in control of our lives with birth control and freer clothing (i.e., no corsets, signified by burning bras). As in all new movements, it was a time of excitement and naïveté, dreams of the future and ignorance of the past, and an optimism for a new world that was combined with an obliviousness to our own prejudices. It was also the most incredible time in history to come out as a lesbian. Loving women was like riding a wave, the wave of feminism. After a brief period of therapy searching for the source of my perversion, I decided that I was the healthiest person I knew and climbed up on that wave.

My personal life and professional ambitions as a counseling psychologist still seemed like separate worlds until I attended a conference in Boulder, Colorado, on Feminist Psychotherapy. About one third of the programs addressed sexual orientation in some fashion. It was the first time that my professional self and my personal self as a newfound lesbian were integrated. On the way home, some of the women I traveled with complained that the whole program was lesbian. When we actually counted the programs, we saw that two thirds were not. This is a good example of when what is invisible starts to become visible, it seems to stand out as dominant. Much effort can be exerted trying to put it back in the shadows in the name of getting back to normal.

That conference was also my first exposure to specific issues for women of color and my introduction to multiculturalism. Issues of oppression and privilege were presented and discussed in terms of the psychological impact and concepts of empowerment. I realized that by coming out, I experienced oppression and stereotyping in a way that I could not have appreciated as a middle-class White woman in America. Both the feminist movement and the LGB movement have been criticized as being White movements. There are some specific issues about worldview, multicultural sensitivity, and politics of power. This critique, however, has also been a way to further marginalize, silence, and render politically invisible LGB and female persons of color.

My feminist consciousness did make graduate school difficult and sometimes painful. There were many examples of rather blatant sexism. For example, I remember watching a lecture on the Strong-Campbell Interest Inventory that was peppered with scantily clad women in different occupations to "spice up the dry content." I hissed from the back row. I remember being angry at most of my instructors and feeling outside the mainstream of my program. I remember surprising many faculty with my scholarship, for they had dismissed me without really knowing or understanding me. They dismissed me because I was not like them and did not seem to share their values and perspectives of the world.

Men dominated graduate programs and university counseling centers at this time. There were usually one or two women, and some had a great deal of influence, but the dominant discourse was male. I was lucky to be mentored by four women who were adjuncts in the department. They were strong, powerful, wise women of the old school and were very important to my early self-concept. They fostered leadership, encouraged women to expand their aspirations and take risks, and nurtured young women to be everything they could image. They understood that relationships were important in life but modeled that relationships should not limit opportunity and achievement. They understood me, nurtured me, encouraged me, and questioned why I had to be so open with my self-definition as lesbian. I do not know how they defined themselves in terms of sexual orientation. They put out strong, nonverbal "stop signs" that discouraged any discussion about their personal lives.

Conversations were sometimes more about what was not said, more nonverbal than verbal. One of my most important mentors seemed to know all about my life from one statement I made as an intern. I said that I could not supervise one of the female practicum students, as there was a conflict of interest. The next summer, when that relationship hit some rocks and

I was back at school, she listened to my innocuous explanation about why I was still there, and she knew everything. She said, "I bet you need a job" and gave me one on the spot. Such communication of essence without the details did have some advantages but was also very difficult. One had to be a really good mind reader, and the possibility of misperception was enormous. So many times I wanted to just ask her directly about so many things. However, silence and invisibility were absolutely necessary in her life, even after the 70s. The most direct those conversations ever came were in the form of advice, but still without open references to her own life, and still in code. Because sexual orientation could not be discussed, I was again left to my own thoughts and imagination and denied the explicit wisdom of those who had gone before me.

I finished my degree in 1977 and accepted a position with a university counseling center. I conducted my job-search in what I like to call the "illusionary closet." I was a bit vague about my personal life and had a vita full of women's issues, women's studies presentations, and some on sexual orientation topics. I was perceived as having a good career counseling background but weak in general clinical work. Even though I had strong credentials in general counseling work, the label "feminist" (and maybe "lesbian") could not be integrated with a social construct of generalist. It was assumed that I could not work with men as clients and possibly with men as colleagues. In my second year, I remember getting complimented on how much I had grown clinically. What had really changed was this man's perception of me, but he needed to see it as my growth. People participating in the dominant discourse do not see its limits (Robinson, 1999). If they see something new, they see it as either an exception or as a change in someone who can then join the discourse.

College and university counseling centers in the 80s were at the frontier in embracing human diversity. To be a cutting-edge center, you needed to seek a gender balance and hire at least one person of color and at least one out LGB staff person. As staff committed to expanding our multicultural skills services, we tended to lead with our desire for political correctness and deal with the necessary changes in values, beliefs, and behavior later. Although I started my career as out to those who could see, which was about half of my colleagues, I was not out to all colleagues and not out in the larger profession. I wanted to be perceived as "Louise" first and then add "who is a lesbian." I did not want to be the "Lesbian Louise." Then, we hired an out gay male intern, and his gayness was what we perceived first. As I addressed people's projections and homophobic comments, I felt compelled to come out publicly at work. It was really a great relief. Let me say that being out for me was not an act of courage. The truth is I was terrible at being in the closet. I like to talk too much. For me, being out professionally has been far more a benefit than a liability. I provided in-service training to a number of counseling centers, presented at conferences, was invited to speak at other schools, and became known.

One of the most rewarding roles in my career is being an out role model. Over the years, I have had those direct conversations with students that I had wanted to have in graduate school. I have written on several topics and have been quite involved in the politics of the profession, serving in leadership roles in several organizations and committees. At some point, I always "out" myself as a lesbian and as a counseling psychologist. I have had the opportunity to touch many students, not all of whom I get to know well. Sometimes when I meet people at American Psychological Association social hours and they refer to my work, I know they are not talking about my work in supervision or career counseling. In some cases, we may talk directly about my LGB work; other times, I just smile back and hope to communicate, "Welcome, there is a place for you here." I suppose this is still code, but at least my visibility shows that one can be out and be professionally accepted. The fact that many students still doubt this suggests that being out is not safe, let alone affirmed, in too many counseling psychology programs.

So what keeps us in the margins? I have also been a voice for embracing LGB issues in the mainstream of the counseling profession. This has been a more arduous task. Lesbian and gay issues have been visible in our profession for about 25 years. I wrote a special-issue reaction for *The Counseling Psychologist,* titled, "Can a Cutting Edge Last Twenty-Five Years?" (Douce, 1998). For me, this is the contemporary core issue. Though we have been visible since the mid-1970s, LGBT scholarship is still seen as a narrow field of study not central to broader issues of human behavior and individual differences. As long as LGBT issues are seen as marginalized against the dominant discourse of White straight Middle America, we are stuck in need of another paradigm shift.

As a profession, we have struggled to determine whether LGBT ("transgender" was added in the 90s) belongs in our multicultural curriculum. Many experts in multiculturalism limit real oppression to characteristics that are immediately obvious and "in your face," excluding sexual orientation that remains invisible until revealed. Other colleagues of color acknowledge LGB oppression, but then state that if I am of the truly oppressed, I should line up behind them for my piece of justice. Still other colleagues are grounded in their own religious perspectives and see homosexuality as a sin, not as a natural normal form of human diversity. All of these perspectives deny the unique oppression that is experienced by people who are LGBT. For those of us who are assumed to be of the dominant, "normal" mainstream until we define ourselves as belonging in the margins, the process of continually choosing when and how to correct mistaken assumptions is just plain tiresome. As long as we can be killed just for who we are and be denied our basic civil rights in the name of God (as defined by the religious Right), then we are oppressed. Furthermore, the experience of LGBT oppression by those who also live with racial and cultural oppression is experienced as oppression squared or cubed. The exclusion of LGBT within group differences in multicultural discourse and curriculum feeds the attempts to push what is now marginalized back into invisibility.

Let us also contemplate what one considers progress. Bringing bisexuality (Kinsey, Pomeroy, & Martin, 1948; Kinsey, Pomeroy, Martin, & Gebhard, 1953) into a visible, viable form of sexual orientation and adding it to our title was the beginning of yet another paradigm shift. The current paradigm shift in queer theory suggests that gender expression and sexual orientation are socially constructed concepts. Those of us committed to LGB pride may be dinosaurs in the next 50 years, as people come to think of themselves in radically different ways in terms of gender and natural forms of intimacy. The discourse on sexual orientation will not be as some of us imagined.

Multiculturalism is also facing a paradigm shift. Current concepts are based in a model of the dominant White Eurocentric majority versus a series of marginalized groups. This model speaks only to the relationship of a specific group to the dominant culture (e.g., Black versus White, Latino versus Anglo, Asian versus Caucasian, female versus male, gay versus straight). The model does not speak to how marginalized groups relate to each other, nor to the reality of multiple identities. We, as counseling professionals trained in the concept of context, need to adopt a dynamic constructionsist view of culture (Hong, Morris, Chiu, & Benet-Martinez, 2000). People are more than one thing; we all have internalized cultural constructs, and sometimes those constructs are contradictory. We also all have sexual orientations. When we embrace this reality, then we will be out of the margins and part of the discourse.

References

American Psychiatric Association. (1973). *Diagnostic and statistical manual of mental disorders.* Washington, DC: Author.

Douce, L. A. (1998). Can a cutting edge last twenty-five years? *The Counseling Psychologist, 26,* 777–785.

Hong, Y., Morris, M. W., Chiu, C., & Benet-Martinez, V. (2000). Multicultural minds: A dynamic constructivist approach to culture and cognition. *American Psychologist, 55*(7), 709–720.

Kinsey, A. C., Pomeroy, W. B., & Martin, C. E. (1948). *Sexual behavior in the human male.* Philadelphia: W. B. Saunders.

Kinsey, A. C., Pomeroy, W., Martin, C., & Gebhard, P. (1953). *Sexual behavior in the human female.* Philadelphia: W. B. Saunders.

Millet, K. (1967). *Sexual politics.* Harcourt Press.

Robinson, T. L. (1999). The intersections of dominant discourses across race, gender, and other identities. *Journal of Counseling and Development, 77,* 73–79.

9

Jewish, Bisexual, Feminist in a Christian Heterosexual World

Oy Vey!

Sari H. Dworkin

California State University

I had just finished my American Psychological Association (APA) approved internship in August of 1985 and was on my way to my first academic job as a counselor educator. Excited and scared, I left a conservative, fundamentalist Christian, agricultural setting for a liberal, progressive state. To my surprise, the university where I was to begin a long and fruitful career was also in one of the few conservative, fundamentalist Christian, agricultural areas in my new home state. Once again, fundamentalist Christian preachers used the outdoor student gathering areas to intone what God considers moral and immoral. Once again, I found myself on the margins as a Jewish, feminist, lesbian (at that time in my life), new faculty member. It was difficult to make a decision about which identity was the safest one to test the waters with. While my vita had listed all of the lesbian and gay professional divisions of counseling and psychological organizations I belonged to, I hadn't begun a program of scholarly writing; so my sexual identity and/or sensitivities were not completely evident. The university did have a Woman Studies Department, and I soon made connections there. A feminist identity was the first "out" identity I had in my new academic setting. Of course, part of the feminist ideology is openness to all sexual identities, so it didn't take long for me to begin to be "out" as a lesbian as well as a feminist.

This narrative explores my journey through the first and only academic position I have held since completing my doctorate. It begins in 1985 and moves to the present. My sexual identity fluidity is explored, as well as my Jewish identity fluidity. I move from lesbian to bisexual and from Conservative Judaism to Reform and Secular Humanistic Judaism. Growing up as a Conservative Jew, I had felt a lack of validation for a nonheterosexual identity and decided to join a Reform temple in the town where I held my academic position. That identity again shifted as I realized that while Judaism was important to me ethnically and culturally, I didn't believe in God. I am now part of the small but international Secular Humanist Jewish movement, although I belong to the Reform temple as well. There aren't any other options in my current community for connecting on a personal level with other Jews.

The Early Years (1985–1990)

Lesbian and gay (LG) students sought me out to become a faculty advisor for the Gay, Lesbian Student Alliance (GLSA) they were forming. At the same time, the Association for Gay/Lesbian Issues in Counseling and the National Association for Lesbian and Gay Psychology (affiliate organizations of the American Counseling Association [ACA] and APA, respectively) sought my active participation. My scholarly writing, a requirement for faculty, began to focus on lesbian and gay issues in counseling and psychology.

My first crisis was with the GLSA. The group was thrust into the local news when its information booth was burned down; the KKK circled the campus during a lesbian and gay student regional conference held on campus, and some students attempted to start an anti-gay/lesbian student group. I was now the most open lesbian in the area and, as yet, untenured at the university. Christian literature showed up on my office door. A student asked to pray with me and prayed that I would give up not only "homosexuality" but also my Judaism, as she hoped I would "accept Jesus as my savior." The chair of my department informed me that calls were received demanding my dismissal. While the faculty all openly supported me, my file for retention, tenure, and promotion (RTP) was questioned. It was suggested that I remove all evidence of the scholarly and professional work I had been doing on gay and lesbian issues from the file. I refused. In addition to problems with my RTP file, some counseling students (especially those with strong Christian religious beliefs) began to question my credibility due to my strong LG-affirmative stance. The only part of my identity that remained unquestioned was my feminism and my work with both the Women Studies Department and the Women's Resource Center. I weathered the crisis by consulting with an openly lesbian faculty member, who advised me to trust the university committees to do the right thing. Her work and her international fame had been rewarded over and over again by the university. I trusted her advice, and neither tenure nor promotion was denied to me. In fact, I received both tenure and promotion early.

The Middle Years (1991–1998)

The climate on campus calmed down somewhat. The GLSA rebuilt their booth and did educational and outreach programming, much of it focused on the AIDS crisis. Anti-gay/lesbian incidents frequently happened, but none as serious as during the early years. I became the token representative of all gay men and lesbians. Added to an already busy faculty job, I've continuously been called upon to join university and local community committees, give presentations and workshops, and help students with papers on lesbian/gay issues. I came out in my classes to mixed reactions, often affecting my student evaluations at the end of semesters. Program faculty encouraged me to develop a course on gay/lesbian-affirmative therapy. Consistently, when I taught this class, I was challenged by one or two students who accused me of biased views and of forcing these views on them. Luckily, faculty supported my affirmative stance. The class has been discontinued due to budget cuts that allow only for core courses to be taught. My scholarly writing on gay and lesbian issues included journal articles, book chapters, an edited book, and many presentations at professional conferences. All of this appeared in my RTP file without problem as I moved up the academic ranks. In addition, I began a private practice that was one of very few therapy practices in the area that reached out to gay, lesbian, bisexual, and, later, transgendered individuals, as well as to those affected by the AIDS crisis.

The local news media still, after 5 years and even when other people were available, often relied on me to respond to anything about gay and lesbian issues that came up either locally and/or nationally. One major news event during this period was the first local gay and lesbian pride march. I was asked to be one of the grand marshals of this march, much to my partner's fear and dismay. My partner was afraid that the KKK would attend and might shoot me. Luckily, I was not shot, although the KKK was there in full drag, as well as some Christian groups that are against "homosexuality." Gay men and lesbians both on campus and in the community were coming out of the closet.

My feminist identity never proved to be a problem. It was my Jewish identity that created some problems and solicited occasional books and pamphlets on Christian religion left anonymously at my office door. Within the local Jewish community, issues often arose concerning separation of church and state, and the local public school system and I were supportive of these issues. For example, members of the Jewish community rallied to protest fundamentalist Christian activists who, in the guise of running benign after-school activities, were actually trying to convert public school children to fundamentalist Christianity. The problems I had around Judaism within the local Jewish community stemmed from my leftist beliefs about the necessity for a Palestinian state and for Israel to leave the occupied territories. I spoke out against the Sharon government's policy of demolishing Palestinian homes when there were suspected terrorists. The labeling of me as an anti-Semitic Jew was painful but not that unusual for the politics around Israel.

Current Climate (1999–Present)

A nonheterosexual identity does not seem to be a problem anymore. I became aware of this profound change in about 2000, when school and university committees openly recognized my identity and the issues of interest to me. I am still called upon to represent the lesbian, gay, and bisexual (LGB) perspective on committees, speak in classes around campus, work with students from programs around the campus who are doing papers on LGB issues, and generally be available for work in this area. Other LGB faculty and students have come out of the closet, making me less of a token and representative of the entire community and giving me room to spread the responsibilities around.

Even the local school districts are more open to LGB concerns, although this is not due to my activism. A gay student with the help of the American Civil Liberties Union sued a school district for not protecting him against harassment. The decision in that case has forced the local school systems to provide sensitivity training on LGB issues. One of the high schools has started a student LGB group. LGB faculty and students from the university and public school systems are helping with this necessary training. Again, I am no longer the only one called when this training is desired.

The current climate in our counselor education program also shows recognition of who I am and what I believe. Students with strong conservative Christian fundamentalist backgrounds ordinarily stay away from my classes, thinking that this is the way to avoid discussing LGB counseling issues. However, other faculty members in the counselor education program are also teaching LGB-affirmative therapy, so I don't worry that the students who stay away from my classes won't get the appropriate training.

In 1992, my sexual identity changed from lesbian to bisexual, and I tried to be very out about this, but few people seemed able or willing to accept this. For many people (both heterosexual and LG), bisexuality doesn't exist, and sexual identity doesn't change. As of 2003, this is still a problem for me. Constantly, I am forced to assert that I am bisexual, not lesbian. My relationship with a woman makes it even more difficult for people to think of me as any identity but lesbian. Not only do I assert the continuum of sexual identity (and other non-LGB counseling faculty also assert this), but I am the only faculty member of the counselor education program to discuss transgender issues. Many of my colleagues do not even know what this term means. This is in contrast with the Women Studies Department, where transgender issues have been infused into the curriculum.

My Jewish identity continues to be a problem. I still receive brochures and notes attempting to convert me to Christianity. The local Jewish community still has problems with my outspoken opposition to the war with Iraq and my opposition to Sharon's policies in Israel. The rabbi of my temple also has problems with my beliefs.

Deconstruction of Heterosexual and Christian Hegemony in Academia

My journey in academia has been a journey of struggling against the heterosexual and Christian norms of the academy as well as in the United States as a whole. This has been a greater struggle for me than the struggle against sexism. The first struggle involved recognition that the sexual identity continuum includes lesbians and gay men. The university had to recognize my research and writing and afford these activities the same merit that they give to research and writing in the other academic disciplines. Many LGB counseling professionals in academia face this struggle.

Once my work was recognized and valued, the difficulty, which still continues, revolved around my being designated as the spokesperson on LGB issues (and now transgender issues). Similar to faculty of ethnic and racial minorities, the workload really increases for LGB counseling professionals when they are seen as the only spokespersons for LGB issues. It is tiring to continuously have to force people to look at diversity in broader than gender and racial/ethnic issues.

When I came out as bisexual, I began to struggle not only with the heterosexism of the academy and community but also with the biphobia of members of the LG community who often refused to acknowledge the existence of bisexuality. The fact that I changed sexual identities and went from a lesbian identity to a bisexual identity made many people uncomfortable; the possibility is threatening that, for some people, sexual identity can be fluid and flexible. Counseling professionals who change their sexual identities will be seen as suspect. Many LG people expect bisexuals to betray them and to take on heterosexual privilege. Sexual identity fluidity also threatens the political theme that LG people cannot change their identities. For heterosexuals, it means that they too might meet a person of the same gender, fall in love, and possibly change sexual identities. Asserting a bisexual identity left me with the support of only the feminist community. Life on the margins can be lonely at times, and counseling professionals must recognize this.

The Christian assumption also creates problems for counseling professionals who are not Christian. Along with heterosexism and biphobia, I had to find a way to handle the perception that everyone should be Christian and that this is a Christian nation. At first, having students pray over me seemed harmless. But that soon changed when I realized that this wasn't a gesture of support but another attempt to change me into what they considered normal and acceptable. Those who had problems with my identities could love the sinner (the sexual identity) but not the rejection of Jesus Christ as the savior (the Jewish identity). The brochures, books, and notes left at my office angered me. Much of this material came from counselor education students. I know this because sometimes they acknowledged this in the personal journals that are required in some classes. This still happens, and it still angers me. Non-Christian professionals need to be aware that deconstructing heterosexism includes the Christian assumption of our nation.

Finally, sometimes even the community where support is expected can be rejecting. For me, it was the Jewish community and their rejection of both my political and atheistic beliefs. Counseling professionals must find a base for support. I have done this by seeking out Jews individually in my community and on the Web who have similar beliefs.

Conclusion

Counseling professionals must remember that identity is complex. Few of us perceive of ourselves as one identity at all times and in all situations. Different aspects of our identities are salient at different times. Counseling professionals bring their construction of identity to the counseling students they teach. It is incumbent upon us to be honest about who we are (a professional value) and therefore to use ourselves as models, when possible, to deconstruct heterosexism. I am outside of the mainstream, on the margin as a woman, a Jew, and a bisexual. In my classes, I am out with all of my identities. For some I am a good role model, and for others I am a threat. My very being forces others, including the counseling students, to deconstruct the power and privilege that come with being male, White, heterosexual, and Christian. This has been my life in the academy and in the community where I live.

10

Becoming Visible

A Balance of Challenge and Support

Susanna M. Gallor

University of Maryland

Beginning this narrative has been one of the most difficult and challenging experiences of my life. I did not know or understand at first why I could not just sit down and "crank this out," as my advisor put it. I have procrastinated and put this off for months, and I have gone to great lengths to explain to myself and others why "I have nothing to write about" and that "I don't know what experiences I have to offer." But after much soul-searching and several difficult discussions with some of my closest mentors, I have realized that I do have quite a bit to write about. I do have quite a lot to share with just about anyone who has ever felt different.

I am a woman. I am a lesbian. I am Hispanic, with Spanish, Cuban, and Middle Eastern heritage. I have never, until writing this narrative, articulated the meaning of these identities together and all in one context. I have told people I am a lesbian, I have described to people some of my cultural history and heritage, and I have discussed with others the role of gender in my life. I have never, however, articulated how these separate identities blend together to form and influence one whole "me," nor have I ever discussed how these identities have interacted with one another to influence my reality and worldview.

The process of planning, thinking about, and writing this narrative has been a significant event in my life, an event that clearly illustrates one implication of the heterosexist dominant discourse (as well as racist and sexist discourses) for my life: There is not and never has been a discourse that adequately captures the complexity of my identity. What exists does not provide me with the language I need in order to express who I am and who I need to be, what I have struggled with and how I have overcome those struggles, what I have experienced and what I have not experienced, how life has brought me joy and opportunities, and how life has shut me out and closed the doors. It is extremely difficult, maybe even impossible, to adequately illustrate how the heterosexist dominant discourse has had implications for me personally and professionally. The main reason for this difficulty is that it is impossible to separate my lesbian self from my Hispanic self or my gendered self from my lesbian self. How do I even begin to describe or even understand what makes me "me" or what is my self and what is the "self" that others see?

In both my personal experience and professional experience as a graduate student and psychologist-in-training within the field of counseling psychology, I have been struck by the centrality of identity in every individual's developmental trajectory. In the most basic sense, identities are representations. As I deconstruct who I am and how my different identities have influenced my life, I recognize how my identities, in isolation as well as considered together, serve as representations that peg me as a certain kind of person. I have often found myself faced with an inner struggle to be both invisible and visible at the same time. For me, being invisible means more than just keeping my sexual orientation hidden or not discussing my cultural background. It means finding ways to remain silent, to stay in the background, to avoid drawing attention to myself. Being invisible allowed me to be closeted, safe, ordinary, "normal." However, without pushing myself to be visible, I would not be where I am today. It is impossible to move forward and upward when you cannot be seen and when you have no voice.

Finding the balance between who I am and who I need to be for others also has been part of this conflict between being invisible and visible. One of the most salient examples of this struggle to incorporate others' expectations of me into my life and decision making is my decision to pursue a graduate degree. Throughout my undergraduate years, attending graduate school was an implied goal. Whether or not it was my own personal goal did not matter. It was what my family wanted for me, and it was what would allow me to have the opportunities and lifestyle I would not otherwise have. My options, according to my father, were to go to medical school or law school. Neither of these appealed to me, and the compromise was to pursue a PhD in psychology.

I made the decision to build my career within the field of counseling psychology partly out of interest and passion for the area but also partly out of a feeling of safety and comfort. Theoretically, counseling psychology was the field where, in contrast to other areas within psychology, diversity was embraced and explored, and multicultural issues were considered valuable areas of inquiry for both research and practice. As a Hispanic, lesbian woman just beginning many developmental journeys, the study of multicultural issues felt like an inevitable part of my future training. I knew that wherever I ended up, I needed to be where I would feel safe, respected, and supported.

I began understanding very early on that I would have to engage in certain strategies in order to be "successful," have options in the future, and stand out from all the others who want to pursue PhDs. Unfortunately, many of these strategies entailed behaviors with which I was not naturally comfortable or inclined to do. Approaching professors and other professionals to find opportunities for research and clinical experience was intimidating. Expressing a certain level of confidence in my ability to engage others, come up with novel ideas, and contribute to projects was challenging. Again, "standing out" meant becoming visible, and this was not yet something I felt safe doing. As a young, Hispanic, lesbian woman with very few similar others surrounding me, becoming visible left me and my differences exposed and vulnerable.

Not having a coherent discourse to understand and express my differences, I developed ways to hide those differences and to fit in. For example, my academic life and my social life were vastly segregated during my undergraduate years. During these years, I became involved with several important research and practice opportunities that allowed me to gain the experience I would need in order to set myself apart from others when applying to graduate schools. Although I found myself surrounded by extremely intelligent, thoughtful, supportive, and friendly professors, mentors, and colleagues, I constantly had to gauge the level of safety regarding any kind of discussion of my personal life. Consequently, I rarely discussed my personal life and relationships or connected the two spheres of my life because I often found the discourse to be one that did not include sexual minorities, much less individuals who have double or triple minority statuses.

Seeking out and gaining these important research and clinical skills as an undergraduate was my first challenge in ensuring the safety and supportiveness of my subsequent training environment. With a full and broad range of experience behind me, I was able to apply to excellent counseling psychology graduate programs, particularly programs that were considered multiculturally oriented. My next challenge, though, was how "visible" to make myself during the application process. Again, finding the balance between who I am and who I need to be was my greatest challenge during this process. A question I asked myself and others very close to me was whether or not coming out as a lesbian (which was a very important part of who I am and what I could offer) would hurt me in any way. One part of me struggled with wanting to remain invisible and safe. The other part of me knew that I needed to be in a place where I could feel comfortable and safe without hiding from or fearing the risks of being out. The influence of my Hispanic identity as well as being a woman added yet more layers to the complex process of deciding, and even understanding, how my identities might influence other people's perceptions of me, as well as their actions toward me. I decided one of the best ways to ensure my safety and comfort was to be as "personal" as possible in my personal statement. Programs that chose not to admit me because of my sexual identity, ethnic identity, or gender were probably programs I wouldn't want to be in anyway.

As a graduate student in counseling psychology, although I have been exposed to a variety of resources as well as a number of amazing scholars and practitioners, I have been astounded by the lack of representation of ethnic and sexual minority professionals and students. I have also been struck by the lack of empirical research addressing the experiences and struggles of ethnic minority gay men and lesbian women. The fact that ethnic minority gay men and lesbian women are underrepresented in the literature has obvious parallels to the underrepresentation of women and racial/ethnic minorities more generally. This underrepresentation also seems to parallel a sense of isolation I have felt at times, both professionally and personally. For example, although my graduate program encourages attention to multicultural issues, research, and practice, I am one of very few students with sexual and/or ethnic minority identities. Here, again, I have been faced with the challenge to stretch myself and make very strong efforts to create the kind of environment that would not only allow for my optimal growth and development but also for my comfort and safety. Recognizing this underrepresentation, I decided to join a fellow colleague of mine, also a student in my program who identifies as an ethnic minority, in working to understand and incorporate the importance of multicultural issues in our training, research, and practice (e.g., attending specific programs at conferences together and starting a research project that will explore the training experiences of minority graduate students in counseling psychology). This collaboration has allowed me the invaluable opportunity to feel connected, inspired, and productive, and I am grateful for the guidance and insight it has provided.

It has become clear to me that part of what makes it possible to have a voice and grow both professionally and personally is a network of similar others who can model, teach, lead, and guide. Although I have encountered very few other young, Hispanic, lesbian women in both my social and professional life, I am unbelievably fortunate not only to have an amazing cohort of open and supportive colleagues but also to have an out lesbian graduate advisor as my mentor. This fact has never been as salient as it was during the writing of this narrative. My advisor helped me explore my fears, once again, of exposure and vulnerability, and she also helped me understand what the heterosexist discourse means for me. Dedicated to multicultural and feminist issues in both her research and practice, my advisor was, and always has been, able to listen and understand and guide me in new directions.

One of my only other opportunities for exposure to and connection with large numbers of other ethnic and sexual minority professionals and students is at national conferences. It has not been easy, however, to find the right meetings and presentations to attend, to seek out the individuals whose work has been integral to my own research and professional activities, and to push myself to become "visible." Moreover, as a presumed representative of several groups and because of the assumptions that persist as a result of dominant discourses, I often have felt pressure to be and become a multicultural spokesperson, researcher, and scholar. Although I actually feel quite comfortable in these roles, the pressure has, at times, contributed to the ongoing battle within myself to find a balance between who I am (and want to be) and who I need to be in others' eyes. Regardless of this struggle, connecting with important scholars and professionals in the field, especially those who are ethnic and sexual minorities, is a vital component of my career development, and this entails an effort on my part to expose myself. With organizations and groups such as the American Psychological Association's Division 44 and Division 17 sections on women, lesbian, gay, bisexual, and transgender (LGBT) issues and ethnic diversity, I have had the opportunity to find homes for myself and places where others support LGBT-affirmative and multicultural research, training, education, advocacy, and practice.

As an ethnic minority lesbian woman, the "unacknowledged reality" (Rich, 1993) of not having the same choices and privileges as persons in the majority could have presented a very different set of experiences than the ones I have enjoyed. In retrospect, it is difficult for me to imagine my reality as one without choices. Thankfully, my life experiences thus far can be described as encompassing important relationships with individuals who have encouraged my growth, fostered my differences, and supported my decisions: a nontraditional mother who has repeatedly modeled for me the true meanings of strength, resilience, and confidence; an older, lesbian friend, also in graduate school, who pushed me to imagine myself as more than "just a college student"; an advisor in my graduate program who has embraced my differences and nurtured my growth; and many others. I don't think my experiences and the relationships I've been fortunate enough to be a part of are the norm. I have come to recognize, however, that it is not merely the chance or luck of these particular relationships that have allowed me to see beyond the parameters of heterosexist, racist, and sexist discourses. I have learned how to create and develop atmospheres of inclusion, acceptance, and "choice" for myself. For example, choosing to pursue my professional degree in the field of counseling psychology and, more specifically, in a multiculturally oriented graduate program located in a diverse metropolitan area has afforded me opportunities not only to create rich circles of friends but also to participate in research projects and practical experiences with diverse populations.

Clinical, empirical, theoretical, and anecdotal literature couched in heterosexist assumptions has clear implications for the developmental experiences of gay men and lesbian women. Further implications exist for ethnic minority gay men and lesbian women who are even more invisible due to sexist, racist, and heterosexist assumptions. The potential risks and threats that result from the heterosexist, sexist, and racist discourse in both my personal and professional life have established the need for me to be very proactive in the decisions I make and the environments I create for myself, and they also have presented me with valuable opportunities and experiences that have been integral to the development of and appreciation for my multiple identity statuses. In many respects, I have really had to stretch myself and all of my various "comfort zones." As an ethnic and sexual minority, my comfort zones developed in part to serve an important protective function, and they were difficult to break down. My minority statuses not only posed a risk for experiencing direct discrimination, they also served as representations that might imply what kind of a person I was and what kind of a life I had. The exposure and vulnerability needed to stand out and express what kind of a person I really am in this very interpersonal field of psychology have often served as barriers that have been difficult to get past. For me, the writing of this narrative has been my latest challenge in finding the right words, along with a good amount of courage, to express who I am and who I have become. Writing these words has been difficult but not impossible. I'm just one step closer to becoming visible.

Reference

Rich, A. (1993). Compulsory heterosexuality and lesbian existence. In H. Abelove, M. A. Barale, & D.M. Halperin (Eds.), *The Lesbian and Gay Studies Reader* (pp. 227–254). New York: Routledge, Inc.

11

From Naïf to Activist

Personal Reflections of an Ally

Jane Goodman

Oakland University

Although there has been increasing attention to lesbian, gay, bisexual, and transgender (LGBT) issues in the counseling literature and in multicultural courses for counseling students, there is still a dominant heterosexist discourse. For example, state licenses are usually for marriage and family counseling. The American Counseling Association's (ACA) "family" division is called the International Association for Marriage and Family Counseling; and many family systems courses are titled "Marriage and Family." (I am proud that my institution has a "Couple and Family" course and "Couple and Family" advanced-specialization course sequence.) Multicultural courses usually address the needs of LGBT students and clients, but students tell me that it feels like there is a competition as to which minority culture gets the most attention—and that LGBT issues often lose out. It appears that even when professors are consciously addressing issues of diversity, heterosexist dialogue holds sway. Elsewhere in this book, elements of the domination of heterosexist discourse have been more systematically outlined. I mention these because they are examples of the sometimes subtle ways in which LGBT counselors and clients can be marginalized, often by well-intentioned but naive colleagues and therapists or counselors. In the following pages, I will discuss my own growing awareness of this marginalization.

I am very flattered to have been asked, as an ally, to write a few pages about my own experiences with LGBT issues. I will write about my awakening knowledge of individuals and their oppressions, my growing awareness of the need for political advocacy within and outside the counseling profession, and my increasing respect for the challenges faced and the discrimination experienced by people whose primary sexual orientation is not heterosexual. Let me talk about this in a series of vignettes.

Some years ago, in the 1970s, I worked with a woman a few years younger than me, whom I will call "Linda" here. Linda was then in her mid-20s. She worked in the counseling agency where I worked. This young woman was struggling with her sexual identity. She was attracted to women, but she believed that if she "worked hard enough" she could change this. This belief was rooted in a family system that held fundamentalist Christian beliefs, as well as in society's general prejudice towards lesbians. To help herself with this struggle, she began seeing a therapist. The therapist shared her belief that she could and should change her orientation. As we got to know each other and became friends, Linda began to share with me her thoughts and feelings about this struggle.

At that time in my life, I did not know anyone who self-identified as LGBT. The level of homoprejudice of the times created the conditions that made this difficult. I was also naive, unexposed to many people different from myself in education and socioeconomic status. My grandparents on both sides were Jewish immigrants who came to this country from Eastern Europe around 1900. Although I was raised in a largely Irish Catholic neighborhood and lived at the time in a community that was largely African American, both of these were middle-class, traditional neighborhoods. People of the same gender who shared houses were called "roommates." It never occurred to me that they had deeper, sexual relationships. And in those days, nobody else, including the couples involved, ever spoke about any other relationship.

It became clear to me very quickly that my friend Linda was indeed a lesbian. The efforts of her therapist to change her orientation were actually rather cruel, although I believe unintentionally so. And they were ultimately, from the therapist's perspective, unsuccessful. From my friend Linda's perspective, however, the decision to terminate her therapy allowed her to be true to herself and develop a loving relationship with a woman. How sad it is to me as a professional that it was necessary to leave therapy to achieve personal growth!

What were my feelings during all of this? First, I became firmly convinced that Linda's therapist was wrong, and I developed a deep and abiding anger at her for this. Although I truly believe that her beliefs were a product of her environment, upbringing, and training, or lack thereof, I found it hard to forgive her for the pain she caused my friend. I believed, and still do, that it was her obligation to learn about the needs of women like Linda or refer her to someone who had that knowledge and understanding.

Why do I think this experience is so important? As I have said, I was naive in many ways. I believed that counselors should always act in the best interests of their clients. This particular counselor was highly respected by most and adored by many. I certainly found myself in the ranks of those who thought she was wonderful. And yet she was so hurtful to my colleague. How do I make meaning of this? It helped me to understand the depth of homoprejudice that existed, how unconscious it often is, and how much I needed to learn. I believe it was the beginning of my understanding that thinking I was not a prejudiced person was not enough: I needed information.

As counselors, we have an ethical requirement to work only with issues around which we have adequate training. Those ethical guidelines were, in my opinion, violated in this case. I suspect that the therapist considered Linda's issue to be a moral one. This only increases her culpability in my mind, since we have also an ethical obligation not to impose our moral beliefs. That Linda was willing to try to change her orientation, for a while, does not exculpate her therapist. I guess it is clear that I still harbor anger, some 30 years later. Some of this probably comes from discovering "feet of clay" in an admired mentor. But more of the anger stems from seeing hurt where help was sought. Reflecting on the power we have as counselors to make a difference in people's lives, I am again aware how our own biases can cause harm.

As I matured both personally and as a professional, my acquaintances among the LGBT population increased. This is probably a result of three factors: (1) as my world expanded, I got to know more people; (2) more people were open about their sexual orientations; and (3) as I got to know more people, I was seen as an "ally," and additional people were open to me. Several years ago, I attended a daylong in-service sponsored by ACA. Association leaders were invited to attend either a day of training on issues of race and ethnicity or one on LGBT issues. About 90%, perhaps more, of the leaders chose the session on race and ethnicity. I and a few others attended the LGBT session, wonderfully led by some of the founders of the Association for Gay, Lesbian and Bisexual Issues in Counseling (AGLBIC). During that session, one of the presenters described being aware from a young age that he was somehow "different" from other children. This resonated with me because, although heterosexual, I also felt "different" from a young age. In my case, it was probably from two causes: I was Jewish in a largely Catholic community, a nonobservant Jew at that, and I was a smart girl. When I was growing up, only boys were supposed to be smart, and people were supposed to take religion seriously. As I puzzle over why so many people are bothered by homosexuality, I wonder whether these early experiences helped me be accepting of difference.

I mentioned earlier that I lived for many years in a largely African American community. In the 60s and 70s it was considered ideal to be "color-blind." Many Black and White people chose to live in our area because of, not despite, its racial integration. We lived there because we wanted to raise our children in an integrated society. In doing so, however, I suspect we glossed over some of the racism inherent in the United States and in our community. Because we were a largely middle-class community and because we were similar in our education and occupations, we found it easy to ignore real differences that existed in the way the rest of the world treated us. At least the White people did! I suspect that many of the African American neighbors were well aware of racism and experienced it in myriad ways I probably can never truly understand.

Why am I talking about this in an article about my experiences with LGBT issues? Because I believe that I was taken in by the same myth in regard to sexual orientation as I was in regard to race. I believed that if I was not interested in you as a romantic or sexual partner, what did I care about your orientation? I missed the point that if the rest of the world cared—if you experienced discrimination—that it mattered even in our relationship. As we know from extensive research on effective counseling, the nature of the relationship between the counselor and the client is the prime determinant of successful outcomes for the client. If our counseling relationship is tainted by my lack of understanding, I am a less effective helper. Charles Willie told the audience at the opening session of the ACA conference in New Orleans in 2002 that effective counseling depends on respect from the counselor and trust from the client. If I am going to demonstrate respect for my LGBT clients, I must be knowledgeable and aware of the effects of the dominant heterosexist discourse and its impact on them. If my clients are going to have trust in me, I must find a way to demonstrate that knowledge and awareness.

I believe that this knowledge is acquired in layers, including both didactic and experiential components. For me, the experiential are usually the most powerful. For example, about 15 years ago, my husband and I took a ferry from Boston to Provincetown, on Cape Cod. As we got off the ferry, we saw same-sex couples strolling along the street, hand in hand. My eyes misted, and I choked up as I realized I had not seen this before, people able to express affection openly—a freedom I had taken for granted. I wondered what it must be like to always wonder how others will react to who you are, even as you go about your normal life business. Perhaps I added at that time another layer of understanding. I hope so.

I have tried to describe in the foregoing my own personal development as an ally along with the implications for me as a counselor. In the following, I will describe some of the impact that I believe this development has had on me in my leadership roles in ACA. I sat on the Governing Council of ACA for 3 years as a representative of the National Career

Development Association before I was elected president of ACA. A resolution was introduced regarding equal rights for sexual minorities. I don't remember the specific content, but what I do remember is that one member of that body opposed it on the grounds of "We have to protect our children." My rage turned to admiration as the AGLBIC representative replied, something to this effect: "We do indeed. And we know that LGBT children have higher rates of suicide, are bullied more, and have a tougher time in school than other children. That is why we must protect the rights of all." I am not doing justice to the eloquence of her remarks, but I hope the point is clear. Her words and the basic decency of the Governing Council prevailed, and the resolution passed easily. But I relearned how vulnerable we all are to bigotry and how vigilant we must be to protect the rights of all.

Two regions of ACA were distressed about this vote, as were some of the divisions, and asked that it be reconsidered. Their avowed reasoning was that they had not had time to discuss the resolutions and give input. The president of ACA, responding to the request, chose to react to the overt statement rather than its potential undertones. She asked me to organize a "town meeting" for the next conference, at which the issues could be discussed. The Governing Council was asked to listen to the input, as requested. I asked two respected past ACA presidents to conduct the meeting. They masterfully allowed full discussion, without any ugliness or rancor. About 100 people were in attendance, and it was my perception that the goals of the meeting were reached. As an example, representatives from the American Mental Health Counselors Association, who were worried about some of the ethical repercussions of saying that reparative therapies were unproven, left after the meeting with representatives from AGLBIC to productively continue the dialogue. The statement that I remember most vividly was one from a member of ACA from Wyoming, who said why he felt these resolutions were important. He stated that he came from a small, homogeneous town, and that one of the reasons he belonged to ACA and participated in its conferences was to expand his horizons, not live within their confines. Again, memory does not do justice to his eloquence, but the power of his statement was his plea for attendees to grow rather than defend preconceived biases.

What are the implications of my personal experiences for counselors? First, it is important to allow ourselves to be open to awareness of oppression in all its forms. It is important to realize that the mantra of "I treat all people the same" doesn't work when you are a member of a dominant group relating to someone who is a member of an oppressed group. The aforementioned mantra has been used to attack diversity training in general. It is the position of its proponents that each client is unique and therefore all should be treated in the same way. It is my hope that this book will help counseling professionals to see the need to be informed about the life experiences of members of oppressed groups. It is also important to consider how many identities we all hold—in my case, female, Jewish, middle class, late middle-aged, highly educated, parent and grandparent, heterosexual, married, and probably others I am not thinking about.

I direct an adult career counseling center. Several years ago I posted signs on the doors that said, "I'm Willing to Talk About:" The list begins, "Sexual Orientation, AIDS, Bisexual, Dating, Pregnancy, Death of a Loved One, Incest, Drugs, Name-Calling, Love, Gay, Neglect, Culture, Parents, Heritage, Harassment, Teachers, Equality, Peer Pressure . . ." The students who worked for me reported that the personal issues raised during their counseling sessions increased and that, in particular, several clients discussed their concerns about the impact of their sexual orientations on their career decision making and job-searching. The learning: People who are fearful of discrimination will be more open when it is clear that it is safe.

I was honored to be in a position to make the motion for AGLBIC to become a division of ACA. There are also now ACA-endorsed advocacy competencies. Let us hope that both new and experienced counselors become aware of these competencies and use them to oppose oppression wherever it rears its head.

As I stated earlier, I learn best experientially. It is my hope that readers of this chapter can learn vicariously from my experiences and can increase their knowledge about and sensitivity to LGBT issues. The U.S. Supreme Court upheld race-sensitive admissions policies at the University of Michigan with the statement that they hoped that 25 years from now such policies would no longer be necessary. It is my hope that 25 years from now the heterosexist discourse will be something only to be read about as history.

12

We Are All Men and We Need Each Other Too

Phillip D. Johnson

Western Michigan University

Having worked for a year after completing my undergraduate education, I was ready to attend graduate school in counseling and had to find a place to live. A former professor from the undergraduate institution I attended just happened to be visiting the city where the graduate school was located, and she told me about two guys, Earl and Robert (pseudonyms), who were looking for a roommate. Both Earl and Robert were already in the program that I was about to enter. I could hardly believe my luck; it took less than a day to get a promising lead on an apartment. Immediately, I called and inquired about the apartment. The conversation went very well; Earl and Robert were happy to get a roommate recommended by someone they knew and trusted, and being an African American male myself, I was glad to be rooming with two African American men who could help me adjust to graduate school and a new city.

When Earl, Robert, and I met in person the first time, I noticed that their speech and gestures seemed effeminate. My unease must have been apparent because after a few minutes, Robert asked me whether I knew that he and Earl were gay. I said, "No, I didn't know that." I was stunned! My former professor never mentioned that they were gay when telling me about the apartment. She only mentioned that they were "really nice guys." The terror I felt inside was masked by the cool, confident front I struggled to maintain. Nothing in my 23 years had prepared me for this moment. As a young boy, I was taught to harass and beat up "faggots." The worst thing a boy in my neighborhood could be called was "faggot," and if someone called you one, that person either had to back down or fight. To be gay was to be inhuman, as in "Oh, he's one of those things." Now, I might be sharing an apartment with two of "them" and looking to them for guidance as I attempted to successfully complete the graduate program I was about to enter.

Earl and Robert explained that if I intended to be their roommate, it was important for me to understand and be comfortable with their lifestyle and them as gay men. They recommended that I accompany them that evening so that I might become acquainted with the world in which they lived. Late that night, Earl and Robert took me to the section of the city where the gay bars were located. Somewhere along the way, we seemed to cross an imaginary line into a world where only men existed, men talking, holding hands, hugging, kissing, arguing, fighting, crying, laughing, dancing . . . living. There was not a woman to be found in this ocean of men. Earl and Robert decided to take me to a dimly lit gay bar where the music blared and men danced, danced together. I was in shock. Earl and Robert checked in to assess my status. Paralyzed with fear, I stood in one place, barely breathing, trying not to make eye contact with anyone for more than an instant, and then redirecting my gaze. Over and over to myself I prayed, "Lord, please don't let anyone ask to me dance." The next day, they asked me whether I still wanted to be their roommate, and I said "Yes."

A month later, Earl rented a U-Haul truck and helped me move the furniture I had stored in Virginia back to our apartment. I knew that my mother and sisters would have a few questions once they met him. Upon meeting Earl, everyone was pleasant and polite; however, every time Earl "switched" through the living room mama looked at me or at my sister who, in turn, just shook her head from side to side. I suspected they thought Earl was gay, but no one said a word, there was only silence. I also had a feeling that they thought I was gay too, because Earl was my roommate, but no one said a word, there was only silence. I didn't want them to think that I was gay; I wanted to make sure they didn't have the "wrong" idea. I also felt anger. So what if Earl is gay, what difference does it make? Why am I so anxious to distance myself from Earl? What does it matter if they think I am gay? In my family, we didn't talk about such things, so that day in mama's living room, I never said a word. There was only silence. Unfortunately, far too many African Americans have been silent about homosexuality and the oppression that African American lesbians and gays experience in Black communities, as well as the steep price we all pay for that silence (Constantine-Simms, 2000; Harper, 1996). Today, I choose to join the ever-growing number of Black men who struggle to create safe spaces for Black men to speak freely about their fears, hopes, strengths, and weaknesses in order that we might be more fully human.

In one sense, it is not very challenging to talk about my experiences with Robert and Earl because it has been more than 20 years since they occurred. The unease that I felt upon learning the two were gay, the homophobic terror that I experienced in the club that night, the impulse I felt to disavow Earl as a Black gay man, and the need I had to establish my heterosexuality and masculinity in the living room that day, all occurred in the past. The "how I used to be but not how I am now; the not-me" is all part of a painful past that supposedly gives birth to a different self, a self free of prejudices and biases, as in "I used to be homophobic and heterosexist, but not anymore." As I assess where I am today, however, I am compelled to ask: Why haven't my understanding and commitment grown more over the past 20 years? Why have I been so reluctant to reflect seriously on issues surrounding lesbian and gay sexuality as a counseling professional? How can I be so committed to racial justice and be so indifferent toward lesbian and gay rights? There seem to be no simple answers to these questions.

Certainly, on an individual level, I could have shown more interest in and taken more personal responsibility for the plight of lesbian and gay women and men. For instance, it troubles me to consider how quickly Robert's and Earl's plight as Black gay men seemed to fade from my consciousness once we were no longer roommates. When I was no longer forced to think about or deal with the harassment and oppression they faced daily, I chose not to. It became their problem and not mine. Even more troubling has been my failure to challenge heterosexist and homophobic talk personally and professionally, not wishing to have my own masculinity called into question or to further jeopardize my shaky position in the club of "real men." However, the failure to care enough or take responsibility only partially answers the questions raised above. Critical though they may be, it is important not to overemphasize such individual factors. To do so is to reduce the political, historical, and cultural to causative factors within the individual, to decontextualize and overpsychologize the origins of my silence. Attention is directed away from the social and material arrangements that make it difficult for me to speak. My silence is also a matter of U.S. history and politics.

Throughout American history, the sexuality of Black men and women has been maliciously attacked (Jordan, 1995). Within the dominant U.S. culture, Black men and women have always been regarded as highly sexualized, wanton beings. Sexuality involves a person's self-image; the way a person defines his or her femininity or masculinity. It refers to one's humanity, and to malign Black people's sexuality is to call into question their very humanity. A major reason Black sexuality has been a primary target is that Black people have been absolutely essential to U.S. economic power, initially as free labor and later as cheap labor (Douglas, 1999). The ability to freely exploit Black bodies has been critical to the labor market. Black sexuality was attacked within U.S. society because it was a way to dehumanize Black men and Black women. Such dehumanization has made it easier to enslave Black people and to treat them merely as property and labor commodities rather than as human beings. It is necessary to impugn Black sexuality in order to suggest that Black people are inferior beings. In the United States, it is the White middle-class family organized around a monogamous, heterosexual couple that is the norm. Sexual practices and groups who do not follow this norm are labeled "deviant" and considered to be threatening. This norm requires stigmatizing African Americans as being deviant, and a primary source of this assumed deviancy can be traced to allegations about Black sexuality (Douglas, 1999).

More than ever, I realize that African Americans are not just silent about homosexuality and the oppression that African American lesbians and gays experience in Black communities. The attacks on their sexuality have rendered African Americans practically voiceless on any matter related to sexuality. Anxious to protect their humanity, they have practically ceased speaking. I have come to understand that my own silence is part of a larger, deeper silence, a silence that has been nurtured over four centuries to protect the humanity of Black people. However, as the oppression of lesbians and gays has become a major human rights issue in the Western world and AIDS continues to ravage Black communities here in the United States and abroad, African American counselors and psychologists can no longer afford to remain silent on matters pertaining to sexuality, and homosexuality in particular. To refuse to engage in an honest, open dialogue guarantees that African American communities will continue to be inadequately prepared to address significant matters of life and death for Black people.

The times seem to demand that African American counselors find ways to help Black people affirm their sexuality in all of its complexity, even as they continue to struggle to liberate themselves and claim their full humanity. Counselors must help create a sexual discourse that will help Black people to understand how dominant U.S. culture has contributed to Black sexuality, a discourse that will offer more life-affirming views and attitudes concerning Black sexuality. The tendency of some African American counseling professionals to position themselves as heterosexuals in a struggle against European American lesbian and gay professionals will contribute little to the realization of that goal. Such discourse does not challenge White lesbians and gays to confront their racism, nor does it force Black heterosexuals to deal with their homophobia.

For me, the first step is acknowledging that there is no way for me to have been reared in a heterosexist society without being affected by it on a personal level. I did not escape unscathed. The assumption that some heterosexism resides in every heterosexual who has been brought up in the United States seems reasonable to me. This does not mean that I am consciously or overtly heterosexist. It does mean that I have these issues to deal with individually. This is my legacy personally and professionally, and I must face it.

I must remember that heterosexism is not only something that exists inside of me as an attitude, a collection of stereotypes, or a bad intention that requires a change in how I feel, think, and behave. It is embedded in an economic system organized around competition over scarce resources, a system that is heterosexually dominated, heterosexually identified, and heterosexually centered. To maintain its own legitimacy, the counseling profession reflects the core values of the larger society. Given this reality, not only must I speak out against heterosexist ideology and practices that guide the operation of most of our social institutions, the heterosexist ideology and practices that guide the counseling profession must be challenged as well. For example, many in our society believe that heterosexuality is universal and unchanging, despite the fact that the concept is only one way of perceiving, categorizing, and imagining relations between the sexes. Unfortunately, the counseling profession has tended to approach the concept of heterosexuality ahistorically, neglecting to study it in historical context. In doing so, the profession has privileged and protected the idea of heterosexuality from challenge. My silence only promotes heterosexual privilege and lesbian and gay oppression.

As an African American counseling professional, I am called upon to join with other African Americans inside and outside the profession who are reexamining their definitions of manhood and confronting their homophobia and heterosexism. Homophobia and heterosexism mean that I allow myself to be robbed of the brotherhood and strength of Black gay men because I am afraid of being called gay myself. Homophobia and heterosexism are terrible barriers to our working together. Hutchinson (2000) makes the point that Black men should be the last ones in America to jettison other Blacks who may be in a position to make a valuable contribution to the struggle for freedom and Black well-being, and I agree. There is no shortage of work to be done. Failed schools, an inadequate comprehensive AIDS education prevention program, the mass incarceration of Black men and women, and the despair and hopelessness that permeate many Black communities across the United States demand immediate attention. It is clear that we share many concerns as Black men. How do we organize around our differences, neither denying nor exaggerating them? In truth, we are all men and we need each other.

References

Constantine-Simms, D. (Ed.). (2000). *The greatest taboo.* New York: Alyson Publications.

Douglas, B. K. (1999). *Sexuality and the Black church.* Maryknoll, NY: Orbis Books.

Griffin, H. (2000). Their own received them not: African American lesbians and gays in Black churches. In D. Constantine-Simms (Ed.), *The greatest taboo* (pp. 110–121). New York: Alyson Publications.

Harper, B. P. (1996). *Are we not men?* New York: Oxford University Press.

Hutchinson, O. E. (2000). My gay problem your Black problem. In D. Constantine-Simms (Ed.), *The greatest taboo* (pp. 2–6). New York: Alyson Publications.

Jordan, W. (1995). *White over Black.* Chapel Hill: University of North Carolina Press.

13

Blessed Be the Ties That Bind

Michael Mobley

University of Missouri–Columbia

Stacey M. Pearson

University of Michigan

In this narrative on the heterosexist dominant discourse, we have decided (after careful weeks of reflection and deliberation) to tell the story of a cultural impasse we experienced during graduate school. A *cultural impasse* is an event resulting from a unique set of culturally based interactional dynamics that adversely affects the optimal functioning of cross-cultural interactions among individuals (Mobley & Trad, 1995).

Background

Stacey: It was the beginning of my graduate school career, and I was quite excited by the prospect of being called "Doctor" someday. Like most students of color, I had heard numerous horror stories about racial oppression in graduate school and the loneliness and isolation from being "the only one." Needless to say, at the first day of orientation, I was delighted to see two other African American students in my cohort of seven. For weeks, we reveled in the beauty of racial solidarity along with brotherhood and sisterhood. At this point, I was unaware of how this bond would be quickly placed in jeopardy between Michael and I.

Prior to this point in my life, my ethnic identity was the primary lens for my worldview, with fleeting attention to my gender identity and certainly no reflection about my sexual/affectional orientation. I began the program unaware of my privilege around being straight and even more ignorant of my own homophobia and heterosexist attitudes and behaviors. In fact, I was reared in an environment steeped in traditional Christian values, and the gay people in my family of origin were out, but we often engaged in unfavorable whispers about them.

Michael: As I embarked on my PhD program, I was quite excited, nervous, and anxious. My excitement was fueled by knowing I was moving toward my goal of becoming a counseling psychologist and focusing on diversity issues. My nervous and anxious feelings were related to wondering whether I would do well in the PhD program. How difficult would the classes and workload be? How would others respond to my openness about being a gay man?

You see, during my doctoral orientation seminar, I introduced myself and consciously stated, "As a gay man, I am interested in gay and lesbian issues." Coming out was not a headline announcement. It simply was making visible an invisible part of my cultural identity. Despite my comfort and ease in being open, I still worried about whether African American students such as Stacey in my cohort would be accepting of me. Within the first few weeks, I discovered that Stacey and I were from the same geographic region of the state. In fact, we carpooled home one weekend and openly discussed and shared our histories, including our families, religion, and my sexual orientation. Our one-way, 4-hour road trip journey forged a feeling of sister-brother bonding for me.

Cultural Impasse

Michael: It was late in the afternoon, and the two of us were working on a presentation proposal that was, as many of us are all too familiar with, to be postmarked by 5:00 p.m. On top of this pressing deadline, Stacey had a scheduled flight departing in the early evening, for which I agreed to drop her off at the airport. As we near completing the proposal, Stacey was responsible for final editing and printing the document while I worked on the title page. As I glanced at the printed document that Stacey had indicated was finished, I noticed a glaring error. Any and all references to sexual orientation were deleted from the proposal. I thought to myself: "What's going on here?"

Stacey: As Michael and I sat and worked on our first conference proposal, I became gradually uncomfortable. I flashed back to various messages I had received during my socialization that opposed the inclusion of sexual orientation in my work unless, of course, it was a heterosexual orientation. Interestingly, the night before this incident, I attended a campus meeting of Christians wherein the speaker shared the reasons why Christians should not be "gay affirming." So here I sat, experiencing major dissonance around my Christian identity, my professional identity, as well as my ethnic identity, given Michael and I were both African Americans. I knew I cared about this man sitting across from me, but I also knew what I had been taught and had embraced as my own beliefs about homosexuality. I decided to maintain silence until I could consult with someone about how I could handle this conflict. However, I was left to make the final revisions on the proposal, so I took matters in my own hands and erased the references made to sexual orientation. We sat to review the proposal one last time, and I sat silently praying I would not be discovered. No sooner than whispering this prayer, I was confronted about the deletion.

Michael: "Stacey, what happened to the references to sexual orientation?" I asked.

Stacey: Anxious, confused, and scared, I parroted the speaker from the night before and stated, "Michael, I cannot be gay affirming." What a relief, I thought, as I said it, but I was unprepared for what followed.

Michael: Hearing this, I was immediately shocked, angered, and felt a deep sense of disbelief followed by an internal rage. My gay cultural identity was being deleted, denied, and dejected in my very presence. And there was a conscious deliberate effort to eradicate the "gay references"—but as I experienced, "my gayness." I feared that Stacey represented one of those African Americans who gave lip service to being friends with an African American lesbian, gay, or bisexual (LGB) person but in reality was obviously not fully comfortable and accepting due to "the church." I had a conscious awareness that a deliberate act was committed in using the cursor key, highlighting segments of text, and hitting the delete button to eradicate signs of gayness. The second level of consciousness as a reflection today is that I felt as if I became Ralph Ellison's *Invisible Man* in front of Stacey. It was shocking. My new African American friend/sister had the power to make me disappear, desired to make me disappear—that is, the gay part of me.

Stacey: The look of horror on the face of this person who had become more than a peer—a friend—hit me so hard I thought I would faint or throw up right there in the computer lab. That feeling of queasiness is still present as I write this piece now, not only because I was outed as an oppressor but also because I had hurt my friend. In my eyes, this offense was much more egregious than any concerns I previously had about being "gay affirming."

Michael: An intense anger surfaced within me. I had to contain my rage and simply state to her, "It's going back in." I felt it was important to be assertive about my position.

Stacey: In an effort to relieve the tension and reconcile the hurting words I had spoken, I quickly acquiesced and agreed that we "put the references to sexual orientation back in."

Michael: Still in shock, I asked myself, "Does Stacey really see me for who I really am? Does she really accept me for who I am, in my totality of cultural identities? Do I become invisible to her when my cultural identity status as a gay man becomes visible?"

Stacey: The intimacies and camaraderie that I had shared with Michael made it hard for me to continue to distance myself from this part of his identity and to continue to hide behind the parts of my identity that were in conflict with him being gay. While Michael was openly gay in our program, it was at this moment that I had to deal with my feelings related to his gay identity.

Michael: Having reinserted "sexual orientation" in our proposal, Stacey and I left the computer lab to get her to the airport. While driving my car, I let Stacey know I wanted us to discuss this matter after she returned. During the following week, the first opportunity we were alone, I stated to Stacey, "We need to talk." I recall her response to me: "I kept saying to myself, I know that Michael is not going to let this go."

Stacey: Feeling afraid of losing the relationship and guilty by the hurt and pain on his face, I committed both to Michael and myself that I would do the work needed to help us work through this issue and points of conflict in the relationship.

Toward Resolution of Our Cultural Impasse

Stacey: Michael and I met to process. I came to the meeting with a plethora of feelings, including confusion, dissonance, fear, anxiety, and guilt, along with my own hurt and pain. I felt rejected. While the rejection was around my beliefs, it was also a rejection of a central part of me. I was also hurt by Michael's anger toward me, along with feeling guilty for causing the pain I saw in his eyes.

We shared perspectives on both the process and content of the cultural impasse. While both of us had very strong convictions, we were able to reach a resolution for the moment. There was no agreement, but we established an increased understanding of our individual perspectives.

Michael: I feared that the bond of trust established between the two of us as African Americans, sister-brother, and doctoral trainees would be broken. Would this cultural impasse stretch our relationship beyond repair? I realized that a safe space had to be created for me to share my "hurt" and hear and understand Stacey's "hurt" as well. We needed to "walk in each other's shoes." For me, I needed Stacey to truly listen, hear, and understand the source of my perceived experience of her act of intolerance, heterosexism, and disrespect of my identity as a gay man. Thus, we were both willing to expose our positions of vulnerability, sources of pain, in order to move toward healing the rupture in our relationship.

Stacey: While some "working through" happened in that meeting, it was the time I put in afterward that brought real resolution for me. The first step for me was to actually begin to take ownership for my homophobia, along with giving voice to my heterosexual privilege. I was able to connect with sexual orientation oppression because of my own experiences with racial discrimination. This act of personalizing oppression removed the distance I had placed between LGB people and me. I also made an effort to understand and respect the culture, history, and struggles of LGB individuals. Last, I consulted others who seemed to have resolved the conflict I was facing.

Over the years, I have continued to explore which parts of my cultural and religious identities are salient and which parts no longer fit. There are days when I am still not sure how to negotiate my religious identity and my identity as an ally. However, what I am sure about is that being affirming of all people, including LGB people, is important and crucial for me.

Michael: Reflection on this experience offers me insight about the power I can have with others as an openly gay man. I was and continue to possess a self-accepting and assertive attitude of my identity as a gay man. From this position, however, I now believe that I may present an unconscious disregard for individuals such as Stacey who may genuinely struggle to accept, affirm, or embrace LGB individuals. My self-empowerment, that is, asserting my comfortableness in being an openly self-affirming and self-accepting gay man, is laced with an unconscious awareness of its potential effect on others in my environment. I contend that my self-empowerment as a gay man at times may represent a form of "righteousness." How dare anyone deny me the freedom to be me? Even if it means that they must stifle or hide their own heterosexism and homophobia in a dark closet, perhaps due to "political correctness." I now recognize the importance of maintaining my power in self-identifying but also affording a safe space for another to respond genuinely while remaining open that a conflict, cultural impasse, may result.

For me, I inadvertently "stepped back" and afforded both Stacey as well as myself an opportunity to reflect on the cultural impasse we were experiencing. I understood that our cultural impasse primarily involved conflicting perspectives related to African American racial identity ego status as well as acceptance and comfortableness with nondominant sexual orientation identity status. In acknowledging that our socialization process generally fosters heterosexism and homophobia, it was crucial for me to meet Stacey where she was, understand her degree of openness and tolerance of me as an African American gay male at this time, and await an opportunity for further growth and change as a result of our continued dialogue and interaction as friends. Equally, I had to displace my indignant hostility and discomfort with her inability to "immediately" accept and affirm me as an African American gay male who also identifies as a Christian. I would need to live with the current cultural tension until we both developed an acceptance of each other's position.

Rewards of Moving Toward Resolving Our Cultural Impasse

Stacey: Thank God for the resolution, because the rewards have been enormous. First and most important, my relationship with my colleague and friend is solid as a rock. We have gone through both the good and bad times with each other, including comps, dissertation, and graduation, but also family deaths and births, the ups and downs of romantic relationships, and joys and sorrows of establishing careers. I believe in Michael and in our relationship, and he serves as a source of inspiration and encouragement for me. Before our relationship, I was unaware that by limiting my worldview to only my racial and ethnic identity I was losing the richness of life outside of this purview. Now, I see the world as more than Black and White, and I am more than Black; but also other parts of my identity, including gender, socioeconomic status, occupational status, a Northerner with Southern roots, straight, Christian, and an ally are equally important and salient in my life. Embracing the totality of all parts of my identity and the identities of others has made me a better clinician, colleague, and friend. In addition, in the past 12 years, I have developed countless other meaningful relationships with people who are culturally similar to and different from me; many of these relationships may not have been created if we, I, had not resolved this significant cultural impasse.

Michael: Today, I am very proud of the depth of our relationship. I am very supportive of each of Stacey's dimensions of cultural identity. I recognize that within our relationship, we openly explore and discuss issues related to sexual orientation, religion, Christianity, gender, spirituality, and romantic relationships. In addition, we integrate an increased awareness of how culture influences our personal as well as professional lives. Indeed, we have created a "shared cultural understanding," respecting, validating, and affirming our unique facets of cultural identities. We would like to encourage those of you with similar backgrounds to continue the exploration process that will allow you to fight for the rights for all people.

In our profession, many individuals may silently act, making decisions resulting in "exclusion" of oppressed sexual minority individuals without ever whispering or shouting a single word. As a participant-observer and recent facilitator of *Difficult Dialogues* at the National Multicultural Conference and Summit II, I truly value and appreciate counseling professionals and trainees who are willing to risk, experience vulnerability, and seek healing as a result of experiencing cultural impasses. Let love abound and honor *all* the ties that bind us.

Process Model for Resolving Cultural Impasses

The goal in resolving a cultural impasse is for both individuals to reestablish cultural affirmation and foster empowerment, defined as "a process of increasing personal, interpersonal, or political power so that individuals can take action to improve their life situations" (Gutiérrez, 1990, p. 149). To meet these goals, we had to first identify and recognize that we were experiencing a cultural conflict. Second, we had to determine cultural influences that created the adverse interaction between us. We noted that Stacey's religious and Christian values were in conflict with Michael's openly, accepting gay posture, personally and professionally. Third, both individuals had to assess his or her own level of sensitivity and cultural knowledge base relevant to cultural impasse dynamics. Fourth, it was critical to select a possible range of culturally appropriate interventions for moving toward resolution of the cultural impasse. We were both in agreement that we needed to meet and, in the words of newly developing counselor trainees, "process our issues." In processing the cultural impasse, a fifth step became crucial, that as individuals we needed to articulate in a respectful and affirming manner our understanding of what specific cultural dynamics had contributed to the conflict.

References

Gutiérrez, L. M. (1990). Working with women of color: An empowerment perspective. *Social Work, 35,* 149–153.

Mobley, M., & Trad, A. M. (1995, August). *Cultural impasses in the therapeutic relationship.* Paper presented at the American Psychological Association Annual Convention, New York.

14

Sexual Orientation, Shame, and Silence

Reflections on Graduate Training

John M. O'Brien

Independent Practice, Portland, Maine

Growing up in a middle-class, Irish Catholic family in a suburb of Boston, I was indoctrinated into a staunchly Democratic, religiously conservative view of life and the world. I was also taught from an early age about the very real and deleterious effects of discrimination. My grandparents spoke with great pride about surviving in a world where job advertisements blatantly stated, "Irish (or Catholics) need not apply." My grandmother would often tell me that my life would be free of prejudice and that I was destined to achieve anything I wanted.

Unlike many other lesbian, gay, and bisexual (LGB) persons, I became aware of my sexual orientation only in my late teens. When I first experienced a same-sex attraction, I labeled it a "close friendship" and proceeded to deny my true self. My upbringing told me that being gay was wrong, "morally depraved." As an only son, I was expected to get married and have a son to perpetuate the family name. How could I disappoint my family? How could I allow myself to give in to "moral weakness"?

For several years, I struggled to maintain a heterosexual identity. I dated women but could never gain intimacy with them. Deep down, I knew "the unspeakable truth," that I was a gay man. But I kept telling myself that it was just a phase. As I entered doctoral training, I knew that I had to make sense of my sexual orientation. Yet I had a deep-seated fear of how the process of coming out would impact relationships with my family. Friends told me that I was catastrophizing and that my family would accept me as I am. My therapist could not believe that my parents' commitment to Catholic teachings would supercede the importance of maintaining a relationship with me.

After coming out, my worst fears initially came true. I lost the support of my parents and initially did not have contact with them. Ultimately, the relationship settled into an uncomfortable silence about my life as a gay man. "Don't ask, don't tell" was the only way to maintain a connection with them. I decided that I was willing to do whatever it took to remain a part of the family, even though this silence perpetuated shame about my life. However, this also meant that I looked to my training and other areas of my life for overt validation of my identity as a gay man.

Graduate School

In my graduate coursework, I was pleased to work with faculty of national recognition. I found my courses to be challenging, intellectually stimulating, and eye-opening in many respects. However, I was often disappointed in classes when sexual orientation was not discussed. Yet I was so caught up in my own process of discovery and struggle with shame that I did not have the internal resources to challenge myself and others to address LGB issues. I didn't need to risk uncovering any other triggers of self-invalidation. I was experiencing enough of this in my family life. So, I found it safer to remain silent. Yet my own silence and the "null environment" that I experienced perpetuated my shame about being gay.

Graduate school included a variety of clinical training opportunities (practicum, internship, etc). I valued each opportunity to develop my skills as a therapist. However, I experienced heterosexist interactions in all these clinical environments. In retelling these experiences, I have made every effort to provide anonymity to the other participants. The value in sharing these stories is not to identify any one site or person but to assist the reader in examining how heterosexism pervades all environments.

I decided to apply for some clinical experiences as an openly gay man. In my deliberations about whether to do this or not, I sought feedback from various sources. I was warned by some people not to be "too gay" and to be subtle in how I presented myself as a gay man. "Let people just read between the lines by reviewing your activities and interests." "Don't look too political. You'll just end up ghettoizing yourself." These well-meaning comments were incredibly invalidating. How openly gay was "too openly gay?" How would I know whether I had "ghettoized" myself?

As I grew more comfortable with my identity as a gay man, I found coming out to others more natural. However, academic and clinical supervisors had power over me (legitimate, expert, reward, coercive), and I was often unsure of their positions on lesbian and gay issues. My ultimate goal of getting through my doctoral program was most important, and I protected myself from homophobia that could derail my aspirations. I struggled with my shame and if, when, where, and how to come out to supervisors and colleagues.

In one site, my supervisor was an openly gay man. He provided me with the support and validation of my clinical work that I craved. However, this clinical experience included group discussions/presentations with a different clinical supervisor. I had noted that when sexual orientation issues were discussed, the group leader framed them as a "phase of sexual exploration" and cautioned us against too quickly concluding that someone was lesbian or gay. I interpreted this as a sign of discomfort with sexual orientation issues since I never heard messages from him that validated sexual minorities. Therefore, my sexual orientation was not something I felt safe to discuss in this group.

Another clinical training site had some very conservative Christian influences, and I remained unsure of how to manage my sexual orientation. I was introduced to other therapists who kept Bibles on display in their offices and drew heavily from them in their work. I figured that I could get good training in this placement and decided to just keep my mouth shut about my life. "Don't ask, don't tell."

In my first staff meeting, the facilitator acknowledged that a tour group would be coming through the office the next day. Members of the organizational leadership would be touring the clinic, and my supervisor was jokingly told to keep quiet about his dissatisfactions with the organization. One staff member said to him, "I know how we can keep them away from you (and your complaints). We'll tell them you have AIDS!" Everybody in the room burst out laughing . . . everyone except me. I froze. As I looked around the room at the laughing faces of the other staff members, I became sick to my stomach. I felt so very alone. My shame silenced me for the remainder of that meeting and for the next few weeks of that placement. I was left struggling with how to continue training in a climate where prejudice seemed to flourish.

In another site, I conducted an assessment on a gay man with AIDS. The client's ambivalence about his sexual orientation emerged from assessment data, and I wanted to talk about this with my supervisor. However, I felt uncomfortable discussing sexual orientation issues with her without coming out. I decided to do so in a supervision meeting as I discussed this case. As I did, I said that I had done so to share this part of my life and to figure out how to integrate my personal and professional identity. Her immediate response horrified me. "Well, if I were you, I wouldn't discuss it at all. I mean, I don't talk about who I sleep with." Blood rushed to my face as feelings of shame, anger, and fear washed over me. However, for the first time, my shame did not silence me. I informed the supervisor that being gay was much more than sexual behavior. "Oh, I know" she said with a wry smile. "I was just kidding."

I was present at a case conference in which this client was discussed. After the conference leader (recognized in his field) interviewed and dismissed the patient in front of those present, he opened up the remainder of the time for questions or comments. One student in the audience wondered about posttraumatic stress disorder (PTSD) as an additional diagnosis, given that the client had lost so many friends to AIDS. The leader quickly responded, "Well, you seem to know a lot about being a gay man with AIDS. Are you one?" The embarrassed student blushed and managed to stammer a "No" before he was drowned out by laughter in the room. I dared not challenge the leader, especially in a room of 75 people. Instead, I sat with a maelstrom of feelings and wondered how I could continue in training.

In another site that had conservative Christian leadership, I became friendly with a coworker who shared my Catholic faith. She became very concerned that I was too focused on just graduate training. She consistently asked whether I was dating any women (to which I replied "No," leaving out the fact that I had a boyfriend) and noted that I really should consider looking for a "good woman." She offered to arrange a date for me. I declined. She remained undeterred and continued to push the offer. This culminated with my colleague cornering me to say, "Look, it's just one date. She's a nice girl from a very good family. And (she whispered), I know she's a virgin." I was stunned. I blushed with shame and anger. I told her that I was not interested in any dates she wanted to arrange for me. EVER! She looked at my quizzically for a moment, then agreed to never bring this up again. I dared not say any more.

Implications

These anecdotes are not reflective of my entire graduate school experience. I was fortunate to have mentors and friends who supported and encouraged me. There were faculty who talked about the experiences of LGB persons in their courses. Yet the overpowering silence of many faculty and supervisors on lesbian and gay issues paralleled my family's unwillingness to share my process of self-discovery.

I continue my struggle to feel validated in my life as a gay man and in relationship with my partner of 5 years. However, I am much more able to do this for myself than I was in graduate school. At that point in my life, I needed my identity more overtly validated. When I experienced silence on the part of supervisors or faculty, I remained unsure of how "safe" it was to come out, and I remained quiet about my life.

Silence in regard to sexual orientation begets the "null environment" described by Betz (1989) in regard to women's career development. The null environment is one that ignores an individual's experience, leaving them at the mercy of other influences (Betz, 1989). In a similar way, silence by faculty and supervisors about sexual orientation leaves LGB trainees confused about their view of sexual minorities. Silence can therefore be assumed to mean that one agrees with the pathological viewpoint of LGB persons. As clinical supervisors, faculty members, mentors, and colleagues, counseling psychologists have an important role in countering the negative messages confronted by sexual minorities who are clients, supervisees, or students.

In my coursework, I felt too vulnerable emotionally to address the lack of coverage of LGB issues. Silence in the classroom on these issues is likely exacerbated by the lack of data on the mental health needs of lesbians and gay men (Rothblum, 1994). Counseling professionals conducting research must attend more to sexual orientation as a variable of interest. Yet in the absence of data, faculty can still encourage discussion of how a lesbian or gay identity may impact the constructs being discussed. Simoni (2000) offers instructors a review of ways to confront heterosexism in the teaching of psychology.

Mentoring relationships were critical in assisting me as I navigated my graduate school experience. Sometimes, the mentor's sexual orientation didn't matter. My academic advisor, a White, heterosexual female, was instrumental in my journey out of shame into self-acceptance. However, I also valued the chance to connect with openly LGB mentors. Kooden (1991) describes the power of role-modeling and self-disclosure to clients by a gay male therapist in enhancing clients' self-acceptance. Mentoring relationships by "out" faculty and supervisors can provide trainees with similar benefits.

At times, I felt as if supervisors and colleagues were "working out" their issues with LGB people solely through our interactions. In my opinion, this is inappropriate. Consultation, training, and peer supervision are effective vehicles to assist faculty and staff to work on their biases. LGB trainees should not be the only way for faculty to work on their heterosexism.

In conclusion, my process of self-discovery as a gay man has not ended. I continue to work on ways to avoid my own heterosexism with clients or colleagues. Yet I am stronger now to challenge null environments that overlook my life and my relationship. Silence equals psychological death. I will not sit in silence and shame any longer.

References

Betz, N. (1989). Implications of the null environment hypothesis for women's career development and for counseling psychology. *The Counseling Psychologist, 17,* 136–144.

Kooden, H. (1991). Self-disclosure. The gay male therapist as an agent of social change. In C. Silverstein (Ed.), *Gays, lesbians and their therapists* (pp. 143–154). New York: W.W. Norton.

Rothblum, E. (1994). "I only read about myself on bathroom walls." The need for research on the mental health of lesbians and gay men. *Journal of Consulting and Clinical Psychology, 62,* 213–220.

Simoni, J. (2000). Confronting heterosexism in the teaching of psychology. In B. Greene & G. Croom (Vol. Eds.), *Psychological perspectives on lesbian and gay issues: Vol. 4. Education, research and practice in lesbian, gay, bisexual, and transgendered psychology: A resource manual* (4th ed., pp. 74–90). Thousand Oaks, CA: Sage.

15

The Evolution of Responsibility

Developing as an Ally

Theresa M. O'Halloran

Adams State College

Hetero—what? Sexism! *Sexism,* now there is a term I knew growing up during the women's rights movement and sexual revolution of the 1960s. But *heterosexism*—it has taken more than three decades for the meaning to become as clear to me.

I am a heterosexual female born into an Irish Catholic, middle-class family in a medium-size city in the midwestern United States. *Moderate, mean, middle:* all terms that aptly describe my experience in childhood and adolescence. Attending Catholic school for 9 years resulted in extremely limited accurate information about sexuality as well as many topics never spoken of but hinted at as "in bad taste." Homosexuality was in that category of "in bad taste" or hush-hush. No priest hollered damnation from the pulpit in our church. If a lesbian, gay, or bisexual (LGB) person was discussed, it was in a hushed, degrading, condescending tone about some stereotypical characteristic.

As a young woman of the 1960s and the only daughter in a male-dominated household, I was committed to women's liberation and freedom, which in many ways centered on sexual freedom. Freedom to choose: choose birth control pills, choose partners, and choose sexual adventure. A key event of this period of initial awareness and fledgling activism took place in 1974 as I wrote my final high school paper, titled "Homosexuality is Not a Disease." The American Psychiatric Association had recently announced the removal of homosexuality from its list of mental disorders after a reevaluation of homosexuality. I wrote a paper citing the research that backed their decision and the history of prejudice against LGB individuals based on religious, social, and political mores. When my parents learned the topic of my paper, they were appalled. My mother refused to type my paper as she had all other papers I submitted in high school and expressed concern over the course of my moral development. The message from my family was not only "You should not be one of 'those people'" but also "You will be suspect and ostracized for respecting LGB folks." Homosexual behavior was wrong and immoral; heterosexual behavior was normal. Despite the clear homophobic and heterosexist messages received from my parents, my resolve to support sexual diversity was cemented as I pecked my way through the 10-page paper.

Ten years later, I made my first attempt at direct advocacy. A young female friend and roommate was dealing with her sexual identity and the process of "coming out." When she discussed her struggle with me, I said something like, "I will support you whatever you choose. It's a choice, and to choose a lesbian lifestyle is the more challenging choice. It may result in rejection by your family, coworkers, and others." Looking at this interaction now, I am appalled at the lack of knowledge and the heterosexist tone with which I offered my support. Preaching choice about sexual orientation ignores the fact that many people do not experience sexual orientation as a choice. I attempted to be supportive but may have confused my friend with my heterosexist belief that one may "choose" to be different than the norm.

Jump another 10 years ahead to a third critical incident in my development into an ally for LGB individuals. Early in my teaching career, it was my good fortune to work among several LGB-affirmative faculty and students who increased my awareness and frequently pushed me to examine my fears, biases, and teaching methods. During one of my first classes, several students were concurrently enrolled in an LGB issues course. As we approached the concept of diversity in my course, students asked: What about research on LGB issues in career? What about the rights of LGB individuals in hiring and in the workplace? So, how does that multicultural model apply to LGB clients? Does it? I did not have answers as I stood in front of the room, and knew I needed to learn more and push through some fears about leading a discussion about homophobia and heterosexism in the workplace. This awareness of my limited knowledge in the area of LGB issues added to my anxiety and sense of incompetence as a novice instructor and pushed me to grow.

In another course, during a student role-play of a gay male client seeking career counseling services, my responsibility as a counselor educator to address homophobia and heterosexism in the classroom was underscored. The client was portrayed with stereotypical and homophobic representations, such as exaggerated hand gestures, lilting voice, a sexual come-on to the male counselor, and the last scene allowed to be portrayed included a statement by the client that suggested he might be sexually interested in young boys. I was aghast and stopped the presentation, went to the front of the room, and asked the entire class take a deep breath while we considered what just transpired in our classroom. Discussion ensued. Forthright emotional reactions were stated by student observers; confusion, explanations, and rationalizations were expressed by the presenting group; and peer education took place regarding sexual identity development and homophobia. I returned from a break in the class with a copy of the ethical codes (American Counseling Association [ACA], 1995; American Psychological Association [APA], 1992) to lead a discussion of ethical responsibility and the importance of working through our homophobic and heterosexist beliefs and our racist tendencies to perform ethical counseling practice.

This class left me shaken and strengthened at the same time. I felt horrified that I had witnessed and allowed such blatant homophobia to be presented in my classroom. I also felt that the full exploration of students' emotional reactions and the ethical code was a powerful lesson. Students learned about fear, respect, and responsibility. I learned that I was not only responsible for managing the learning environment but I also had responsibility for pushing counseling students to explore and consider their homophobic and heterosexist reactions to clients and counseling issues.

Reflections

Writing and reflecting on my slow and uneven development as an LGB ally leaves me with a sense that my work has just begun. Over the last 30 years, I have gained greater knowledge and sensitivity. My early adulthood sense of activism has been renewed in my role as a counselor educator and LGB ally. Broido's (2000) application of Jackson and Hardiman's social identity development model to heterosexual ally development consists of five stages: naive, acceptance, resistance, redefinition, and internalization and is based on the belief that oppression is learned and thus can be unlearned. Movement from one stage to another is motivated by dissonance between one's current worldview and conflicting logic, practicality, self-concept, or self-interest. Although this model lacks empirical validation, it is a useful framework to reflect upon my development as a LGB ally.

Naive is the natural stage of social identity development from birth, until homophobic and heterosexist social conditioning makes an imprint in early childhood. The second stage, *acceptance,* can be passive or active. Passive acceptance involves unconscious acceptance, while active acceptance is conscious acceptance and incorporation of the dominant group, or heterosexist, message. Like most people in our culture, I appear to have passively accepted heterosexist notions throughout my childhood and adolescence.

I feared the unknown and the dark shadow surrounding homosexuality until my development as a feminist and sexual young adult collided with the taboos. As I moved into the *resistance* stage, I had increased awareness of the impact of oppression against LGB individuals. I experienced fear and anxiety about speaking out against the oppression and carefully chose the venues for my resistance. I seem to have spent my early adulthood in this passive resistance stage of feeling powerless to make any major difference in heterosexism. I was aware and yet acted only in small ways by writing a controversial term paper and supporting my friend in private.

During the active resistance stage, one deliberately confronts heterosexist and homophobic social norms and actively dissociates oneself from the dominant group. I entered the active resistance stage as I transitioned from being a doctoral student to a faculty member. My responsibility as a counselor educator to develop multiculturally competent counselors clearly includes exploration of heterosexism and homophobia, along with racism, sexism, and other biases (ACA, 1995). In the last 6 years, I have included reading and discussion of sexual identity development as part of the multicultural component of my courses. Competence arises out of knowledge, experience, and self-exploration; therefore, in my classes I use both homosexual and heterosexual case study examples for use in and outside the classroom. I urge students to examine heterosexist biases in language (e.g., wife, husband), assumptions, and behavior during the intake and counseling process. And I confront the mistaken notion that counselors can just "refer" if not comfortable with a client's sexual orientation while at the same time cautioning them to "do no harm." Discussion includes the heterosexist and homophobic sexual orientation conversion therapies in use today and APA's (1997) strong stance against such harmful, unproven treatment that is based on the mistaken notion that LGB individuals are mentally ill due to their sexual orientations.

As my sense of responsibility and power to change attitudes about heterosexism has evolved, I have moved into the *redefinition* stage. In the last couple of years, as I respond to literature, research, students, and clients, I have considered sexual orientation. I have provided visible, active support by attending pro-LGB rallies on campus. In addition, I have considered how my privileged status as a White heterosexual female impacts LGB persons. With every freedom comes responsibility: The freedoms I experience as a privileged person result in responsibility to be active in my alliance with LGB individuals in my personal and work life. I am uncertain what form the next critical incident in my development will take. I am certain only that there will be another as I increasingly release my fears and move toward *internalization* of my identity as a LGB ally.

Since Broido (2000) suggests that heterosexual ally development is motivated by dissonance, those of us who teach counselors and psychologists need to expand our knowledge, experience, and self-exploration related to heterosexism. Instructors need to become familiar with sexual identity development, the research on homophobia, and the ethical practice standards of our fields related to sexual orientation. Beyond knowledge, instructors need new experiences to develop dissonance in our heterosexist beliefs. Instructors should invite panels of LGB students to discuss issues in class, engage in training provided by LGB support groups on campus, attend public discussions of homophobic and heterosexist attitudes and laws, and gain an ally voice by raising these issues in the classroom and in their personal lives. Self-exploration regarding heterosexism should include both professional and personal practices. Instructors should review their courses for bias in language and focus, breadth and currency of research, and sexual orientation of case study examples with attention to less overt heterosexist teaching practices. Review of personal practices of heterosexism could be accomplished through introspective writing and an assessment of personal relationships with LGB individuals.

The personal growth of counseling and psychology instructors impacts students. If we address our heterosexist tendencies through gaining increased knowledge, experience, and self-exploration, our students can benefit from new course content, experiential exercises, and incorporation of hetero-sexist beliefs in self-exploration components of their training and move toward becoming more multiculturally competent practitioners.

References

American Counseling Association. (1995). *Code of ethics and standards of practice.* Alexandria, VA: Author.

American Psychological Association. (1992). *Ethical principles of psychologists and code of conduct.* Washington, DC: Author.

American Psychological Association. (1997). *Resolution on appropriate therapeutic responses to sexual orientation.* Washington, DC: Author.

Broido, E. M. (2000). Ways of being an ally to lesbian, gay and bisexual students. In V. A. Wall & J. Evans (Eds.), *Toward acceptance: Sexual orientation issues on campus.* Lanham, MD: University Press of America.

16

Through Racism and Homophobia

An Ally's Journey

Ruperto M. Perez

The University of Florida

My parents immigrated to the United States from the Philippines when I was 8 months old, so I never knew of my cultural homeland growing up. As the oldest of five siblings, my parents wanted us to learn and appreciate U.S. culture. As much as my parents wanted my brothers and sister and me to be fully immersed in U.S. culture, they also kept us tied to our Filipino heritage. They would often talk to us about our relatives in the Philippines and their own childhood memories. One of the main ways we remained tied to our Filipino heritage was through the foods that my mother (and grandmother, when she lived with us) would make. Food was a unique and strong cultural tie for all of us to the Philippines. My fondest memories of home were the foods that my mother and grandmother would cook; dishes like "pancit," "lumpia," "guinataan," or "dinuguan" kept our family tied to our Filipino heritage.

Targets of Racism: Being Filipino

As much as I felt a part of the United States during my childhood, I also felt different and excluded. Because I was not of Anglo descent and because I did not view myself as a White American, a part of me did not feel a belonging to mainstream White America. This was in large part due to growing up in the southern United States during the early 1960s and 1970s, when racial tolerance, acceptance, and affirmation were not the highpoints, but rather the low points, of that era. I remember the effects of racism growing up in the

South and the impact of those experiences on me. I remember our family being targets of racist comments and actions. I remember experiences of being laughed at and made fun of because I looked different. And I remember the feeling of being regarded as less of a person because of my race. I learned racism not only from these personal experiences but also from the social and political climate when the South was in tumult during the civil rights struggle by Black Americans and the entire country was in the grips of the war in Vietnam. But I also remember feeling accepted for my skin color by some, only because I was not Black. And I accepted this.

It was about that time too, in elementary school, when I first heard the word "fag." I remember a classmate of mine who was teased because he did not show an interest in playing baseball, wrestling, or other "boyish" activities that the rest of my classmates and I took part in. I had no idea what "fag" meant, but I do remember having it explained to me as someone being a "sissy" or "like a girl." And in second grade, there was nothing worse than being treated or seen as being like a girl by the rest of your classmates. And so I learned that being masculine was the accepted way to be as a young boy and that if some did not accept me as being Filipino, at least I could find acceptance in my masculinity.

So it came to be with me for a long time that I played down my racial identity, an experience similar for many Filipino immigrants in the United States (Rimonte, 1997), and immersed myself in my masculine gender role identity and being accepted for it. I felt my racial and cultural identity becoming "invisible" (Pido, 1997) as I played down even talking about being born in the Philippines and trying to understand more of my cultural ties. Only after a pivotal return back to the Philippines did I reclaim my own cultural identity and, in the process, come to understand what oppression was really about.

My first reaction upon arriving in Manila and seeing the city for the first time was one of a literal culture shock. It was a shock for me to be back in my own homeland, and I remember how ironic that felt for me—there I was standing in the place of my birth, and how out of place, how not at home I felt. But slowly I started to feel at home as I reconnected with relatives whom I knew and connected for the first time with relatives whom I never knew personally but had only heard about from my parents. I began to feel a belonging and a tie to my homeland that I had never felt before. And I remember, at the end of our trip, feeling proud of my heritage, my identity as Filipino.

The realization of my cultural identity also brought with it a feeling of guilt that I had regarding my "disaffiliation" with being Filipino and also the realization of how deeply acculturated into Western U.S. culture I had become. This realization also brought to me how much I had also bought into the values of racism, heterosexism, and homophobia. Though I had been aware of racism and had been taught by my parents not to be prejudiced against others, I realized my subtle racism toward others, which was influenced by my Western acculturation. And yet I also remember when I made my personal commitment to not be the one to oppress as I had been oppressed because of my race: It was the first time (and only time) I witnessed a rally by the Ku Klux Klan, while I was an undergraduate in college. I remember my feelings of fear but also my stronger feelings of rage. And I remember committing myself to not be "one of them." However, it would not be until graduate school that I realized other ways in which I was "one of them" in oppressing others namely, that I held homophobic and heterosexist beliefs and although I was aware of them, I did not know what to do to address them or how they affected me or my work with clients.

An Ally's Journey

I remember the extreme negative images of mostly gay men as portrayed by the media during the 1970s. It was the rise of Christian fundamentalism as a political force and the influence of the media and Anita Bryant on the portrayal of lesbian, gay, and bisexual (LGB) people as socially deviant. I remember being a part of that oppressive thinking and adopting the prevailing heterosexist and homophobic social attitudes of the 70s. My awareness of these beliefs would not be raised until I began my graduate studies in counseling psychology, and the intersection of these beliefs with my experiences of racism.

In my first master's practicum experience at a university counseling center during the mid-1980s, I felt that I was generally prepared to deal with a wide range of developmental and personal issues that students typically presented. I could not have been more wrong. One of my first clients was a lesbian student facing issues of depression and emotional abuse. As much as I believed (and hoped) that I was helpful to her, our relationship was of incredible significance to me. She was the first lesbian person that I had known in any of my relationships, and she remained patient with me through my blundering of interventions, my heterosexist biases, and my cultural assumptions. Supervision during this time was enormously helpful to me to start to confront my biases and my homophobia and to help me begin to see the ways in which my biases and homophobia could hinder my work and connection with my clients.

My major growth as an ally, though, was during my internship year, when I decidedly wanted to dedicate the focus of my training and experience to working with LGB clients and to continue my own exploration of my role as a nongay counselor with my LGB clients. A pivotal experience for me was addressing my homophobia in supervision when dealing with issues of attraction toward me from one of my gay clients. Through thoughtful, challenging, and encouraging supervision and education, I realized that the stereotypes I held about LGB people were the mirror of the cultural biases and prejudice that had targeted me because of my race. I painfully realized then that my biases and homophobia were the same oppressive forces as the racial discrimination and prejudice that I experienced. And I realized that as long as I subscribed to my own heterosexism and homophobia, I was also an oppressor of others and "one of them."

I felt both a professional and personal need to undo my biases, not only through education and supervision but by action as well. During my internship, I immersed myself in the existing literature on counseling LGB clients and also became involved in outreach to the LGB student group on campus. I also became connected to LGB professionals in the area and in professional organizations. I began to become better attuned to the issues that LGB people face in their lives. To this day, one of my most rewarding experiences during internship was facilitating a group for LGB students, one that was significant for me in being seen and accepted as an ally.

I have since continued my dedication as an ally and my interest in working with LGB clients in my current career; however, my dedication seems to have moved on from alliance to activism. Though I continue to work with LGB students in counseling as well as consulting and reaching out to our campus LGB groups, my activity has extended to the local community as well as my professional community. Becoming openly involved in the politics of advocating for LGB people both on my campus, in my community, and in my professional organizations has been the cornerstone of my work as an ally. My involvement with the American Psychological Association (APA) Division 17's Section on Lesbian, Gay, and Bisexual Awareness has offered me opportunities to not only be active within my profession but also contribute in meaningful ways through collaboration in program presentation and research.

Counseling Profession: From Alliance to Action

As counseling professionals, our history has defined us in part through our role in social advocacy and prevention. Our challenge is to continue our role as agents of social change and advocacy to LGB people in ways that focus our efforts to directly confront the negative, sometimes violent, effects of the oppression of LGB people—efforts that go beyond alliance and reach out to activism. To do this, however, it becomes even more important that counseling professionals also examine areas of bias and prejudice within our own profession and the ways in which individual biases and prejudices influence our relationships with our clients and our colleagues. If the counseling profession is to become truly active in addressing the social diseases of heterosexism and homophobia, our profession also needs to turn the mirror on to ourselves, to ask the difficult questions, to examine the ways that heterosexism and homophobia are present in the counseling profession, and to work actively and visibly toward ways to disarm their effects.

One way to begin this self-examination is to begin to ask difficult questions and initiate difficult dialogues to look at the ways that the counseling profession has historically and presently acted to oppress LGB individuals. How has the counseling profession either overtly or covertly reinforced heterosexist bias and homophobia or biphobia? In what ways has our profession marginalized our LGB colleagues? In what ways might our profession subscribe to multiple levels of oppression (e.g., race, ethnicity, age, ability) of LGB individuals?

Initiating difficult but useful dialogues within our profession can give rise to useful and creative ways to drive awareness into action and advocacy for LGB people. One of the ways that this work can begin is to fully use the *Guidelines for Psychotherapy With Lesbian, Gay, and Bisexual Clients* (Division 44/Committee on Lesbian, Gay, and Bisexual Concerns Joint Task Force, 2000) in our research, training, and practice. These guidelines are groundbreaking in outlining concrete ways that counseling professionals can integrate principles of ethical and sound practice and research in working with LGB clients and their concerns.

Another avenue in which the counseling profession can become active is in its research. There is a need for an active agenda of quantitative and qualitative research that can guide our theory development and counseling practice with LGB clients. Moreover, publication of this research in counseling journals (e.g., *Journal of Counseling and Development, Journal of Counseling Psychology, The Counseling Psychologist*) and in textbooks (e.g., *Handbook of Counseling and Psychotherapy With Lesbian, Gay, and Bisexual Clients,* Perez, DeBord, & Bieschke, 2000) can raise the visibility of the counseling profession as taking an active role in disarming the oppressive and harmful effects of homophobia, biphobia, and heterosexism.

My journey as an ally to the LGB community has been marked by the challenge to become aware of and understand my personal biases and homophobia in the context of my own experiences of racism and oppression. The struggle has been to confront the realization of my own oppressive role as a result of my homophobia and to undo those same biases and oppressive beliefs that were born of the same prejudices that targeted me because of my race. Yet it was also through this journey that I have found my professional relationships enriching and my personal relationships more rewarding as close friends have come out to me. Through this journey, I have experienced affirming experiences and relationships as an ally that have also given rise to my sense of responsibility to give back to the LGB community in ways that are visible and oftentimes political. And yet this journey could not have begun until I felt my own sense of acceptance and pride in my own racial and cultural identity.

The counseling profession has much to be proud of in its historical efforts toward social advocacy and social change. However, much more can be done in the way of social change and social justice by examining the ways in which the counseling profession has acted (and currently acts) to reinforce heterosexism, homophobia, and biphobia. By acknowledging and becoming aware of our own professional and personal biases, the counseling profession can move toward becoming a strong and visible ally to LGB people by integrating our awareness into action and advocacy for our LGB colleagues, clients, and the LGB community.

References

Division 44/Committee on Lesbian, Gay, and Bisexual Concerns Joint Task Force on Guidelines for Psychotherapy With Lesbian, Gay, and Bisexual Clients. (2000). Guidelines for psychotherapy with lesbian, gay, and bisexual clients. *American Psychologist, 55,* 1440–1451.

Perez, R. M., DeBord, K. A., & Bieschke, K. J. (2000). *Handbook of counseling and psychotherapy with lesbian, gay, and bisexual clients.* Washington, DC: American Psychological Association.

Pido, A. J. A. (1997). Macro/micro dimensions of Filipino immigration to the United States. In M. P. P. Root (Ed.), *Filipino Americans: Transformation and identity* (pp. 21–38). Thousand Oaks, CA: Sage.

Rimonte, N. (1997). Colonialism's legacy: The inferiorizing of the Filipino. In M. P. P. Root (Ed.), *Filipino Americans: Transformation and identity* (pp. 39–61). Thousand Oaks, CA: Sage.

17

Being Bisexual in the Counseling Professions

Deconstructing Heterosexism

Julia C. Phillips

The University of Akron

In preparing to write this narrative, I have felt myriad emotions. I am proud to have been asked to do so. I am nervous about what people will think. I am hopeful that I have something to say: something that will contribute uniquely to the ongoing development of the field of counseling, as one that truly understands diversity issues, not only on an intellectual level but on an emotional one as well. The field has been enormously facilitative of my identity development in the context of my heterosexist upbringing. Still, heterosexism in the counseling profession contributes to the artificial dichotomization of sexual orientation, which has been difficult, isolating, and often tiresome for me as a bisexual woman.

I grew up in Shaker Heights, Ohio, living the privileged life of a White, middle-class kid. The community was known as a model of racial and religious integration, and I was exposed to several types of diversity early on. As I reflect on this upbringing, the fifth grade stands out in my mind because of Miss Jones, my first African American teacher, whose lessons about civil rights were not only factually informative but emotionally powerful as well. In the same year, amidst much fanfare, we also had sex education. However, this education taught us nothing about lesbian, gay, and bisexual (LGB) people. My English heritage also contributed to a sense of shame related to sexuality in general.

Around this time, my best friend and I were inseparable. I adored her, and sometimes we would lie together in bed and kiss. She said we did it to practice for our future boyfriends. I just remember that I liked doing it. We also delighted in holding hands as we walked in public. Holding her hand was something that came so naturally that I didn't think much about it. That is, until a couple of older friends began to make fun of us, calling us "Chocolate" and "Chip." When they did so, it was with scorn, and they would laugh at us and walk away. We were confused about these nicknames and, of course, they wouldn't tell us what they meant.

I remember the day we began to understand. We were walking along, holding hands, as our friends walked in front of us. They turned, saw us holding hands, and the taunting began. One said, "Chocolate and Chip, holding hands!" and the other responded, "Oh gross, what lez-bos!" Today, I know that they were derogatively referring to us as lesbians. Back then, we had to demand to know, "What are you talking about?" Finally, they gave us a hint, saying that we were two of the same thing, like a chocolate chip cookie, and that it was disgusting. We should not hold hands because we were both girls and doing so made us "lez-bos." I was more ashamed. So, we stopped holding hands, and I desperately hoped that no one would find out about the kissing.

In my teenage years, there were several boys I liked, and I fell easily into a heterosexual identity. While I harbored my secret of same-sex attraction, I was fairly good at suppressing it. Other things occupied my mind and my life as I recklessly rebelled in the face of family crises. I saw a psychologist at that time who probably saved my life. I told him most of my secrets, but there was no way I would have ever brought up my same-sex attraction; it was simply too shameful. And he never asked nor showed any signs of being LGB affirming. Also in my high school years, I took a powerful class called "Oppression." We learned about racism, sexism, anti-Semitism, and the Holocaust. I vaguely recall hearing the teacher talk about gay men, only to be met with snickers of disgust from my peers.

I consider myself very fortunate to have had the upbringing that I did. The roots of my openness to diversity were planted early on, allowing me to later more fully confront my stereotypes and prejudices with an increased understanding of oppression. I only wish that I had had the chance to learn that in the world there were also LGB people leading fulfilling lives but who had also been oppressed by a societal "ism." In college, I got the chance to be educated about gay and lesbian issues by psychologists and feminists. I learned that even heterosexual people sometimes had same-sex attraction. Still, it seemed as if one was either lesbian or heterosexual, and I continued to be attracted to men. Thus, the identity I brought with me to grad school was that of a heterosexual woman who was sometimes attracted to women.

In my counseling psychology graduate program, diversity was defined broadly. The definition included not only gay men and lesbian women but bisexual people as well. I confronted many of my ism's during my training, including my own biphobia. I remember being challenged in a values clarification exercise during which I had indicated that I would not date a bisexual man. Uncomfortably, I explained that I knew a woman who had dated a bisexual guy who had run off with another man. My overgeneralization was pointed out to me, as were other irrational ideas I held about bisexuality. The exchanges led me to more fully contemplate my own myths and stereotypes about bisexual people and to consider bisexuality as an option.

I also found role models of women whose sexuality was more fluid and who identified as lesbian and bisexual in my graduate program. I remember when one of my peers came out to me as bisexual. My response was, "Really? I think that I might be, too." So, I began to immerse myself in gay and lesbian literature, and I occasionally ran across something about bisexuality (e.g., Klein & Wolf, 1985). Programs put on by counseling professionals from the university counseling center offered me a safe place to more fully explore, accept, and value my same-sex attraction. Had I not been exposed to positive images of bisexuality, I imagine that I would have defaulted to either a lesbian or heterosexual identity. As I continued to integrate my same-sex attraction with my heterosexual attraction, I found a comfortable home in bisexuality.

After I left graduate school, I began to recognize that heterosexism was more of the norm elsewhere. I joined a terrific group of counseling center staff whose original purpose was to promote ethnic diversity but seemed to advocate for diversity broadly defined as the years went on. During one meeting, we all shared a moment about when we first knew that we were somehow different. Everyone supportively listened to each other's stories, mostly about race, but also about gender. When my turn came, I worked up my courage, told the Chocolate Chip story, and came out as bisexual. Then, I noticed that only a few people in the room were looking at me. Most eyes were down on the floor or looking away. I felt hurt, confused, rejected, and angry. I wished I had said nothing. I later thanked those who had offered their support with their eyes, and I took some comfort in having been an activist by coming out. In the coming years, I also began to better understand the negative feelings that people of color may experience when LGB folks relate their struggles to those who have been oppressed by racism.

As a new professional on a very conservative campus, I enjoyed my work with LGB clients, I was out to my supportive colleagues, and I advocated for LGB students. I also married the man I had been involved with, following serious conversations about what my bisexuality meant for our relationship. At that time, I felt isolated professionally as a bisexual woman. I also became more aware of the relative lack of inclusion of bisexual issues in the field of counseling, and I sometimes wished that I were either lesbian or heterosexual. It was difficult, but I found strength in reading books on bisexuality, most of whose authors were not connected to the counseling professions (e.g., Hutchins & Kaahumanu, 1991). I was disappointed that the pioneering special issues on counseling LGB clients of two major counseling journals did not include bisexual people in any meaningful way (see *Journal of Counseling and Development,* 1989, vol. 68, no. 1, and *The Counseling Psychologist,* 1991, vol. 19, no. 2) but appreciated the reaction paper that noted the importance of bisexual people, nonetheless (Betz, 1991).

Later, I began to research and collaborate with other counseling professionals on projects about LGB issues. I have been told I am a leading voice speaking for the inclusion of bisexual issues in lesbian- and gay-related projects. I experience others to be genuinely open to my feedback. Still, I do sometimes feel like a one-hit wonder on a broken record. It often seems easier for counseling professionals to add "bisexual" to the label of "gay and lesbian" and/or to advocate for inclusion of bisexual issues than it does to know how to integrate bisexual issues in meaningful and nonstereotypical ways.

In 1995, I started a study examining the extent to which psychology doctoral programs taught students about bisexuality. It turned into a larger study examining how programs taught gay and lesbian issues as well. I began another research project similarly. A review of articles in major counseling journals was originally intended to focus on bisexuality but turned into a review focusing on lesbian and gay issues as well. Although comprehensively examining LGB issues was a good choice, I occasionally wonder whether the results that bisexuality is neglected in counseling psychology training (Phillips & Fischer, 1998) and literature (Phillips, Ingram, Smith, & Mindes, 2003) get lost when others look at the big picture. For a long time, I wondered whether an article on bisexuality would be seen as worthy of publication in a major counseling journal. Recently, I was encouraged by the publication of two articles on bisexuality in major counseling journals in 1999 (see Phillips et al., 2003).

I am often mistaken for lesbian or heterosexual. Recently, a gay male colleague assumed that I was lesbian, despite my public acknowledgement of bisexuality. At the time, I was too tired to set the record straight, so to speak. Some of those who have known me since grad school know Tim, my husband. And they may be surprised to find out about my bisexuality. Others know I am bisexual and may be surprised to learn about the "married to a man" part. I don't begrudge people making assumptions, especially since I occasionally make those mistakes myself, but it is interesting to note that I don't remember a single instance of anyone in the counseling professions assuming that I, or anyone else for that matter, was bisexual.

I can handle heterosexism from heterosexual colleagues much more easily than the possibility of rejection from gay and lesbian colleagues, especially when I disclose that I am married to a man. My marriage puts me in a privileged position, and people may have negative feelings about that. Still, it hurts to be rejected by those I see as my strongest allies. The myths and stereotypes about bisexuality are typically unspoken. It is hard to know who subscribes to them and who doesn't, and it's probably not that simple, anyway. I usually assume that counseling professionals don't subscribe to the myths and won't reject me, but I sometimes get the feeling that they do and they might. Does this person think that I am sitting on the fence or just trying to be trendy? Telling people that I came out before I got married has helped to counter that belief. Does this person think I am hypersexual or nonmonogamous? Once, when I came out to a trainee, she exclaimed with wonderfully honest dismay, "WHAT? You're bisexual? But how do you do that? You're married!" So, I willingly explained about what being bisexual and being married meant to me with respect to my (and his) feelings, thoughts, and behaviors. It can be tiresome to wonder about the true attitudes of others and to have to ponder how much to disclose and when is the most appropriate time to do so. It takes up space in my mind that could be better used. Lately, I have been working on letting it go.

Implications for Counseling Professions

My narrative offers a glimpse at some of my experiences as a bisexual woman in the counseling profession. While not exhaustive, I offer my reflections to stimulate thought and action in the professional realm. At the same time that my experiences in the field have helped me to value my same-sex attraction in the context of my heterosexist upbringing, they have made dealing with my bisexuality more demanding. Most of the people in my doctoral program responded to the dominant discourse of heterosexism by challenging it. That bisexuality was valued was unique at the time and is probably still somewhat so today.

The prevailing model of sexual orientation in the counseling professions has been the dichotomous model in which one is either gay/lesbian or heterosexual, resulting in the marginalization of bisexuality (Firestein, 1996). Marginalization creates the need for identity management, which can be tiring for people. Firestein proposed that research on bisexuality would result in a paradigm shift away from the essentialist dichotomous model, and Linda Garnets (2001) presented similar ideas at the National Multicultural Conference and Summit II. I also believe we are in the midst of a paradigm shift and that my mixed experiences as a bisexual woman reflect this ongoing shift. The lack of inclusion of bisexual issues in counseling in a meaningful way creates, at best, a null environment. To counteract that null environment, people will need to be more proactive in showing support for bisexual people.

Another implication for counseling professionals is that they need to educate themselves to think more complexly about sexual orientation. It does a disservice to bisexual people (clients, students, colleagues) to assume that their experiences are the same as those of gay men and lesbian women. The unique issues facing bisexual people should be known in the same way that the unique issues facing lesbian women and gay men are known. In addition, remember that there is great variability among bisexual people with respect to their feelings, values, behaviors, lifestyle choices, and identities. Reading up on bisexuality provides not only information about bisexuality itself but also about issues that are applicable beyond the bisexual population. For example, Paula Rust (1996) wrote an excellent chapter on managing multiple identities.

Another implication that emerges from my narrative is that individual actions can have great influence when they are affirming and inclusive of bisexuality. Consider your attitudes and challenge yourself to recognize whether any discomfort, bias, or stereotyping exists and consider ways to be bi-affirming. Challenge yourself to not only avoid heterosexist assumptions but to also consider that someone might be bisexual, whether they are single, partnered with someone of the same sex, or heterosexually married. Furthermore, remember that identities may not match behaviors. Finally, as social activists, counseling professionals can be extremely powerful in counteracting the damage done by heterosexism in society at large as well. You can make a critical difference by defining diversity broadly and advocating for LGB people when interacting with schools, businesses, governmental bodies, and organizations.

References

Betz, N. E. (1991). Implications for counseling psychology training programs: Reactions to the special issue. *The Counseling Psychologist, 19,* 248–252.

Firestein, B. A. (1996). Bisexuality as paradigm shift: Transforming our disciplines. In B. A. Firestein (Ed.), *Bisexuality: The psychology and politics of an invisible minority* (pp. 263–291). Thousand Oaks, CA: Sage.

Garnets, L. (2001, January). Sexual orientation in perspective. Keynote address at the National Multicultural Conference and Summit II, Santa Barbara, CA.

Hutchins, L., & Kaahumanu, L. (1991). *Bi any other name: Bisexual people speak out.* Boston: Alyson Publications.

Klein, F., & Wolf, T. J. (1985). *Two lives to lead: Bisexuality in men and women.* New York: Harrington Park Press.

Phillips, J. C., & Fischer, A. R. (1998). Graduate students' training experiences with gay, lesbian, and bisexual issues. *The Counseling Psychologist, 26,* 712–734.

Phillips, J. C., Ingram, K. M., Smith, N. G., & Mindes, E. J. (2003). Methodological and content review of lesbian-, gay-, and bisexual-related articles in counseling journals: the 1990s. *The Counseling Psychologist, 31,* 25–62.

Rust, P. C. (1996). Managing multiple identities: Diversity among bisexual men and women. In B. A. Firestein (Ed.), *Bisexuality: The psychology and politics of an invisible minority* (pp. 53–83). Thousand Oaks, CA: Sage.

18

Crashing Through the "Lavender Ceiling" in the Leadership of the Counseling Professions

Mark Pope

University of Missouri–St. Louis

I am a Native American gay (two-spirited) man who is physically disabled and currently works as a faculty member at a large, urban, land-grant university in the Midwest. As I said when I began my acceptance speech for the American Counseling Association's Kitty Cole Human Rights Award, I grew up as "a poor gay Cherokee boy from southeast Missouri." That alone should qualify me for some type of cultural diversity award.

What follows are stories from my rise to two of the top leadership positions in the counseling professions, filtered through the lens of oppression. I will focus my observations through a primary lens of heterosexism; however, it is impossible to fully separate my native Cherokee ancestry, my lifelong disability, my rural upbringing, and all that constitutes my personal cultural identity from any of the others. When I turned 50, my fellow tribal members welcomed me into Elderhood within our St. Francis River Band of Cherokee with the presentation of a beautiful handmade quilt. Each panel was fashioned by a different tribal member and was hand-sewn together by members of our Women's Council. I mention that quilt because my identity is similar to it. Each part of that cultural identity is distinct yet truly part of a whole that has developed over these past 50 years.

Some History and Context

First of all, you should know that I was elected to my first leadership position when I was in the ninth grade at my high school. I was elected to the post of parliamentarian of the Fisk-Rombauer High School Library Club, a rather auspicious beginning, followed shortly by honor society president for two terms, senior class vice president, student council president, and state vice president of the honor society. I always felt special, and my mother in particular supported that perception. I was always an overachiever and felt that there was not anything that I could not do. But I also knew from a very early age that I was different—not like my peers, although I struggled mightily to blend in and be accepted, and I was generally successful. But I was not "out" in high school. In fact, I had many opposite-sex dates and even married my high school female sweetheart, thinking that I might be able to escape my sexual orientation. The stories I will share here are about my leadership work in the counseling professions as an openly gay man and thus are quite different in context from my early days; however, the stories are still about the larger issue of having to deal with heterosexism in my leadership journey.

It takes many years of sustained work in the professional associations in counseling to be elected president, and only a few lesbian, gay, bisexual, and transgender (LGBT) people have successfully attained these important and highly visible leadership positions. In this chapter, I will discuss some of the heterosexist issues that I have encountered in my rise to the presidencies of both the National Career Development Association (NCDA) and the American Counseling Association (ACA). Very relevant to my rise to these presidencies is the notion of the "glass ceiling," which was brought into the popular and professional lexicon in part by Morrison and colleagues (Morrison, White, Van Velsor, & the Center for Creative Leadership, 1987; Morrison & von Glinow, 1990). It is there, and it stops your advancement, but you never really see it. If you coat the glass in the ceiling with a light purple color before you install it, you then get a "lavender" tint. The term "lavender" is in general usage by LGBT groups and has a long history throughout time and culture referring to LGBT people. For example, the mixture of blue (traditional color for males) and pink (traditional color for females) creates a fusion of genders referred to as "two-spirited" or "twin-spirited," which are Native American terms for LGBT persons. The term "lavender ceiling" was applied to the inability of LGBT employees to fully enjoy career development and promotional advancement because they are, or are perceived to be, LGBT (Friskopp, Silverstone, & Silverstein, 1996). These authors identified the lavender ceiling, homophobia, and heterosexism as issues that impact both the emotional and financial well-being of LGBT employees. Whatever makes you different from the dominant group of that culture is the barrier, or "glass ceiling," to your ever achieving membership in the top leadership echelon of that institution, be it a business or a professional association. To continue developing my professional advancement and leadership, I needed to crash through the "lavender ceiling" within the counseling professions.

In 1997, I was elected by the 5,000 members of the NCDA to be their president from 1998 to 1999. Later, I was also elected to the presidency of the 60,000-member ACA from 2003 to 2004. Only 52 people have been elected to the ACA presidency, and breaking into such a small group takes perseverance, hard work, a vision, some talent, and luck. Only a very few openly gay or lesbian leaders have been able to attain these offices in the counseling professions. As far as I and others can assess, I was the first "openly" gay man to be elected to either the NCDA or ACA presidency.

Along the way, there were mentors who aided the process and those who provided obstacles. Thankfully, the former are by far the large majority, but you always remember those who provided substantive barriers to your work. Two very specific heterosexist incidents have been quite defining for me.

First Incident

In 1994, my partner (Shahri Kadisan) of 13 years died of complications from HIV disease. I was quite distraught by the death of my longtime partner, and within hours of his death I wrote a poem about Shahri and our tremendous relationship. I organized a memorial service for him at the hotel where he had devoted his talents as a restaurant manager, and all of his coworkers attended to express their sorrow at his loss. He was buried in Malaysia next to his grandfather in his *kampung* (village) Muslim cemetery, where I still visit him regularly.

I was at the time of his death serving at the beginning of my term as president of a local/regional professional association. I had decided that since I was receiving so many inquiries concerning his death from many of my colleagues, I would inform them in my column in the association newsletter of what had happened. There, I shared my feelings about his death and a poem I had written. I also let them know that I was doing alright. It seemed the right thing to do, and I never questioned it for one instant. Months later, I received a telephone call from a close supporter and friend of mine to let me know that a past leader of the same association had let my friend know that she felt that sharing this information was inappropriate. This past leader stated that a poem celebrating a gay relationship should never have been published in this venue. It was acceptable for opposite-sex couples to grieve and to share their grief, but, since this was a "sin" and immoral, all I was trying to do was to convert them all to a positive stance on "homosexuality." She stated that this had been my "agenda" all along when I ran for the president of the association and that she was sorry that she had supported me during that time because what she had feared had indeed come to pass.

Second Incident

It is a time-honored tradition in ACA that one of the current ACA presidential leaders (the ACA president, president-elect, president-elect-elect, or immediate past president) attends certain organizational meetings on certain occasions. I was the person from among the ACA leadership who was designated to attend the meeting of a certain organization. One week before the organizational meeting was scheduled, the current ACA president received an e-mail message from a leader of that organization requesting, or demanding, that anyone from ACA leadership other than myself be sent to attend the organizational meeting. The tone of the e-mail message was hostile. The organization had military sponsors, and the organization leader attacked my criticisms of the military's discrimination against LGBT people as "self-serving" and "ignorant." The clear communication to the current ACA president was that my presence at the meeting would be harmful and that the organization leader would rather not have an ACA representative at all than to have me in attendance.

The ACA president felt it was important to share this e-mail message with me and ask me what I felt would be an appropriate response. After much discussion, I decided that I would not attend the meeting, and the president decided that no one would attend the meeting. As I wrote this narrative, I reread an e-mail I had sent to a supportive colleague. It was clear, that at the time, I was just barely keeping it in perspective. I felt the stark contrast of being barred from this organization's meeting for my work with sexual minority issues—and at the same time getting an award from the ACA sexual minority division for my work with sexual minority issues. I was most disgusted that as a longtime member and supporter of this organization and its issues, I personally was treated with such disrespect. I felt that if it were just my support of barring the U.S. armed forces from participating in professional associations because of their policy on discharging armed forces members whose sexual orientation does not match majority culture, I might have understood the person's disagreement with me politically. However, another heterosexual colleague in the ACA presidential leadership, who openly shared the same political position as I, was welcome to attend. So, I had to assume it was obviously more than just this. I had to face that the person who made this demand was simply homophobic.

Implications

In this section, I wish to address how I have survived these types of incidents that, although few in number, do take a psychic toll. Let me first say how difficult this was to write. I am not characterologically a whiner or a complainer. I am a very positive person who refuses to dwell on the negative aspects of the human existence. I acknowledge that such negative incidents occur at times, yet my personal approach is to move forward and not devote a lot of time to the negative. I also do not submerge when confronted directly with the negative, nor do I discount such events as unimportant in my life or in the lives of others. While maintaining an initial consciousness of such incidents, I choose to not focus on them nor spend a large amount of my personal energy or time searching for reasons. I accept that different people have different attitudes, cultures, awareness, and ways of coping; I simply prefer mine for me. This survival mechanism I would call being realistic and maintaining perspective.

It is very important to point out that these incidents are anomalies in my experience, yet they obviously represent a certain segment of the counseling profession as well as our society. In each of the incidents that happened to me, I received a tremendous amount of personal and professional support from many others, support that I continue to appreciate. In the first incident, the friend who called me wanted me to know that the person who had seen my acknowledgment of loss as inappropriate did not reflect the views of any of the other association members with whom she had talked. In fact, every person had said how tremendously important it had been that I shared my grief with them. My friend also told me how important it had been to her personally because it made her realize how important it is to live every day cherishing each moment you have with your chosen partner.

In the second incident, it was a combination of personal and organizational support that helped me. I was extremely angry at first, wanting to lash out at the perpetrator personally and politically. I, however, have learned very important lessons from my two partners, both quite introverted and patient. It is always best to think first and then act, natural for them but a developed skill for those of us who prefer extraversion, like me. So, I called a couple of supportive colleagues and talked. That process helped me gain perspective. Particularly important was a conversation I had with another leader of the organization that had barred me from speaking. I had decided to not broach this heterosexist incident with this person but was very gratified when he opened the issue himself and apologized honestly and directly for the attack on me. I was very appreciative of his forthright handling of this incident, and I felt supported by him. It was very kind and caring . . . and unexpected. Later, during the national convention, I was approached repeatedly by others who expressed their support for me and their disdain for the behavior directed toward me. After the convention, I also received several calls from individuals expressing their support.

In addition to the support and opportunities to discuss with others, some personal mechanisms have also assisted my process in responding to heterosexism. In both instances in this narrative and in my life generally, I have developed a willingness to look at myself honestly and directly, an appreciation (always) of the importance of congruence based on a sense of self, a strong personal and cultural identity, a knowledge of how I fit into the world, of hope, of having a positive outlook, of taking responsibility for the part of my existence that I have some control over, and of knowing the difference. I have also developed a keen sense of humor. For me, an important way of surviving such attacks discussed in this narrative is humor. Humor is one of my personal qualities that is also most culturally derived—both from my Native American and gay experience—and that allows me to transcend the anger and hurt. I have a rather dry intellectual wit that allows me to not take anything too seriously, especially myself, while always remaining passionately convinced that I am always right.

As you have no doubt noticed, this narrative is filled with feelings. It was not always the case that I have had the power of my feelings available. I learned early the male stereotype to hide and deny my feelings from others and myself. Through the process of counseling, I learned the power of reclaiming the awareness of my own feelings and ways to share them with others should I choose to. The first part of this was a battle at the personal level. The process of "coming out" is first and foremost a process of turning inward to battle your own personal, familial, cultural, and socially imposed demons. Furthermore, I have found that when you have survived the death of the most important person in your life, you can truly survive anything. Consciousness of self is the foundation upon which a true personal identity and then cultural identity are formed—first, to recognize the feelings, acknowledge them honestly and directly, and then decide what to do with them.

I also want to acknowledge and further emphasize that few ever do this alone. I have had two magnificent partners in my life: Shahri, my partner who died, and now Mario, my love for the past 8 years. Then, there are my mother, who always loves me unconditionally (she is an unconscious Rogerian); my grandmothers, both paternal and maternal; my three brothers, their partners, and my nieces and nephews who have taught me about the importance of patience and perspective; my teachers and counselors; my friends and sex partners. Finally, there are my mentors and my colleagues at work and in the counseling professions who have told me how great I am and also offered constructive feedback, both on an as-needed and regular basis. I have actively sought these mentors, who have assisted and supported my work in the counseling professions. As I started making a list of those who have mentored me and had a profound effect on me and my career, I observed that many of them had been heterosexually oriented and most gay-positive. I had only a few formal or informal mentors who were sexual minorities, mostly due to the dearth of such individuals in the leadership of our profession.

In my work in the counseling professions, I know that there is a critical need for such mentoring, and I have actively tried to provide this for many people but especially for sexual minorities who were also racial/ethnic minorities in the United States—people like me. In my counseling practice, I have actively sought such individuals as I recruited associates for my counseling and consulting firm as well as for leadership positions in the counseling professions. I have always wanted to find a place for people like me in the counseling professions, and there were many years when it seemed there were none where I wanted to be. I am doing my best to change that. I did not just break through the lavender ceiling that existed in ACA for over 50 years and in NCDA for almost 90 years—I crashed through it. I hope it will not take an equal amount of time for the next LGBT person to reach such positions.

References

Friskopp, A., Silverstone, S., & Silverstein, S. (1996). *Straight jobs gay lives: Gay and lesbian professionals, the Harvard Business School, and the American workplace.* Carmichael, CA: Touchstone Books.

Morrison, A. M., & von Glinow, M. A. (1990). Women and minorities in management. *American Psychologist, 45,* 200–208.

Morrison, A. M., White, R. P., Van Velsor, E., & the Center for Creative Leadership. (1987). *Breaking the glass ceiling: Can women reach the top of America's largest corporations?* Reading, MA: Addison-Wesley.

19

Fluidity in the Disclosure and Salience of My Identities

Jennipher Wiebold

Western Michigan University

I am of European ancestry and was born with septo-optic dysplasia, a rare congenital disability that impacts endocrine and visual functioning. Therefore, I am 4'10" tall, with low vision and panhypopituitaryism. I identify with, and socialize in, Disability/Blind culture. In addition, I came out to myself as a lesbian at the age of 14 but remained closeted to my friends and family until I was 19. At 19, I became an active member in the lesbian, gay, bisexual, and transgender (LGBT) community. I have "passed" as both sighted and straight in various work settings. However, for the past 10 years, I have chosen to live "out" as both identities: I am a lesbian with low vision. I have had an opportunity to work in a variety of rehabilitation counseling service provision roles as both closeted and out.

One of my first experiences as a rehabilitation service provider was in a rural community at a facility for persons with mental retardation. The facility was opened as a result of the deinstitutionalization movement and was designed to assist persons with mental retardation to reintegrate into the community. At this early point in my career, I was working as a paraprofessional and, as stated previously, I have low vision. I was assigned to work with consumers with deafblindness. The rationale for this placement was justified as a safety precaution by supervisors. More specifically, I was told that the risk of incurring an injury due to maladaptive behaviors was lower because "they" could not see me. Given my low vision, I might have a chance to "get away" before I was injured. I found this rationale offensive, but I was happy to find an employer who was willing to accommodate my visual impairment. Prior to this placement, I rarely found an employer who was willing to conduct an interview with a person with low vision.

During this time in my life, I was living as a "semi-out" lesbian. I was out to my parents and a small group of friends. My hair was short, and, in a rural community, this stereotype of lesbianism was revered as truth. While working at the facility, I was sent into the community to assist a consumer, Sandra, with an exercise program and to purchase a positive reinforcer. Sandra was a person with deafblindness and mental retardation. It was a windy Saturday afternoon, and there were one-and-a-half-miles to walk to the convenience store. I was providing sighted guide, as Sandra did not possess orientation and mobility skills. Thus, Sandra was holding my arm at the elbow and following behind and to the side of me a half step. On the return route, we were passed by the same pickup truck three times. Each pass was a little more suspicious. I positioned myself between the street and Sandra, moving her as far away from the street as possible. I was becoming concerned about our safety. We walked as quickly as Sandra was able, and I contemplated the potential impact of my lifestyle on consumers. Escape routes were limited due to Sandra's mobility limitations. On the fourth pass, the truck slowed down, and the passenger of the truck threw beer cans at Sandra and I while yelling, "DYKES!!" Fortunately, the truck continued on, and we safely returned to the facility. I was afraid, I was angry. I was angry about jeopardizing the safety of Sandra. As a result of this incident, I made what I thought was a sound career decision: I would take every necessary precaution to ensure the well-being of consumers I serve. If this required sublimating my identities in the work place, then that is what I would do.

This experience and decision stayed with me well into my practice as a rehabilitation counseling professional. My identities were critical aspects of my personal life; however, I sublimated those identities in pursuit of career advancement, service provision, and consumer quality of life. I required health insurance to absorb the costs of regular medical appointments with specialists and costly, life-sustaining daily medications. For me, unemployment (i.e., no health insurance) due to discrimination had the potential to be life threatening. This interaction of my identities occurred in small, conservative rural communities enmeshed with heterosexism, sexism, and ableism.

Later, when I began working at a rehabilitation agency, the prejudicial environment strained my relationships with managers and coworkers. I was the only lesbian with a disability at the agency. I was also the youngest member of the team by almost 20 years. Thus, given the organizational climate and my fears of discrimination, I was closeted regarding my sexual orientation. Coworkers were knowledgeable in the area of blindness and low vision but had difficulties grasping my overall experience of disability. For example, an administrator at the agency would, in the presence of others, often ridicule me with sizist and ableist comments. The end result was a sense of disempowerment. Much of my energy was consumed by image and damage control.

Given these experiences, I was certain that coming out would not be favorably received. While recognized at work as a person with a disability, I was able to pass at work as someone who had a "good friend" who visited regularly. However, this farce created an atmosphere of availability. As a result, a male supervisor on the management team began asking me out to dinner, movies, and so on. How could I avoid drawing attention to myself while discouraging him from pursuing me? Although I was out to my family and friends, they encouraged me to go on one date. Perhaps he would not ask again; I could remain closeted, and the problem would be resolved. If it had only been that easy! When he arrived for the date, I had on jeans and a sweatshirt. Instead of a steak dinner at an expensive restaurant, I expressed interest in burgers and a game of pool. I conducted myself in what I assumed to be a very unattractive manner. I swore and I belched. Unfortunately, my efforts did not dissuade advances. I spent the next 3 months traveling or having "company" on weekends to avoid being available for a date. This was my first professional job, and I did not want to jeopardize my career or my access to health care.

Questions regarding previous boyfriends, current boyfriends, and my desire to have children were on the rise from my colleagues. In addition, I was invited to express opinions regarding "controversial" topics such as gay rights, same-sex marriage, and same-sex parenting. Did I know any of those "dykes, queers, and candy-ass faggots"? Previously, issues of this nature were often commented on but not "discussed," until it became more obvious that I was not interested in relationships with the opposite sex. I feared the questioning was because my coworkers suspected I was a lesbian. The manager continued to express interest, and I felt enormous amounts of guilt for what I perceived as deception. I was now not only concerned about how I would be received in the workplace if my lesbian identity were revealed but also about the backlash I would experience from the manager and his longtime friends, my coworkers. I avoided places in the office where I might encounter him. I eventually found it necessary to explain my lack of interest due to my sexual orientation. The conversation was emotionally draining and escalated my fears. We attempted to establish a friendship but interactions remained strained. My fears were confirmed when I left the agency a few months later and received negative exit evaluations based on disability-related and coworker "relationship issues."

This experience taught me the importance of being genuine not only with myself but also in relationships with colleagues. I learned that the cost of passing and the effort required to pass were not productive for me in the work environment. I decided to honor myself as an individual: an individual who is female, lesbian, and a person with a disability in the counseling profession.

Later in my career, I became a rehabilitation counselor educator at a university. Again, I found myself in a very conservative, rural community. Given my previous life and employment experiences, I was keenly aware of my evolving value of living "out," whether it was related to my age, gender, sexual orientation, or disability status. I accepted the position with the assumption that not all of my identities would be understood or accepted. However, I would live "out" as a lesbian with low vision. Much to my surprise, I found a number of colleagues who identified as LGBT and/or persons with disabilities. Furthermore, I met heterosexual colleagues who were advocates of gender, LGBT, and disability issues. My experiences in this new setting were much different than the exclusionary environments of the past. For example, I was invited by fellow faculty and staff members to attend LGBT cultural events, and efforts were made to include me in the local LGBT community. This was an amazing experience for me!

My commitment to being "out" was both recognized and valued by my colleagues. I appreciated their recognition of my partner and our life together. This open acknowledgement and LGBT culture in the workplace facilitated the integration of my identity as a lesbian in the workplace. Fears of homophobia-related repercussions impacting my career generated by past employment experiences began to dissipate. I felt my identity as a lesbian was no longer viewed and treated by others as an anomaly but as a life-enriching individual difference. I found congruence between my life as a lesbian and as a counseling professional. The energy I had previously invested in passing was now accessible to invest in my contribution to the counseling profession.

My colleagues demonstrated LGBT competencies that created an inclusive environment, yet the issue of ableism was a subtle undercurrent that was, for the most part, void of intention yet synonymous with exclusion. Many counseling professionals I encountered in this position were limited in their awareness of disability issues. However, of these individuals, I experienced a distinct split in their willingness to address issues of ableism and acquisition of disability competence. For example, I was given a nickname that contains a reference to my small stature and, I suspect, to my sexual orientation. On a more positive note, the instances of seeking knowledge far outweighed the prevalence of ignorance. In many instances, the willingness to acquire knowledge was demonstrated through seeking consultation regarding disability-related counseling issues and strategies for providing reasonable accommodations for myself, students, consumers, and other faculty and staff.

Although disability competencies were demonstrated or pursued in the workplace, the transference of awareness, knowledge, and skills to work-related social events was sporadic. More specifically, many colleagues adapted to my vision loss by offering transportation assistance, environmental information, and verbal cues rather than body gestures. For example, when I encountered colleagues in the community, they would approach me and verbally identify themselves rather than waving from a distance. However, different levels of awareness were demonstrated with other disabilities. My partner uses a wheelchair for mobility, and this added another level of complexity to the social aspects of the organizational environment. For example, departmental celebrations and events that included significant others were often hosted in inaccessible environments. The failure to attend to additional disability-related accessibility issues resulted in an air of exclusion. I felt conflicted between my identities as a (a) person with a disability, (b) partner, (c) disability advocate, and (d) counseling professional in an organization. The concept of ableism was understood by colleagues in regard to low vision, yet transference to other disabilities required facilitation. Openness of colleagues to discussion of ableism raised consciousness and remediated, for the most part, the exclusionary practices.

My lesbian and disability identities were not only "accepted" within the counselor educator setting but also considered to be assets of diversity by my colleagues. As such, counseling professionals in the university setting invalidated my false assumptions regarding understanding and acceptance generated in previous employment experiences. Although I was cautious in disclosing my identities, I found not only a supportive environment but also a rich, diverse environment that recognized me as an individual, a counselor educator, and a lesbian with a disability. Through the newly found freedom from the fear of marginalization and discrimination, I was encouraged by the efforts of the counseling profession to recognize LGBT and disability as diversity issues.

Two interactive points of emphasis for counseling professionals are woven through this narrative. The first point of emphasis highlights the struggle to be closeted or out as both lesbian and as a person with a disability. The second point of emphasis encapsulates the fluidity and complexity of identity. Situation and state of being in conjunction with environment all interact with identity and disclosure as each moment passes. For example, in interactions with colleagues, my identity as a lesbian may be in the forefront, while less emphasis is placed on my identity as a person with low vision. Yet at other times, the salience of identities is fluid within the context of interactions with colleagues. For example, I may be walking through the building discussing a theoretical construct in counseling (my counseling professional identity) with a colleague who uses a wheelchair (my disability community identity). As we wait for the elevator, I encounter a gay male colleague (my lesbian identity) who states his name to aid in my visual recognition (my low-vision identity) before sharing information with me about an upcoming LGBT community fundraiser (my LGBT community identity). More specifically, the salience and disclosure of my identities emerge as situations dictate.

In conclusion, counseling professionals promote self-awareness and develop knowledge and skills that facilitate a supportive and diverse environment. As such, we need to continue to promote the profession by continuing our efforts to recognize the interaction of diverse identities and experiences within each of our colleagues.

Section II

Narrative Perspectives on Special Issues

The second section of the book, comprising Chapters 20 and 21, was developed to address two major issues that became apparent during the process of developing the narrative approach of this book. Through conversations with several chapter authors, we discovered that the widespread and public disclosure concerning sexual orientation required by authoring a personal narrative in the prior section of this book systematically excluded the stories of many counseling professionals. The decision of a counseling professional to disclose a minority sexual orientation is a complex, multifaceted process. A decision to "come out" publicly through telling one's narrative in a professional book is a highly personal one, affected by many factors, including culture, multiple oppressions, degree of heterosexism in one's professional and personal contexts, and differing understandings of public and private self. The narratives in this book inherently involve a type of self-disclosure that does not fit well for some professionals due to the aforementioned factors. Yet the discourse on sexual orientation in the counseling professions could not be fully explored if we excluded the voices of such professionals. Thus, for Chapter 20, seven narratives from counseling professionals were collected anonymously and analyzed by the chapter authors to enlighten the often "untold stories" of counseling professionals who do not openly disclose their sexual orientations in all of their professional contexts.

When the Sage multicultural counseling series became the leading contender as a publication outlet for this book, this highlighted the second major issue, addressed in Chapter 21. When sexual orientation is considered within the wider context of multicultural counseling, important and sensitive issues often arise concerning whether multicultural counseling should focus on diversity issues extending beyond race or culture. On one hand, perspectives that focus on race and racism issues may fail to capture the complexity of how sexual orientation and race interact and may reinforce the invisibility and marginalization of lesbian, gay, and bisexual (LGB) people and issues. On the other hand, perspectives that focus on sexual orientation or other issues of human diversity along with race may "obscure the understanding and study of race" and "allow us to avoid addressing problems of racial prejudice, racial discrimination, and systemic racial oppression [by shifting focus to other issues of oppression]" (Sue, 2001, pp. 791–792). Chapter 21 describes this dilemma as it is currently manifest in the counseling professions and then focuses on narration of the chapter authors' own attempts at navigating the sometimes rough waters of race and sexual orientation in multicultural counseling.

Reference

Sue, D. W. (2001). Multidimensional facets of cultural competence. *The Counseling Psychologist, 29,* 790–821.

20

Untold Stories

Voices From the "Closet" of Counseling Professionals

Mary A. Fukuyama

University of Florida

Marie L. Miville

Teachers College, Columbia University

Jamie R. Funderburk

University of Florida

"To be, or not to be (*out*) . . . that is the question." This chapter was conceived as a means for illuminating the experiences of counseling professionals who, for a variety of reasons, might not share the stories about their own sexual orientation in a nonanonymous professional publication. The question may be raised, "Why is a chapter on the closet included in a book of narratives by professionals who speak openly about their sexual orientations?" Indeed, in an ideal world, this chapter would not be necessary. However, the decision for a counseling professional to disclose personally about his or her minority sexual orientation in a professional venue is a complex issue, taking into consideration variables such as cultural context, multiple oppressions, and identity. Stories about the heterosexist discourse from counseling professionals who make choices not to widely disclose their lesbian, gay, or bisexual (LGB) or ally status, stories "from the closet," so to speak, need to be heard. These stories are a key to better understanding the depth of the problem of heterosexism and homophobia in the counseling profession and to shedding light on avenues for healing and change within the profession.

The use of the term *closet* connotes a restrictive stance in the world surrounded by unhealthy secrecy. That is neither our intention nor meaning for the word. We offer a different perspective; that is, to view these stories as if they are coming from the edge or margin of a marginalized group. We were not interested in bringing to light the stories of mainstream "out" LGB professionals, nor the stories of professionals who hide their sexual orientations completely. We were interested in the stories of counseling professionals who, after having given significant thought to disclosure, at times choose not to disclose or to remain closeted.

We would like to begin by defining the closet as those times or situations in which an individual chooses not to disclose his or her sexual orientation (or LGB-affirmative stance if one is a heterosexual), sometimes for protective reasons and sometimes for other reasons, which we will discuss. We recognize that the closet might reflect a range of feelings and choices related in part to one's own acceptance (or lack thereof) of one's own and others' sexual identities. Our focus, however, is on the variety of other contextual variables that influence decisions about the coming-out process professionally. In addition, we believe the very fact that a person must indeed choose to come out by itself signifies the painful choices surrounding one's survival as an LGB person or ally in a potentially hostile world, including the world of professional counseling.

Feminist and narrative therapists advocate the value of "giving voice" and "breaking the silence" regarding experiences of oppression (Brown, 1994). As a result of the now-famous statement that imbued the women's movement of the 1960s and 1970s, "The personal is political," there are pressures or expectations that professionals use their personal lives as a way to fight oppression. Nowhere is this seen more poignantly today than in choices surrounding to live in or outside of the closet. As helping professionals, we recognize that avenues for self-expression about experiences of oppression are important and that such expressions encourage personal and professional awareness and facilitate growth and social change. Coming out about a personal aspect of one's life (i.e., sexual orientation) in a professional forum, however, necessarily entails vulnerability related to one's professional career, even livelihood. Thus, choices related to this area center not just on self-acceptance but on economic and professional survival in a potentially rejecting world. Indeed, sometimes it is hard even to predict the source and reasons of anti-LGB hostility or fears encountered as one copes with an educational and professional world that purportedly represents itself to be accepting of all.

Given this reality, the closet in the counseling profession indeed still exists. Sometimes it exists in covert, even invisible ways (e.g., choices of self-silencing, so that LGB topics do not even surface for open discussion). Other times, it is framed by overt hostile reactions by persons in power (who, sadly, have administrative and supervisory responsibilities). Unfortunately, the closet often exists for some of the more vulnerable members in our profession (e.g., students and trainees, and persons with multiple oppressions). To the credit of the editors of this book, it is groundbreaking in the field of counseling to provide an outlet for the voices of LGB counselors and their heterosexual allies to be heard. It is essential that the voices heard in this book also include those professionals who must speak from the closet. Only with the inclusion of these often-vulnerable voices can this book succeed in fully illuminating the nature of the sexual orientation discourse in the counseling professions.

To more fully accomplish such inclusion, we first present a collection of brief anonymous essays from graduate students and professionals who have encountered heterosexism in the field of counseling. After each essay, our commentary focuses on illuminating the dilemmas of being an LGB counseling professional, particularly those dilemmas associated with the continued existence of the closet in the counseling professions today. Then, in the final part of the chapter, we provide additional commentary on how multiple oppressions and cultural factors can be key contextual variables that influence choices about the "closet" in the lives of counseling professionals.

The Narrative Essays

Volunteers who were invited to share their stories were sought among counseling professionals known personally by the chapter authors, and such potential volunteers were asked to "pass the word" to others about this project. Volunteers also were sought through a "call for submissions" announcement on professional counseling listservs on the Internet. Narratives and demographic data were submitted to the chapter coauthors via surface mail. All identifying information was separated from the narratives to protect anonymity. Potential volunteer narrative authors were asked, "Would you be willing to share anonymously a personal or professional experience of heterosexism that you would like your colleagues to know about through professional publication?"

A total of seven narratives were received. Demographic descriptions of the participants are provided in aggregate format to protect anonymity. The demographics of the contributors include the following: (a) five women and two men; (b) a mixture of racial/cultural backgrounds: one White, one White Jewish, two biracial persons (Asian/White; Native American/White), one Chinese American, one Mexican American and one Jewish Canadian; (c) a range on sexual orientation: two heterosexuals, one bisexual, three lesbians, and one gay male; (d) an age range from 26 to 44 years; (e) the following professional titles: three graduate students, one postdoctoral fellow, two clinicians, and one assistant professor; and (f) the primary employment setting was a university setting (six persons), and one individual worked in a hospital setting. All contributors indicated that they personally faced more than one form of oppression from among sexism, heterosexism, racism, ableism, classism, and homophobia. The narratives are presented in their near entirety and are followed with commentary by the chapter authors.

In these narratives, the experiences of heterosexism in the field of counseling are described from both graduate school and in the workplace. The narratives will be presented in a chronology that begins with student trainees and finishes with professional practitioners and faculty. A primary theme present in most of the narratives is the intensity of experiences of both overt and covert heterosexism and homophobia. As the following stories portray, regardless of the reasons for the closet, these situations are accompanied by intense negative reactions that also may harm the professional's development.

Narrative 1

I realized I was bisexual shortly before I started graduate school in counseling psychology. I moved to a midwestern college town to begin a PhD program. I wanted to explore my bisexual identity but was quite nervous about it. My cautious first step was to tell another new student in my program. I was taking classes and studying with her and starting to consider her a friend. I did think she was very cute, but I wasn't ready to think about whether to consider dating her. When I disclosed to her that I was bisexual, she stopped being willing to study and talk with me. I felt hurt and rejected and felt much more cautious about coming out. In fact, I didn't come out to anyone else in my program until my sixth year, when I told the instructor and students in my multicultural practicum and got a very warm and accepting response.

I think that the rejection from my classmate was a large factor in my not forming friendships among students in my program but going elsewhere for friendships instead. I always felt "other" and not quite accepted among my peers. I still find bisexuality a challenging identity. Because I am attracted to both men and women, I was able to choose the easier route of dating men, thereby avoiding most overt heterosexism, dealing with my family, and so forth. And because I am monogamous, once I finally found a life partner and got married (because that's legally sanctioned), I have found it quite difficult to explain my sexual orientation. So, there are only few people in whom I've confided it: mainly close friends, but very few colleagues in my workplace, and none of my family of origin. I was thrilled to have such a supportive and affirming coming-out ceremony at the Association for Women in Psychology (AWP) conference a couple of years ago. It's great to know that in AWP, it's okay to be out with my identity.

Commentary on Narrative 1

Of the three labels for minority sexual orientation, lesbian, gay, and bisexual, bisexuality is probably the least understood or discussed. In her book on bisexuality, Firestein (1996) brings visibility to bisexuality and its "multidimensional, fluid, and evolving nature of sexuality and its expression over the life cycle" (p. xix). In our dualistic society, the bisexual person is caught between heterosexism of the heterosexual community and biphobia of the lesbian and gay community.

This narrative also focuses on the vulnerability of graduate students. The fear of rejection by peers is a powerful force for staying closeted, particularly with classmates. In addition, this person expended a lot of energy screening her friends in order to maintain some sense of safety and acceptance. The fact that a professional organization like AWP provided a safe space in which to affirm bisexual identity is significant and provides hope for change and healing in the mental health profession. The social needs of graduate students are discussed similarly in the next narrative.

Narrative 2

My account involves an experience with fellow students in my program. The situation that served as the catalyst for this episode involved two friends (Authors' note: Names have been deleted and represented by X and Y). X, an individual of the same gender whom I had feelings for and (prior to this incident) was uncertain of her sexual orientation, and Y, an opposite-gender heterosexual classmate with whom I was close. Y was aware of my feelings for X and about some of the "hazy" situations that had occurred between us, X and me. One night at a party, Y met X and they "hung out" for the majority of that night. At the end of the night, X ended up going to Y's place and having sex. Although what had occurred between them, especially considering that Y knew about my feelings for X, was upsetting, the far more hurtful and damaging part of this experience was the dissension that occurred. When other classmates found out, some were upset at Y, yet many "sided" with him, saying things to me such as,

This is your fault. You put yourself in this situation.

You should have known better than to have had feelings for a straight woman.

Y had every right to do that because nothing could have happened between you and X anyway.

I was very shocked at the individuals who felt I had no reason to be upset or that it was "my fault" I was in the situation that I was in. With multiculturalism being the current wave in our field, I suppose I had taken for granted that my classmates would be sensitive to the impact that an oppressive environment has on an individual of a marginalized group. It is very difficult being at school here because this is a small city in a very conservative state. Thus, the lesbian, gay, bisexual, or transgender (LGBT) community here is very small and mostly closeted. I felt that my classmates were blaming me for being in my situation, where I really don't know who is or isn't gay and my lack of prospects is due to some personal attribute. It seemed that many of them just assumed that I had the same opportunities and privileges they have when it comes to the dating scene.

The personal impact of this incident . . . is that it has made me distrustful of my classmates. I felt very misunderstood, invalidated, and unsupported by many. Since then, I have distanced myself from the program and from being involved in many of the social activities. Moreover, it has made me dread this place even more than before and has made me consider dropping out in order to move to a more affirmative and caring environment.

Commentary on Narrative 2

As in the previous narrative, graduate students often look to each other for social support, particularly if they are alone in an unfamiliar community. To be sure, graduate school is coupled with other developmental issues of identity and relationship building for many. The circumstances in this narrative illustrate the negative emotional valence of heterosexual prejudice and bias that reinforced the disregard of the social and sexual needs of this graduate student. Even more important to note is the impact on the student socially. To be as uncomfortable as to think about moving to a less conservative part of the country is no small matter.

Such circumstances raise the issue of regional prejudice in the United States. There is quite a range in social acceptance for LGB persons in the United States. Examples range from conservative regions such as Florida, where it is illegal for gay or lesbian parents to adopt children, to progressive communities such as San Francisco, which has domestic partner benefits. Some parts of the country are also known for conservative attitudes; for example, states such as Oklahoma continue to have archaic laws outlawing behavioral practices related to being LGB (although state sodomy laws were recently declared unconstitutional by the U.S. Supreme Court). The cultural context of regional prejudice and legislated restrictions are real threats to the faculty, community, and students, who may be relatively isolated in these situations. In such cases, the counseling closet exists within a larger social context of perceived threat and lack of safety. Even though this student appeared to be comfortable with her sexual orientation, the social context lacked support, understanding, and affirmation. One could guess that if she were to complain, she would be discounted or might be rejected further. Student awareness on these issues seems to be a repeating theme as we consider the next narrative.

Narrative 3

During my second semester as a doctoral student, I was given an opportunity to facilitate a group of master's students in the experiential component of a group counseling course. Over the course of the 15 sessions, the group underwent many stages typical of a group, discussing issues and offering support to one another. While members may have had some difficulty reaching deep levels, they remained supportive and in tune with the presenting needs of the week. Toward the end of the semester, one of the group members unwittingly identified herself as a minority in terms of sexual orientation when the question of race and ethnicity was posed to the group. It became immediately apparent that after the disclosure, this member withdrew from the group and other group members colluded with her silence by addressing other racial/ethnic differences while failing to address the "coming out." As part of the course requirement involved journals regarding the group experience, I was able to read their thoughts and feelings each week. As I had suspected, the group member who had revealed her sexual orientation expressed great distress after doing so. She wrote about feeling ill, sweating, wanting to be in a different place, and she hoped that the others would treat her as invisible. Much to my dismay, this not only occurred within the group, but only one other member in a group of seven mentioned the disclosure in her own journal. Naturally, the experience was quite distressing for me, and I did not want group members to have the privilege of avoiding a sensitive topic. I felt torn between respecting the wishes of the group member who did not want additional attention and the knowledge that the avoidance was unacceptable. Several weeks went by without the issue coming up again, and, finally, the one member who had written about the incident in her journal brought it back into the group.

Initially, group members were uncomfortable, evidenced by their use of euphemisms, such as, "When X said what she said," and "the disclosure," rather than naming the actual event. When I took the opportunity to point this out, group members seemed to dismiss my observation. Members then started referring to "lesbianism," clearly uncomfortable with the term, both by spitting it out as though it were a disorder and by labeling the student, who had never come out as a lesbian herself. It then became evident that group members did not want to address either the reality that they had bypassed the initial coming out or the current status of the group member, as they kept changing the subject by bringing up "new" issues. Again, I felt frustrated and angry with the group and made extra efforts to keep them on task. They began to attempt supportiveness by asking how the member needed help and "What's most distressing about being a lesbian?", again pathologizing her sexual orientation rather than responding to any particular distress. When the member requested feedback from the group rather than an exploration of "life as a gay woman," members again became agitated and were not satisfied with this request. They were merely interested in understanding the "problem," an approach that has seemingly been abandoned in ways of understanding identity development.

The experience left me feeling angry, and sad, as this group of counselors-in-training in a program that emphasizes multicultural training has a great deal of trouble and discomfort with the invisible minority status of sexual orientation. I felt cornered and ashamed of their accusations that my interest stemmed from my own sexual orientation (even if this was, in fact, the case) and at their resistance to explore the heterosexism and homophobia that they were helping to perpetuate. At the end of the semester, the group member who had been at the center of the discussion came up to me and thanked me for my efforts, expressing her disappointment with the group's response to her, and society in general. I was never able to share with her how upset the experience had left me but thought that it is an important issue to be mindful of in terms of training. The silencing or pathologizing of LGBT students and issues may not always be noticeable, but is harmful, nonetheless.

Commentary on Narrative 3

This narrative reveals some of the delicate balances of self-disclosure around sexual orientation in a nonsupportive environment, particularly for someone in a helper role; in this case, a group facilitator. When is it appropriate for a helper to self-disclose sexual orientation, and when is it appropriate to be an advocate? In this instance, the group comprised trainees who were apparently ignorant about sexual orientation and pathologized it. The group leader, also a student, was vulnerable along with the group member (although they were at different levels of identity development). This presented a double-bind predicament, a "Catch-22," or no-win situation. It raises the following question: What is the role of a group facilitator in the face of overt oppression when he or she is a also target, whether implicitly or explicitly? Although this student understandably wanted to intervene, she felt powerless to do so. We wonder what sort of supervision this student had available to process such challenging issues. We could imagine that, under the circumstances described, she felt as isolated as the group member and that the pressure of conformity to heterosexual norms was overwhelming. Another issue raised in this narrative (as in the previous one) is the assumption that multicultural training includes LGB awareness training. In this case, the writer wished that the students had transferred their knowledge of racism to understanding the dilemma of invisible minorities such as LGBs. Dealing with multiple oppressions, particularly regarding the issue of openness in professional settings, is an important educational issue (see Alvarez & Miville, 2003). If these issues are not addressed in multicultural courses, where are they addressed?

Narrative 4

I told somebody not long ago that the worst prejudice, if you will, that I have encountered has been from my own family. Of course, that is not the focus of this study, but it is important to note. Important to note because I believe that it has colored my perception of the world. I am reticent to share my personal side because if my own family cannot accept me, how can others? It really isn't that simple, I know, and yet it is. So goes the greatest struggle of my life. . . .

I have been partnered for nearly 15 years, since I was 21 years old. I knew her before that for almost a year. We have grown up together. We don't fight about the house or chores or things like that because we were so young when we got together, we have compromised over time. It is just how "we do things." Recently, we made the decision to have a child. Very scary to tell the parents. But, we did it. Now, we have a beautiful 3-year-old (Authors' note: name deleted and represented by X) who is the center and focus of our lives. What a great decision!

I started my master's in counseling prior to her birth. Everything in our lives is now "BX" and "AX"—before X and after X. I didn't tell anyone I was gay, one, because they didn't ask. I am sure they suspected. But no one knew for sure, and I didn't feel the need to tell. . . .

In my first practicum, I was placed under a very religious man who didn't mind telling anyone who would listen about the "right" ways. We worked at a hospital for children with behavior problems. I smelled trouble early, and my instincts did not betray me this time. One night, he asked me to stay late and "talk" with him. Of course I did. He ate dinner at his desk in front of me and began a seemingly innocuous conversation about TV. It turned to "that show, you know the one, about the queer lady. . . ." He went on a rail about Ellen, her filth, her corruption of kids, and so on. Then, he asked me what I thought about her. Stunned, I said I thought the show was funny but I didn't watch much TV. A lie. I watch a lot of TV, and I darn sure watched *Ellen*. He then went into how queers were fine, going to hell, but fine, but they had no place counseling kids, or being around kids for that matter. . . .

Trust me. I got the message. But you know, I was a first-semester practicum student with no prior experience. I didn't know about ethics or anything else for that matter. All I knew was that my "career" was sunk before it was started. I was going to get screwed by this guy because I was gay. I didn't tell anyone for a long time, a few weeks. But I was so bothered by the incident on two levels. One, I was afraid my career was over. But, two, why didn't I stand up and tell him he was full of it, and yes I was gay, and he was wrong, and did he have something to say to me, and anything else that could come to mind? Why didn't I? Was a career worth my self-esteem? Evidently, yes. Finally, I talked to my supervisor on campus. She was very calm and supportive in words, but the message was clear here, too. We weren't going to make a stink about it because this was a paid practicum site that we didn't want to lose over an issue like this. "Like this?" What does that mean, "like this"? Meaning not a real issue, a minor issue, a gay issue? What the hell did that mean? Again, I sat silently and kept going to that place. In the end, my grade was fine, it wasn't mentioned overtly again, and my career continued. But I have worried and thought about that experience a million times since then. I still do not believe I did the right thing, and I am scared to death that I would do the same thing over again.

When I interviewed for doc schools, I wondered whether I should tell from the beginning or not. I could put up a very convincing case for either side. In the end, I decided to bring it up only if it "came up." Here's a shock. It didn't. Once again, I hid behind rhetoric. My first week there, X was born. I missed a party because she was being delivered. I "had" to tell the reason when I called to say I wasn't coming. Imagine that shock! The faculty was comfortable, I think, with it. They sure tried to make me feel they were. But there is always that sense of disbelief in others' sincerity. Waiting for the other shoe to fall, even when it never does. It isn't so much about what they do or don't do, it is internal. This internal sense of distrust. It was a year or more before I spoke openly about my family to my peers and the faculty. . . .

Another time, one of my peers was having difficulty with a gay couple and brought it up in supervision in practicum class. It was so hard for the person to talk about it with me in the room. I really don't know why. Just choking on every word, so afraid to say something "wrong" or offensive to me. . . . Later, I wondered if it was all in my head. Was the person really checking me from the corner of the eye? Was there really uncomfortable silence? Or was it just me overreacting? Another surprise here. . . . I am not sure even today. . . .

As I read over this, I cannot say I get a positive, well-adjusted sense from it. In my day-to-day life, I plug along. We have fun, do things together, and in general live well. But if I sit down and think about this issue, discuss it, it is still a wound for me. One that may never heal, I guess. It is not going to kill me, or stop me, but it is always there. Always. Act one way and feel another, and so it goes. . . .

Commentary on Narrative 4

The internalization of fear and denial that saturates the workplace and academic environment is palpable in this narrative. Again, the vulnerability of graduate students is clearly stated, and the tendency toward self-doubt and blame in the face of oppression in a hostile environment is evident. Here is an example of both overt and covert heterosexism that illustrates the importance of advocacy and affirmation from faculty and allies at a systemic level. Silence or avoidance of taking an affirmative stance had an incredible impact on this student. One of the more poignant aspects of this narrative is the second-guessing that nagged this individual and the feelings of pain and frustration at both being in the closet (silenced) as well as speaking up (the supervisor refused to make a big deal about it). This narrative illustrates the grim reality that coming out is not necessarily well received nor a panacea to the problems endemic with homophobia. This writer also points to a dilemma of "act one way and feel another." Such internalized dissonance may act as an inhibitor to the coming-out process as well, in which previous negative experiences influence the course of future actions.

We can hope for a supportive environment in academia, although that is not always the case. Similarly, the workplace in the community may be unsafe. Consider the following narrative in which the workplace was the primary source of heterosexism.

Narrative 5

I graduated from college in the 90s, and for a couple of years explored different jobs and tried to figure out what it was I wanted to do with my life. I identify as a lesbian, and I was looking for a workplace where I could openly identify as a lesbian and be accepted. Up to that point, it had been difficult for me to be out at work, and I didn't specifically mention my female partner unless I was directly asked. The incident I want to relate happened when I applied for a job for which I went to interview. The interview started out smoothly enough, although it became readily apparent to me that the interviewer knew nothing about state laws regarding what can and cannot be asked as part of a job interview, which I knew from my work in human resources. . . . Anyway, his ignorance extended far beyond asking illegal questions . . . as he turned to more personal matters. He asked if I was married. I had trepidation about answering. I wanted the job, as it sounded interesting, but I really couldn't respect someone asking me questions that were clearly irrelevant to the job and my qualifications. If I lied and was hired, however, I knew I could never keep up the act, nor would I want to. I indicated I had a partner and left it at that. I hoped that he would get the hint and leave it alone. Thankfully, he dropped that line of questioning, and we talked about the job, but later in the interview he came back to the subject.

"When you said earlier that you had a partner, do you mean a male partner?" By this time, I knew I did not want the job. This was not the supportive workplace environment I was looking for. Since I figured I had nothing to hide, I replied truthfully, "No, my partner is a woman." He frowned and shook his head. "Well, I want to know if that's going to be a problem. I mean, we can't have you bringing your sexual orientation in to work everyday and flaunting it around. This is a place of business, and there's no room for that kind of display here."

The sick feeling in my stomach that had started earlier when he asked the original question intensified. I couldn't believe I was hearing what I was hearing. I had reached a turning point—either I could nod my head, get through the rest of the interview, and get the hell out of there and never go back, or I could take the risk and speak my mind. For one of the first times in my life, I chose the harder option. "I can't believe you just said that," I said in a controlled voice. "What difference does it make what my sexual orientation is? I have never been so offended in my life, and there's no way I would work for you." I carefully got up and walked to the elevator. I had to force my legs not to shake as I stepped in. I didn't look back.

As horrible a situation as that was, I look back now and can see the impact that it had on my vocational choice as a counseling psychologist. Why? Because my bigoted, prejudiced, illegal-question-asking interviewer was a licensed, clinical psychologist. This did not happen in the 70s, 80s, or even early 90s. This did not happen in a rural area. This was in the late 90s in a major metropolitan city in the Midwest. I decided that I needed to know whether he represented the field of applied psychology. I applied to graduate schools and was accepted into and entered a counseling psychology doctoral program. I am glad to report that he is not representative of the psychologists I have met and worked with thus far. However, most people who have prejudice are far less forthright about it than he was; to protect myself, I continually analyze my interactions with people to determine whether there is any heterosexual bias.

Commentary on Narrative 5

As in the previous narrative, decision points about disclosing one's sexual orientation continue to arise throughout one's career, sometimes in uncertain environments. As with other social oppressions, such as sexism, racism, and ableism, people may make ignorant or sometimes hostile comments. When such negative comments come from persons with credentials (i.e., power and privilege), the impact is even greater, and in this instance contributed toward forming another social bias (of not trusting clinical psychologists). As with other writers, the vigilance that is developed to screen for safety is an ongoing phenomenon. The use of vigilance as a survival strategy is reminiscent of posttraumatic stress responses of hyperarousal and hypervigilance in an effort to cope with perceived danger. In this instance, the writer elected to come out with a person whom she perceived to be unsafe, to make a point. Even so, the physical and emotional stress of the disclosure was memorable. It seems that only in deciding to let go of hope or desire for that particular job was the writer able to speak out courageously about the heterosexist comments and, in so doing, feel empowered. Unfortunately, many counseling job applicants, employees, or graduate student trainees don't feel they have the choice to confront and speak out about heterosexist comments due to economic needs or the power differential inherent in their relationships. A similar incident follows, which involves a supervisor's behavior and his impact.

Narrative 6

Because of my doctoral program's training experiences, which were sensitive to LGB issues, I had assumed that psychology's practitioners were LGB affirming. This impression was shattered as I ventured out from my program. I interviewed at a predoctoral internship site which was a community agency. During the interview, I was asked whether there were special populations with which I felt comfortable working. I described my interest in and work with the LGB population during my doctoral practicum experiences. At the time, I thought I noticed a couple of the interviewers twitching or making faces in reaction. As a result, I did not want to match with this internship, but I did end up attending this site.

One of my supervisors was a psychologist whom I'd noticed twitching during my interview. From the beginning of the internship, I thought that this supervisor was treating me with mild hostility. For example, he would joke with and act sweetly toward the two other female interns, but he would address me with cutting remarks. I was uncertain about whether this behavior was due to my racial background, my interpersonal style, or something else. In retrospect, I believe it was due to his heterosexist attitudes.

Upon starting internship, the caseload I inherited from previous interns and staff members included about 10 clients, all of whom identified as lesbian or gay. Difficulties with two of my gay clients brought my supervisor's heterosexism to light. After my first session with an older gay male client, this client complained to my supervisor about me and requested reassignment to another therapist. In supervision, I tried to discuss what I thought went wrong in my interaction with this man with bipolar disorder and personality disorder diagnoses. My supervisor dismissed my speculations and questions and instead attributed this client's difficulties with me to my identity as a young woman. My supervisor explained that I represented sexuality issues that this client was afraid to face. Although I was willing to entertain this possibility at this point in supervision, I found his hypothesis more unlikely than my hypotheses about my relative inexperience in working with personality disorders or about my expectations about therapy frequency being different from the client's. However, discussion of my hypotheses was not allowed, as my supervisor was convinced about the correct nature of his conceptualization of the client. This experience was my first hint about my supervisor's heterosexist attitudes, but it was somewhat covert given that I could make many interpretations of his conceptualization, some of which seemed to have clinical validity.

Shortly after this experience, I began to witness overt expressions of racism, xenophobia, and heterosexism in the agency. For example, within earshot of the waiting room, therapists would speak in derogatory terms about the foreign clients who did not speak English very well. One day when my flamboyant, gay, male client went into the restroom, I witnessed my supervisor broaden his chest and tug up on his pants as he joked with another male therapist, "Do you want to go in there and make a man out of him, or do you want me to do it?" I was mortified and terrified that my client would hear these therapists bantering right outside of the restroom door.

My intake with this same client followed immediately after this interaction. He talked about his presenting concerns and asked for a letter supporting his application for disability. I consulted with my supervisor, who immediately became reactive and described my client's "manipulative" behavior by using all sorts of expletives. He instructed me to follow him back to meet with the client and to watch how he taught this (expletive) a lesson. When he entered the room with the client, my supervisor attacked my client verbally and completely berated him.

After the client left, my supervisor continued to talk to me about the situation. He explained that all gay men are dramatic and that this manipulative behavior is to be expected from them. He further explained that people are homosexual because they fear the opposite sex and they cannot overcome this fear in healthy ways. When I told him that his explanations were offending me, he laughed a little bit. Then, with a glare and a chuckle, he said, "I'm dying to know what you are, but I know I'm not allowed to ask." My reaction was intense anger and intense fear. I was, and I still am, embarrassed that I succumbed to his scathing pressure and told him I was straight. I was so relieved that I could truthfully identify as straight in that moment. I could not imagine how much more horrible this experience would have been for someone who identified as lesbian, gay, or bisexual.

The semi-happy ending to the story is that I told my training director about this experience. She responded by immediately scheduling a meeting with this supervisor and confronting him on his behavior. I was assigned to another supervisor, and my interaction with my initial supervisor was minimal throughout the rest of the internship year. I had great sadness that he continued to supervise and to influence others who had less training and exposure to LGB issues than I. Unfortunately, my disillusionment about the LGB sensitivity of psychologists continues. I feel fortunate that my doctoral program provided meaningful training and modeling in relation to LGB sensitivity. . . .

Commentary on Narrative 6

Here is another example of workplace prejudice and the predicament of both overt and covert heterosexism. When the cues were subtle, the narrator was left guessing. When the cues were made overt, she had to deal with direct confrontation with a person who had more authority (a supervisor). Given the power differential between intern and clinical supervisor, it is surprising, and likely the exception, that this student would speak out about being offended by the supervisor's behavior and remarks. This intern's behavior is an excellent example of the risks an ally may take in advocating against heterosexism in the context of a hostile environment, and the important function of this advocacy. The support of the training director as an ally also was incredibly important in order to validate the trainee's experience and need for safety for her and her client. This narrative illustrates the need for training in encountering heterosexism; for example, learning how to respond as LGB and as an ally (see Evans & Wall, 1992). The fact that this intern had training in LGB issues and support in her doctoral program provided her with the knowledge and courage to speak out when she experienced heterosexism and unethical behavior during her internship.

We can only imagine that the coming-out process here is complicated further if the person is a member of multiple minority group statuses, such as being female, lesbian, and a woman of color. In an ideal world, fighting oppression may lead one to have skills to fight another. However, the reality often suggests that dealing with oppression such as racism may deplete the individual's energy and resources, making it difficult to resist yet another form of oppression (such as sexism and heterosexism).

Narrative 7

I have multiple professional identities as a faculty member, two of which are being a counseling psychologist and a multiculturalist. . . . In the courses I teach, I attempt . . . to help students better understand how a multiculturalist perspective changes the classroom discourse. Recently, I taught a course called "Advanced Multicultural Theories," in which we discussed various issues related to multiculturalism. . . . At the end of the course, the students pair up and present a workshop on their multicultural topic of choice to the class.

One of the pairs presented on issues related to the gay, lesbian, bisexual, and transgendered community (GLBT). The objective of their workshop was to sensitize undergraduates to the GLBT community. The pair chose to show a clip from the cable series *Queer as Folk,* in which two gay men were kissing. After the clip, the class was asked to respond. As the students and I were responding, the interaction felt strained and awkward. It felt as though people were not sure what to respond to in the clip. However, as the interaction progressed, we started to compare the two men kissing to two women kissing. The interaction in the class became more engaged as the discourse focused on the acceptability of two women kissing over two men kissing. Eventually, the entire discussion, to the end of the class, was focused on two women kissing, pornography, and how two women kissing reinforced heterosexism among potential participants in the workshop. The two presenters became quiet in the ensuing discussion, and the class ended politely.

After the class, it is my custom to replay the class discussion and to critique my performance and participation. This class felt strange and awkward, but it took me some hours to decipher my feelings and cognitions around the interaction. It came to me that the reason for my awkwardness and uneasiness following the class was my participation in changing the discourse of the classroom from a difficult conversation around homophobia and heterosexism to the dominant discourse of pornography and sexuality in a heterosexist sphere.

The following week when my class met again, I presented to them my discomfort with the previous week's class and invited discussion. It seemed that my self-evaluation and critique resonated with several others in the classroom who had also walked away from class somewhat confused about what had occurred. During our discussion, we were able to talk about critical pedagogy and how they can be more aware of themselves and how discussions flow and change as people alter between comfort and discomfort. At the conclusion of the class, we had a fruitful discussion of my own complicity as a teacher in the discourse and how my subtle displays of power, as well as their own concessions to my power, allowed us to move from understanding our own homophobia to understanding heterosexism.

I think this experience was helpful in allowing me be open and honest with my students. The discussion also helped me to articulate to the class how the subtle effects of the teacher's power often can change the discussions in a class and reinforce dominant discourses. It also, in my mind, helped me to model to my students the acceptability of making mistakes and learning from potential pitfalls.

Commentary on Narrative 7

Comfort versus discomfort, invisible power, and collusion with dominant culture are issues not often openly recognized in the classroom. The honesty and genuineness of this faculty member was critical in order to examine heterosexist bias. This story powerfully illustrates how part of "teaching" is "learning" and that admitting mistakes is necessary in order to move on from them. The faculty member, rather than taking an expert role and using his power to suppress dialogue (i.e., hide his mistakes), chose instead to take a facilitator role and open up discussion, owning his biases and furthering the learning of his students (see Alvarez & Miville, 2003).

This narrative illustrates the importance of a willingness to deconstruct the dominant discourse and to examine subjugated texts and hidden motivations. Such ongoing analysis is important, especially when one is in a position of power as a counseling professional. This faculty person had the courage to be fallible, to speak out, and to role-model for students the honest exploration of internalized homophobia and heterosexism. This example illustrates the difficulty of making changes in a system that is often invisible and pervasive.

Concluding Commentary on the Narratives

These narratives tell stories that represent harmful experiences more common than our profession would like to admit, particularly to those who are vulnerable in the field (e.g., students, trainees, clients, and persons with multiple oppressions). Waldo (1999) found that LGB people who had experienced heterosexism in the workplace exhibited more health-related problems and psychological stress and were less satisfied with their jobs. A number of the narratives presented here clearly demonstrate the emotional and psychological pain associated with homophobia and heterosexism in the workplace, including training settings. Indeed, words used to express the writers' reactions were strong and poignant, such as feeling embarrassed or mortified, or experiencing fear, terror, shock, hurt, or rejection ("I couldn't believe I was hearing what I was hearing"). They also experienced secondary reactions such as withdrawal, avoidance, increased caution, and sadness. Such intense reactions suggest that there are ample reasons why counseling professionals may be reluctant to disclose personally or to take an explicitly LGB-affirmative position.

For a number of contributors, choice points relevant to coming out of the closet in response to the incidences occurred at various times. For some, this occurred in the moment of the offending or homophobic behavior (e.g., job interview), whereas, for others, it took time (e.g., next class, group, or supervision session), even years, to risk disclosure and confrontation. Critical themes for most writers included a need for support to confront heterosexism as well as the importance of taking time to process the experiences within oneself and with others. Obviously, this implies the importance of dialogue and education to eliminate ignorance about LGB issues (Chan, 1996).

On Multiple Oppressions, Culture, and the Closet

In the beginning of this chapter, we suggested that the process of coming out professionally may be influenced by a number of contextual variables. A brief discussion here will touch on themes of multiple oppression and cultural factors related to sense of self (personal identity). We focus primarily on the experiences of LGB people of color as a prime example of intense and sometimes conflicting realities based on multiple oppressions (race/ethnicity and sexual orientation).

Despite advances in understanding multiculturalism, the psychological literature, research, theoretical paradigms, and clinical practices are imbued with Eurocentric cultural biases (Sue & Sue, 2002), which largely have overlooked the impact of multiple oppression. Themes for LGB people of color in the United States include managing the dilemma of visibility versus invisibility, understanding cultural complexity, and managing multiple oppressions; for example, racism, heterosexism, homophobia, and biphobia (Fukuyama & Ferguson, 2000). Indeed, coming out may not be the healthiest option for some LGB people of color (Greene, 1997). The decision to come out professionally in public ways (including in professional publications such as this book) is affected by many variables, including one's culture (past and present, personal and professional), social status within cultural identifications, and differences in definitions of self, such as individualistic versus collectivistic identity or public versus private self (Fukuyama & Ferguson, 2000).

For some persons, it is not salient to use sexuality as the defining variable in one's identity. For others, an LGB identity may be more associated with middle- and upper-middle-class White American culture, and acculturation or assimilation may influence the degree to which individuals identify with being LGB. These variables influence the different ways of negotiating the coming-out process professionally.

In addition, the concept of self (e.g., identity development, self-esteem, and self-concept) is influenced by group memberships. The relationship of self to one's reference group and to the dominant culture affects this identity development process. For people of color, collectivistic identities (derived from family and ethnic community, or shared experiences of oppression and discrimination) may be more salient than an individualistic identity.

Therefore, it is important to examine the dynamics and interactions of multiple cultural group identities and the accompanying social statuses and stigmas (Fukuyama & Ferguson, 2000). In some instances, cultural context is more important in defining presentation of self than any individual identity descriptors. Thus, dominant cultural biases in the counseling profession must be systematically identified and deconstructed to provide a safe context to facilitate the integration and inclusion of counseling professionals and trainees with multiple oppressed identities and orientations.

For example, a prevailing model for minority identity development suggests that individuals go through developmental stages of self-denigration, dissonance, immersion, and integration of a more positive minority identity (e.g., sexual orientation, gender, or race) (Cass, 1979; Downing & Roush, 1985; Helms, 1990). Some of the biases of these models include the assumptions that individual identity is more important than group identity and that the individual is dealing with only one minority status. Research that has examined the relationships between collective and personal (ego) identity confirmed the importance of the former in understanding the latter (Miville, Darlington, Koonce, & Whitlock, 2000). Other theorists have posited that in dealing with multiple social identities development may progress unevenly or independently of each other (Oetting & Beauvais, 1990–1991). If a professional is coming from a monocultural or ethnocentric viewpoint, that is, there is "only one right way to be," he or she may not understand why other professionals do not come out in the same way.

Let us imagine a case example (fictionalized): Rosa is a 30-year-old Latina who identifies herself as bisexual. When she visits her family, who lives near the Mexico-New Mexico border, she finds herself speaking Spanish and fulfilling the traditional female roles at home. She brings home her "significant other" (be that male or female), and her family is warm and accepting; however, they do not talk about her sexual identity, as there are no words for this discussion, and it does not come up overtly in extended family or community conversations. In fact, the only words to describe her sexuality in Spanish are negative and pejorative. When Rosa returns to her home in the city and her job as a mental health counselor, she sometimes participates in LGB social events, but she does not come out in her professional setting. When she attends professional conferences, she attends the Women of Color Coalition, which often meets at times that conflict with LGB meetings. Her LGB professional colleagues wonder why she is not more forthcoming because she seems to be comfortable with her sexuality. She comments, "My sexual identity is not as important to me as my Chicana identity. I feel a sense of loyalty to my family first."

Another "minority" status that conflicts with coming out deals not so much with a demographically based identity but one's level of training or position in the workplace. That is, as a number of the stories here illustrated, being a trainee or early professional adds a layer of vulnerability related to power status that at a minimum creates internal dissonance, inhibits feelings of acceptance, and impacts the healthy development of social relations. An assessment of the workplace, including training sites, must involve creating safety for beginning professionals.

Persons of color may feel particularly vulnerable to discrimination or increased oppression in response to speaking out or coming out related to their sexual orientation status. Add in the experience of being a trainee or otherwise vulnerable person in the workplace, and it becomes an understandable choice to remain anonymous regarding LGB issues in the professional setting. Historic models advocating the benefits of the coming-out process and of speaking out to promote change may not consider the contexts and consequences of these actions for individuals with multiple oppressed identities and nondominant culture identifications. Privileges bestowed to White-American-identified LGB counseling professionals, as for anyone with privilege, are likely unexamined as a context that enables and supports the speaking-out and coming-out process. The reality of homophobia and heterosexism that infuses American culture and therefore the counseling profession is inevitably institutionalized in training programs and work sites and adds understandable trepidation to all LGB individuals and allies.

In summary, our point in offering this chapter has been to illustrate that the coming-out process for counseling professionals is complex and multi-faceted. Cultural context and multiple oppressed identities, both in the moment and across time, are just two of the many facets of that complexity. As a profession, we have a responsibility to deconstruct the dominant ethnocentric cultural messages regarding identity development, hetero-sexism, and sexual orientation. We humbly acknowledge that the field of psychology is a relatively young and evolving science. Similarly, the counseling profession is an empirically informed art embedded within multiple subordinate and dominant cultural contexts. We need to understand and respect life choices and differences of counseling professionals and trainees who have socially oppressed identities.

In closing, we would like to acknowledge and thank the contributors of these personal narratives who made this chapter possible. We respect that the process of coming out takes many forms, and it is a continuous and life-long process. For all of the counseling professionals who are not out in their communities, workplaces, or professional associations, we offer support and encouragement. For all of the counseling professionals who are out, we thank you for your courage and leadership. And to the editors of this book, we thank you for the opportunity to give voice to these untold stories.

References

Alvarez, A. N., & Miville, M. L. (2003). Walking a tightrope: Strategies for teaching undergraduate multicultural counseling courses. In D. Pope-Davis, W. Liu, & R. Toporek (Eds.), *Handbook of Multicultural Competencies in Counseling and Psychology* (pp. 528–547). Thousand Oaks, CA: Sage.

Brown, L. (1994). *Subversive dialogues: Theory in feminist therapy.* New York: Basic Books.

Cass, V. C. (1979). Homosexual identity formation: A theoretical model. *Journal of Homosexuality, 4*(3), 219–235.

Chan, C. S. (1996). Combating heterosexism in educational institutions: Structural changes and strategies. In L. Bond & E. Rothblum (Eds.), *The prevention of heterosexism* (pp. 20–33). Thousand Oaks, CA: Sage.

Downing, N. E., & Roush, K. L. (1985). From passive acceptance to active commitment: A model of feminist identity development for women. *The Counseling Psychologist, 13,* 695–709.

Evans, N., & Wall, V. (1992). *Beyond tolerance.* Lanham, MD: University Press of America.

Firestein, B. A. (Ed.). (1996). *Bisexuality: The psychology and politics of an invisible minority.* Thousand Oaks, CA: Sage.

Fukuyama, M., & Ferguson, A. (2000). Lesbian, gay, and bisexual people of color: Understanding cultural complexity and managing multiple oppressions. In R. Perez, K. DeBord, & K. Bieschke (Eds.), *Handbook of counseling and psychotherapy with lesbian, gay, and bisexual clients* (pp. 81–105). Washington, DC: American Psychological Association.

Greene, B. (1997). Ethnic minority lesbians and gay men: Mental health and treatment issues. In B. Greene (Ed.), *Ethnic and cultural diversity among lesbians and gay men* (pp. 216–239). Thousand Oaks, CA: Sage.

Helms, J. E. (1990). *Black and White racial identity: Theory, research, and practice.* New York: Greenwood Press.

Miville, M. L., Darlington, P., Koonce, D., & Whitlock, B. (2000). Exploring the relationships between racial/cultural identity and ego identity among African Americans and Mexican Americans. *Journal of Multicultural Counseling and Development, 28,* 208–224.

Oetting, E. R., & Beauvais, F. (1990–1991). Orthogonal cultural identification theory: The cultural identification of minority adolescents. *International Journal of the Addictions, 25,* 655–685.

Sue, D. W., & Sue, D. (2002). *Counseling the culturally diverse: Theory and practice* (4th ed.). New York: John Wiley.

Waldo, C. R. (1999). Working in a majority context: A structural model of heterosexism as minority stress in the workplace. *Journal of Counseling Psychology, 46,* 218–232.

21

Race and Sexual Orientation in Multicultural Counseling

Navigating Rough Waters

James M. Croteau

Western Michigan University

Madonna G. Constantine

Teachers College, Columbia University

Analyses by several authors indicated that a number of different perspectives appear consistently in multicultural counseling literature (Carter, 1995; Carter & Qureshi, 1995; Helms & Richardson, 1997). The tension between two of those perspectives represents what has been called one of the "the most problematic" definitional issues in multicultural counseling (Sue, 2001, p. 791). On one hand, there is a "focused" or "race-based" perspective emphasizing issues of racism, race, and/or ethnicity (e.g., Carter, 1995; Helms & Richardson, 1997; Locke, 1990). On the other hand, there is an "inclusive" or "broad" perspective which focuses across an array of sociodemographic factors that result in groups of people being socially devalued or privileged (i.e., race and ethnicity, along with gender, sexual orientation, economic class, disability-ability status, etc.) (e.g., Constantine, 2001, 2002; Fassinger &

Richie, 1997; Fukuyama, 1990; Lowe & Mascher, 2001; Pope, 1995; Pope-Davis & Coleman, 2001; Robinson, 1999; Robinson & Howard-Hamilton, 2000). We contend that the tensions between these two perspectives are a source of great discomfort and, at times, direct conflict in the lives of counseling professionals engaged in multicultural and diversity issues.

This book employs the narrative voices of a diverse group of counseling professionals about their experiences with sexual orientation to serve as the basis for deconstructing the discourse on sexual orientation in the counseling professions. The book editors explicitly instructed all chapter authors to ground their writing in multiculturalism and considerations of race, ethnicity, and racism. Because sexual orientation is considered in its racial context in a book that is part of Sage Publication's multicultural series, it seems inevitable that reactions to this book will involve the tensions between race-based and inclusive perspectives on multicultural counseling. This chapter is an exploratory tool for counseling professionals in explicitly and constructively addressing those tensions.

In the first section of this chapter, we describe the inclusive and race-based perspectives as they have previously been discussed in the multicultural literature. In the second section, we outline the tensions between these perspectives and how they are manifest in the lives of counseling professionals, concluding with an assertion that despite these tensions, both perspectives are crucial and needed. To embrace both perspectives, we suggest a diunital or "both/and" balancing approach (Reynolds, 2001a, 2001b; Sue, 2001) to navigating the tensions and conflicts between these two perspectives. In the third and largest section of this chapter, we turn to the method that is central to the rest of the book— narrating stories of our own personal and professional experiences. We give some background information about our own journeys concerning race and sexual orientation and explore the tensions between race-based and inclusive perspectives that we have experienced in our professional lives. We discuss our navigation of those tensions and how we are beginning to see ourselves struggling with their reconciliation through the adoption of a "both/and" approach to race-based and inclusive multicultural perspectives. In the final section, we conclude the chapter by suggesting that our narratives are primarily useful as stimulus material for counseling professionals to reflect on their own navigation of race and sexual orientation. We attempt to give some context for such reflections by commenting on the contrasts, similarities, and limits of our two stories. We end by offering a series of reflective questions that might help other counseling professionals explore their own struggles in navigating the often rough waters of race and sexual orientation in multicultural counseling.

A Review of Inclusive "Versus" Race-Based Perspectives on Multicultural Counseling

The race-based perspective on multicultural counseling is primarily focused on racism, race, and/or ethnicity, although not denying the existence of other social inequities (e.g., Carter, 1995; Carter & Qureshi, 1995; Helms & Richardson, 1997; Locke, 1990; Sue, 2001). This perspective is consistent with the historical roots of the multicultural counseling movement, which grew largely out of efforts of professionals of color to challenge the racist and ethnocentric nature of the counseling profession. A race-based approach assumes that race is "superordinate" in the United States and that the "racial group transcends/supercedes all other [group] experiences" (Carter & Qureshi, 1995, p. 251). Race is, therefore, the "ultimate measure of social exclusion and inclusion" because racism is deeply embedded within the culture and history of the United States (p. 251). In the race-based multicultural literature, the superordinate nature of race and racism has sometimes been defined in reference to degree of psychological or social salience. For example, Helms and Richardson (1997) said that "in our experience, issues of race, ethnic culture, and ethnicity generate more consistently strong, negative, and unpredictable responses from counselors in training (and our professional colleagues) than virtually any other aspect of personhood" (p. 70). At other times, the superordinate nature of racism has been defined more from a cultural point of view. Carter (1995) argued that the socially defined classification of race and the application of oppression and privilege based on that classification (racism) are central to the overall culture of the United States. Carter presented an overview of the historical and political underpinnings of race and racism in the United States, pointing to how these are the central constructions by which difference and oppression are defined in the culture of the United States and thus in the consciousness of its people.

Inclusive perspectives in multicultural counseling have really emerged only in the last decade, but there is now a wave of multicultural literature that is intentionally inclusive of a range of diversity and social oppression, sometimes including sexual orientation (e.g., Constantine, 2001, 2002; Croteau, Talbot, Lance, & Evans, 2002; Fassinger & Richie, 1997; Fukuyama, 1990; Hays, 2001; Lowe & Mascher, 2001; Pope, 1995; Robinson, 1999; Robinson & Howard-Hamilton, 2000). Authors who take an inclusive approach have argued that multicultural counseling "has focused on individual aspects of identity (most often race and ethnicity or both)" and that consideration of multiple issues of oppression, identity, and their convergences have been "missing" (Robinson & Howard-Hamilton, 2000, p. iv). The inclusive perspective can be summarized in three tenets. First, individuals are confronted with systematic societal oppression (or privilege) based on their membership within a variety of sociodemographic groups, including but not limited to racial or ethnic groups. Thus, all forms of oppression and privilege need to be considered. For example, people with disabilities are systematically discriminated against and devalued at individual, social, and institutional levels. Individual attitudes, social norms, and physical facilities systematically advantage able-bodied people and disadvantage people with disabilities. Second, nonracial sociodemographic groups have characteristics that are cultural or at least subcultural. For instance, there is a lesbian, gay, and bisexual (LGB) culture that includes unique social norms, customs, artistic expressions, and so on. Third, an individual can be fully understood only in a holistic manner that includes understanding the influences and interactions of the individual's multiple sociodemographic groups, some or all of which may be salient "identities" for the individual. Thus, multiple social group memberships can be salient, can be the basis for identity, and can interact with one another in shaping experiences. To illustrate, gender and race may both be salient identities for a White female counseling professional. Furthermore, being a woman shapes some of her experiences of White culture and privilege, and being White shapes some of her experiences of sexism and being female.

To further elucidate the contrasts in race-based versus inclusive perspectives, we will review some of the arguments made for each perspective. The arguments for an inclusive perspective focus on establishing the validity of the three tenets discussed in the preceding paragraph. A number of authors have made the case for specifically including sexual orientation within an inclusive perspective on multicultural issues (e.g., Fassinger & Richie, 1997; Garnets, 2002; Lowe & Mascher, 2001; Pope, 1995). In the context of providing a comprehensive and current synopsis of sexual orientation for the multicultural literature, Garnets provided data showing how LGB people face sexual prejudice, including stereotyping, discrimination, hostility, and violence. She further provided a summary of the ways in which sexual orientation intersects with other aspects of diversity, particularly with race and ethnicity. Lowe and Mascher noted that there is a need to approach multicultural work from an integrated perspective that considers both race/ethnicity and sexual orientation. They discussed the system of dominance that is both racist and heterosexist and emphasized how adequate understanding and intervention with LGB people of color requires such an integrated perspective.

Pope (1995) argued explicitly for "an inclusive definition of multiculturalism" that includes lesbian women and gay men (p. 301). He asserted that lesbian women and gay men (a) have identity issues similar to those of racial and ethnic minorities, (b) are a cultural minority, and (c) need counselors with multicultural skills. Furthermore, he specifically countered the notion that the relative invisibility of sexual orientation negates or lessens the oppression, explaining how the ability to pass as heterosexual comes with negative psychological costs. Fassinger and Richie (1997) argued that "sex matters": that gender/sexism and sexual orientation/heterosexism are major factors that should be included in multicultural counseling and training (p. 84). They contended that heterosexism is a "non-conscious ideology" that results in oppression (p. 84). Furthermore, they showed how the framework for developing multicultural competence involving skill, attitude, and knowledge acquisition applies to work on sexual orientation issues.

The arguments for a race-based perspective focus on distinguishing race from other issues of oppression, arguing that race is more primary or superordinate than other issues, and/or making the case that including a broad array of oppression allows racism to be avoided or minimized (e.g., Carter, 1995; Carter & Qureshi, 1995; Helms & Richardson, 1997; Locke, 1990; Sue, 2001). Sue explained that an inclusive multicultural perspective can obscure differences between the dynamics of race and racism and the dynamics of other forms of oppression. Locke (1990) argued that it is flawed to assume that "racism is not different from the problems experienced by White persons who suffer from social devaluation" (p. 20); an inclusive perspective "tends to minimize the relative importance of different reference group memberships by conceptualizing them as equal" (p. 23). Furthermore, as previously stated, race-based authors have argued that in the United States race is more primary in terms of psychological, social, and/or cultural salience (e.g., Carter, 1995; Carter & Qureshi, 1995; Helms & Richardson, 1997; Locke, 1990).

In addition, perspectives that focus on an array of issues of oppression in addition to race may allow issues of race and racism to be avoided or ignored. Both Locke (1990) and Sue (2001) cited examples in teaching and training in which racism was avoided by attending instead to other issues of oppression/privilege. In short, these authors argued that often, professionals and students feel "greater discomfort" in response to race and racism as opposed to other forms of diversity and oppression (Sue, 2001). Thus, in situations in which diverse forms of oppression are being considered, attention is shifted away from the area of most discomfort, race and racism, and toward other diversity issues. To put this argument in stark terms, an inclusive multiculturalism provides professionals and students, particularly those who are White, with another avenue of "White flight" from the realities of racism that are so difficult to examine.

Inclusive Versus Race-Based Tensions in Navigating Race and Sexual Orientation

In our experience, there is often unease, mistrust, and/or conflict when counseling professionals are faced with both racial and sexual orientation concerns. We further believe that the difficulties are often connected to tension between inclusive and race-based perspectives on multicultural counseling. Indeed, we agree with Pope (1995) that the tension about the inclusive versus race-based nature of multiculturalism plays out most sharply around issues related to the inclusion of sexual orientation.

On one hand, tensions arise because an inclusive perspective can, and often does, result in the minimization of the cultural centrality of race and racism in the United States and in the avoidance of racism all together by shifting the focus to other issues of oppression, such as heterosexism. An undercurrent of mistrust often exists when a perspective that is inclusive of sexual orientation is taken. Professionals committed to work on race and racism may fear that racism will again be discounted and denied by focusing on another issue that will be inaccurately portrayed as similar to racism. A narrative by a multicultural pioneer contains a sharply worded observation of her colleagues' behavior at a recent multicultural conference, which exemplifies the powerful reactions that occur when racism is avoided by this means. "I was aware, for instance, of how much easier it was for participants to assail a participant for his regressive views on sexual orientation than for them to talk about race and racism at all" (Helms, 2001, p. 28).

On the other hand, tensions arise as a race-based perspective can, and often does, result in the exclusion or minimizing of other issues of oppression/privilege, as well as in the neglect of the significance of the complex intersections across race, ethnicity, sexual orientation, class, disability-ability, gender, and so on. In our experience, there is often an equally palpable undercurrent of mistrust in many situations when the focus is on race and racism, and professionals committed to work on sexual orientation fear that heterosexism will be ignored or even sanctioned by neglect. A narrative by one lesbian counseling professional in this book contains a statement that explicates the powerful feelings and reactions about the exclusion of sexual orientation in multicultural counseling:

> Many experts in multiculturalism limit real oppression to characteristics that are immediately obvious and "in your face," excluding sexual orientation that remains invisible until revealed. . . . As long as we can be killed just for who we are and be denied our basic civil rights in the name of God (as defined by the religious Right), then we are oppressed. (Douce, Ch. 8, this volume)

Conference discussions and panels relevant to these tensions have certainly been "difficult dialogues" (see Adams, Ch. 2, this volume; Bingham, Porche-Burke, James, Sue, & Vasquez, 2002; Croteau, 2001; Lowe & Mascher, 2001). We believe difficult dialogues around these tensions also arise frequently in the everyday lives of counseling professionals who are committed to multiculturalism. For example, these tensions arise at a group level as faculty or training staff must decide how to structure the requirements for a student multicultural work portfolio. Will the focus be on issues of race and racism, or oppression along a variety of dimensions? Will the inclusion of nonracial issues such as sexual orientation allow students to avoid a focus on race and racism? The tensions also arise at an interpersonal level among counseling professionals in collegial and supervisory relationships. Imagine the rough interpersonal waters between two colleagues when one is focused more on being vigilant about the use of sexual orientation to avoid dealing with race and the other is focused more on being vigilant about whether sexual orientation will be seen as a legitimate multicultural issue. We believe that both race and sexual orientation are always present and often relevant in clinical work, training and supervision, outreach, consultation, scholarship and research, professional organization work, and collegial relationships. Confrontation with the aforementioned tensions, therefore, is a common experience for counseling professionals with adequate awareness to notice issues of race and sexual orientation in their work.

We do not think that advocating for one perspective *to the exclusion of the other perspective* is productive. In one form or another, several authors have explicitly supported the idea that counseling professionals must be able to take both race-based and inclusive perspectives (e.g., Locke, 1990; Reynolds, 2001a, 2001b; Sue, 2001). Reynolds (2001a) envisioned race-based and inclusive views of multiculturalism "existing side by side as a symbol of the diunital (i.e., both/and)" approach that she believes "is necessary to the creation of a psychology and world that fully embrace multiculturalism" (p. 104). Such a "both/and" approach seems workable to us when considering the basic tenets of each perspective, as we find ourselves in strong conceptual agreement with both inclusive and race-based perspectives. We believe that multiple social groupings result in psychologically and socially potent privilege and oppression and that many social groups have culture-like characteristics. We also believe that the multiple social groups to which every person belongs can have psychological salience and that multiple salient social group memberships can become identities that interact in significant ways. Nevertheless, we also believe that race and racism are central, or superordinate, in the history and the current cultural ideology of the United States. Furthermore, we believe that efforts to challenge racism are so threatening to many White people that attention to other issues of diversity and social oppression often serve as a way for them to avoid or dilute attention to racism. In essence, at a conceptual level, we hold to tenets of both inclusive and race-based perspectives.

Race-based and inclusive perspectives are of necessity in competition with one another only from a limited-resources model, in which there is only so much of the "counseling profession pie" to be allocated for multicultural counseling. Thus, each slice of the pie that goes to one perspective is one less slice for the other perspective. We suggest that multicultural counseling must not accept the limited-resources model (see the work of "The More Pie" initiative in the Society for Counseling Psychology, e.g., Toporek & Gerstein, 2002). There is room in multicultural counseling for both perspectives, and we believe both perspectives must be nurtured.

The task for individuals who are attempting to hold a diunital or "both/and" approach is one of "centralizing race while considering other important social identities" (Reynolds, 2001b, p. 836) or "balancing" the acknowledgment of nonracial issues of diversity and oppression and the tendency of such acknowledgments "to dilute the importance of race" (Sue, 2001, p. 792). This is no easy task, especially given the sensitivities born from a history of struggle around issues of sexual and racial oppression. But we believe that a "both/and" approach is possible and is one viable way for counseling professionals to navigate the rough waters involved in considering both race and sexual orientation in multicultural counseling. To illustrate and explore the possibilities and the struggles of a "both/and" approach, we turn to the method employed throughout this book: the telling of our own personal narratives.

We offer our two personal stories not as examples of successful approaches but as an exploration of the possibilities and practicalities of a "both/and" approach. We hope that our stories will serve as stimuli for other counseling professionals in reflecting on their own navigation of the race-based/inclusive conflicts that occur when both race and sexual orientation are considered. In each of our narratives, we first provide background about our context and history in dealing with race and sexual orientation. Then, we each discuss our own struggles toward incorporating both race-based and inclusive perspectives into how we navigate race and sexual orientation in our personal and professional lives. We conclude with a description of the ways we grapple with making sense of this "both/and" approach for ourselves at the current point in our multicultural journeys.

Our Stories in Navigating Race and Sexual Orientation

Madonna's Story

Background and Context. I am a Black, heterosexual, middle-class, 40-something-year-old woman who grew up in a medium-size, predominantly Catholic city in Louisiana during the early 1960s. My nuclear and extended family members lived primarily within an eight-block radius of each other, and I grew up in a largely Black working-class neighborhood. I was reared as a Catholic, attending private Black Catholic schools from elementary school through college. This intentional "academic segregation" occurred because my parents wanted to isolate my four siblings and me from experiencing overt racism and discrimination on the part of school administrators who believed that Black children were inherently academically inferior to their White counterparts. My parents believed that my siblings and I possessed a reasonable amount of intelligence and ability to succeed at traditional academic tasks, so they did not wish to risk having their children placed in school settings where they would receive second-class treatment in their exposure to academic curricula and educational opportunities. As such, my exposure to Whites and other individuals who differed from me along some cultural dimension (except for sex/gender) was quite limited.

When I was growing up, I remember having occasional interactions with one or two classmates whom I suspected were gay. I remember thinking that these individuals were somehow "different" from me, but issues of sexual orientation were never openly discussed between any of us at that time. As a child, I also remember having Black male neighbors and a female cousin who were each living with a "friend," a word frequently used by many of my family members and adult neighbors as an acceptable term for a romantic or life partner. I soon learned that many of my family members believed that being gay was not tolerated in the Black community and that they were not willing to accept my cousin and her partner's relationship as a "valid union." In fact, I saw my cousin and our neighbors being largely ostracized by the local community. I remember thinking that my cousin and her partner seemed to be constantly subjected to ridicule for the ways they expressed their love for and commitment to each other. Although I believed this marginalization was wrong and unfair on many levels, as a child, I was unable to articulate specifically what was disturbing about the attitudes and actions of my family and neighbors.

Struggles in Embracing a Diunital Approach to Race and Sexual Orientation. As I think back to my early experiences related to the intersection of race and sexual orientation, I realize that in some ways it seemed easier for me to assume that most of the Black people I encountered were heterosexual. It appeared that individuals who did not self-identify as "heterosexual" seemed destined to suffer a miserable existence within the Black community. Again, this seemed wrong, and it reminded me of the discrimination I had experienced as a child during the limited times I interacted with Whites when I frequented stores and playgrounds. Over the years, it has become abundantly clear to me that many of my early experiences related to race and sexual orientation have profoundly shaped my current perspectives and values regarding my own understanding of the importance and intersection of these cultural group memberships, along with other salient sociodemographic variables.

As I consider my early struggles related to adopting a race-based versus a more inclusive approach to multicultural counseling, I realize that much of my initial thinking in this regard was based on my own experience of race being the most salient cultural group membership in my life. Thus, I expected that others would also view racial group membership and identification as the primary cultural variable in their own lives. Only after I entered a doctoral program in counseling psychology in a large city in the mid-South region of the United States was I substantially exposed to White individuals and other persons who differed from me along cultural dimensions such as social class, religious affiliation, ethnicity, and sexual orientation. In particular, during this time I became even more aware of sexual orientation issues because a male member of my program had confided to me that he was "closeted" in his true sexual orientation and behaviors. At that time, my peer was married to a woman, and he was afraid to "come out" to his spouse, other family members, our peers, and his close friends.

While sitting with my friend as he shared his struggles about this situation, I remember questioning (to myself) why he felt so comfortable discussing these issues with me, when it seemed clear that I was proudly and blatantly heterosexual (i.e., I was dating a couple of men at the same time and was enjoying my newfound freedom from a prior 5-year romantic relationship). I was also attending a Catholic church at least twice weekly and identified strongly with my religious group, so I figured he had a pretty good idea that most practicing Catholics believed that marital infidelity and "homosexual" behavior were "mortal sins in the eyes of God." During my Catholic upbringing, I had learned through catechism readings and priestly sermons that having a "homosexual" orientation was not necessarily considered "sinful" in the eyes of the Catholic Church, but that *acting* on this orientation was deemed sinful. I knew that I did not actually buy into this religious perspective, especially because of my early beliefs about the unfairness of discrimination and oppression. I also had to admit that I admired my peer's courage in struggling with issues surrounding his sexual orientation. I knew he was fundamentally trying to do "the right thing" by attempting to come to terms with his sexual orientation. In general, I was proud of myself for "having an open mind" about gay, lesbian, and bisexual orientation issues despite my conservative Catholic upbringing and some of the negative messages I had received growing up in reference to these issues. I also learned quite a lot about my own heterosexism in the context of this relationship. I became embarrassed about my own bigotry in this regard, and I worked actively to engage in personal reflection about ways to combat my own intentional and unintentional prejudices.

If I were to be completely honest (which my coauthor has appropriately challenged me to do), I would admit that I think it is somehow (at least a bit) easier to exist as a gay individual than to live as a Black person in this country because sexual orientation is a variable that often is not obvious to most people. In other words, having the choice not to come out as gay *seems* easier than having some people view you as "substandard" or "inferior" based on issues such as Black skin color, for example. One often can exist as a gay person without others necessarily knowing about one's sexual orientation, even though being closeted in this regard likely would cause an individual much internal turmoil and distress over time. I do not believe that the option of being "closeted" with regard to their racial group membership is a real one for most Black people in this country because of the obviousness of Black skin color or phenotype.

A primary concern that I and many other people of color have related to equating sexual orientation oppression with racism when an inclusive approach to defining cultural oppression is used, is that some people ignore the unique experience of racism in order to focus on broader issues of discrimination. It is undeniable that many gay, lesbian, bisexual, and transgender people have been subjected to unspeakable oppression at the hands of others. It is not my deliberate wish to poise one form of cultural oppression against another, yet I feel fairly certain that understanding and experiencing discrimination based on same-sex sexual orientation is not equivalent to understanding and experiencing racial discrimination. Moreover, being an openly identified gay individual or even an ally with regard to same-sex sexual orientation issues does not necessarily ensure that one is free of racism and other forms of oppression. I believe that the tendency of some White people, for example, to broaden the discussion of race and racism to other forms of oppression (e.g., heterosexism and homophobia) seems to be an immediate reaction in the face of the discomfort that many of these individuals often feel related to racial issues. However, such a defense, which can often be used to mask feelings such as anxiety and guilt, may leave many people of color feeling bereft of having true and honest dialogues about racism and its unique impact in people's (especially White people's) lives. Feeling "cheated" out of having such tough discussions has often left me feeling frustrated and mistrustful of individuals of any race or ethnicity who avoid engaging with me or other people of color at this level.

Many of my professional experiences as a teacher and trainer of graduate students in counseling psychology and as an organizational consultant regarding cultural diversity issues have focused on helping individuals to gain awareness of the salience of race and ethnicity in their own and in others' lives. Because of cultural lenses regarding my own race and ethnicity, it seemed natural to me to approach the understanding of cultural issues in these contexts primarily from a race-based perspective. At various points in my professional and personal life, however, I have struggled with getting in touch with how sexist experiences directed toward me have affected me as a woman and, specifically, as a Black woman. For example, as an administrator in my professional life, I was challenged to deal with sexism in a colleague's tendency to bypass me or minimize my professional authority. Instead, this colleague often went to the administrator directly above me (who was a man) for the "official word" regarding how to address certain issues related to the unit for which I was the administrator. The colleague had disclosed to me that side-stepping me to consult with the male administrator was a behavior that stemmed from "ingrained cultural values" related to viewing men as the "ultimate" authority figures and deeming women as holding relative positions of powerlessness. This colleague also professed that relating to a man interpersonally was simply "more comfortable" and that the behavior directed toward me was "not intended to be taken personally."

Such experiences are clearly difficult for me and countless other women who represent authority figures to individuals who struggle significantly with sexism. However, some of the challenges I have experienced related to others' sexism have allowed me to "make room" for my own personal explorations and informative dialogues with others regarding experiences of oppression based on my membership in a cultural group that was not racially based (i.e., gender). Such explorations and discussions have been critical to me in better understanding how the salience of one or more cultural group memberships in my own life and in other individuals' lives depends largely on issues such as social location(s), situational context(s), previous experiences, and a host of other variables that affect perceptions and experiences of discrimination and oppression.

Current Perspectives Regarding Adopting a Diunital Approach to Race and Sexual Orientation. I believe that race and ethnicity serve as vital cultural foundations for how people understand and articulate their worldviews, values, perspectives, and experiences. Because every person has a race and/or ethnicity, all can participate in dialogues about how membership in any given racial or ethnic group can create the potential for either being oppressed or serving as an oppressor. I view other cultural group memberships, such as gender, sexual orientation, social class, and religious affiliation, as social locations that interact with and add complexity to understanding individuals' unique experiences based on their racial and/or ethnic group memberships. *All* of these cultural memberships are important. Thus, I believe it is vital to adopt a diunital approach to understanding how race and other facets of culture are experienced and expressed in people's lives.

I also believe, however, that much of the work related to addressing issues such as oppression and discrimination seems to occur when individuals are truly in touch with various forms and levels of racism and are then willing and able to work to combat these issues in their own and in others' lives. I do believe that membership in an oppressed racial or ethnic group in the United States is more likely than other aspects of culture to draw consistently unfavorable and unpredictable reactions from individuals who have a vested interest in maintaining the status quo (Helms & Richardson, 1997). Much of my professional experiences have focused on identifying and instituting antiracism interventions among the populations with whom I have worked. These experiences, I believe, have strongly shaped my predominant use of a race-based approach to understanding others.

The aforementioned points notwithstanding, I must also admit that I believe in the multidimensionality of all individuals. That is, we are not simply racial or ethnic beings, although these cultural identities may comprise important parts of who we are. I believe it is important to recognize the intersections of cultural group memberships that shape individuals' unique backgrounds, perspectives, and experiences. Because the intersections of race, ethnicity, gender, and sexual orientation (as examples) determine individuals' overall personal identities at least to some degree, focusing exclusively on one particular dimension of culture (to the neglect of other cultural groups) leads to an incomplete picture of identity (Constantine, 2002; Robinson, 1993). The intersection of race, ethnicity, gender, and sexual orientation seems to be most apparent to individuals who face oppression as a result of membership in more than one marginalized cultural group (Reynolds & Pope, 1991; Weber, 1998). However, I believe we must all strive to understand others and ourselves more holistically as individuals who could simultaneously hold memberships and social locations in both dominant and oppressed cultural groups.

I value and appreciate the interconnectedness and importance of all living things. Such a perspective has allowed me to fully embrace and seek exposure to a wide range of human diversity in that I see all of us as being truly interdependent and vital to the effective "workings" of this world. In this vein, I have attempted to value both similarities and differences among individuals and to build bridges where chasms exist. In a particular effort to achieve this latter goal, I have found myself being challenged at times by students, colleagues, close friends, and even myself to see heterosexism and homophobia as forms of oppression that are on par with racism. This, of course, is easier said than done in the case of a Black heterosexual woman who has experienced very painful racist episodes. In my mind, which at times is considerably narrow, I still find it hard to believe that heterosexism and homophobia could be as painful or difficult to bear as racism.

It is never easy having discussions about oppression, regardless of its nature or source, but having such dialogues propels us toward self- and other-valuing, a necessary component for peaceful coexistence. Admittedly, obtaining a complete consensus may be idealistic and improbable; yet an increased understanding and a strong commitment to uncovering the complexities of and problems associated with oppression need to be crucial outcomes. Are having a same-sex sexual orientation and being a member of a racial or ethnic minority group fundamentally similar experiences in the levels of discrimination and oppression that individuals associated with these cultural group memberships experience on a daily basis? From personal experience, my perspective holds that they are not, but I have never been told that my membership in the Black racial group was "immoral" and "pathological." Perhaps one day I could be convinced that they are nearly equivalent experiences. Nonetheless, I cannot deny that being a member of any oppressed cultural group is sometimes much too painful and intolerable for words.

At this point in my life, I believe it is crucial to embrace both race-based and more inclusive perspectives to conceptualize others' experiences because there is room for both approaches in working with clients in counseling and in interacting with others in general. Although one perspective may take center stage over the other at different times (and, quite realistically, should), the ability to employ both perspectives allows for a much fuller and richer understanding of how "culture" is constructed and operationalized in individuals' lives. Ongoing awareness of the fluid, complex, and multidimensional nature of the salience of cultural group memberships in people's lives is a critical component of multicultural counseling competence.

Jim's Story

Background and Context. I am White and grew up during the 1960s and early 1970s in a predominately White middle/working-class neighborhood in suburban Memphis, Tennessee. Despite the civil rights movement around me, I was immersed in the kind of privilege that allowed a White young man to be insulated and isolated from any contact with racial issues and racism that seemed personal or "about me" in any way. I also grew up gay and, quite literally, hating myself for being so. I was determined to keep my sexual orientation a deep, dark secret and was living in what writer Paul Monette called the "coffin world of the closet," with a life that was emotionally gutted (Monette, 1992, p. 2).

I entered graduate school insulated in White privilege and emotionally overwhelmed with internalized heterosexism and homophobia. While there, I experienced the few, sparse signs of LGB affirmation that were present in a few graduate programs of the time. "I was so desperate for a way out of the closet, that those small affirmative signs, combined with the program's demand for genuine self-reflection, were all it took to bring the walls of my self-hatred tumbling down" (Croteau, 2001). Since my coming out in graduate school, I have had my share of homophobic and heterosexist assaults directed at me in my professional life, ranging from a "Die faggot" note in my graduate school mailbox, to comments on teaching evaluations accusing me of "flaunting" my sexuality, to social discomfort and ostracism from colleagues. For me, however, neither the overt nor the subtle discrimination could ever equal the misery of my former closet of self-hatred.

Struggles in Embracing a Diunital Approach to Race and Sexual Orientation. In my training and early in my career, I thought purely from an inclusive perspective, thinking similarly about all issues of diversity, including sexual orientation and race, and believing that all these issues deserved equal professional attention. In practice, however, I was often so immersed in undoing my own first heavy layer of internalized heterosexism and homophobia that I barely had enough emotional energy left to deal with the most basic academic and professional requirements, much less for taking on racial self-examination. I recognized that racism existed but saw racism as an injustice that some "bad" Whites perpetrated on people of color, and it seemed to have little to do with me.

Around this time, I and several fellow graduate students made a complaint about a newly formed multicultural student services office that was focused exclusively on race/ethnicity and was not inclusive of sexual orientation. This is an example of White people who face oppression along some dimension of diversity calling for attention to their issue of oppression in a manner or circumstance that will dilute and divert much needed attention to race and racism (see also Carter & Qureshi, 1995; Locke, 1990; Sue, 2001):

> Like is all too common of a mistake for those of us who are White and LGB, we were essentially trying to "appropriate" the struggle against racism to serve our own purpose, without having worked or invested anything in that struggle against racism. (Croteau, 2001)

I was challenged on my attending to sexual orientation and not attending to race as I became more involved in multicultural-training environments. Despite my "inclusive" belief that racism deserved equal attention to heterosexism and homophobia, I was ignorant about my own racism and very scared of acknowledging and dealing with it. I remember once in my graduate training, when it was time to express supervisor preferences, I requested to not work with a particular clinical supervisor because I felt unsure of where that person was with LGB issues. I gave no thought to the racial dynamics of that request from a White supervisee about a supervisor of color. I failed to understand the feedback about possible racism and racial dynamics that I received. I wrote about another incident that occurred around this same time, when I received feedback about a pattern of my behavior that some of the staff at a training agency considered racist: I was "walking on eggshells with the people of color on staff . . . so excruciatingly careful to appear nonracist to people of color that I was avoiding, closing off, distancing myself" (Croteau, 1999, p. 30). My own view of racism at that time as "an unacceptable individual moral or psychological failure" (p. 30) had left me little room to respond to feedback and learn from these mistakes.

Within an inclusive multicultural perspective is an emphasis on how different issues of oppression and privilege interact with one another. One of the first sources of progress in my racial journey involved a process that participants in a recent study described as translating from one's own experience of being oppressed (or privileged) to achieve greater understanding about the experience of oppression (or privilege) of a group to which they do not belong (Croteau et al., 2002). I knew what oppression felt like as a gay man, and I began to use that experience as a window to generate empathy or some limited understanding of what it might be like as a person of color facing racism.

This was sufficient progress to motivate me to join a diversity-training program. The "training of trainers" in this program focused on multiple issues of oppression and was intensely challenging. In this training, I participated in small-group discussions about collective group experiences with others who belonged to my same social and cultural "home" groups. My earlier discovery of a common experience with other LGB people was reinforced, and I discovered for the first time a common experience with other White people (as well as other men, other temporarily able-bodied people, etc.). After these "home" group discussions, the small groups would report back to the larger, more diverse group. Reporting back my collective experiences and listening to the collective experiences of other people's "home" groups was very powerful. My sense of gay pride soared, and I also began to be motivated to work against racism. I was growing in my gay identity and for the first time beginning the process of developing a White antiracist racial identity. The inclusive approach in this program, which focused on all forms of oppression, including both heterosexism and racism, was significant to my growth. While I was finally ready to examine racism and racial identity, my own sexual identity development still needed nurturing and attention. I would not have been able to set aside sexual orientation concerns and focus totally on racism and White identity.

As I gained greater empathy for racial injustice, I began to formulate a beginning commitment to working against racism. Furthermore, the notion of coalition became very important to me. I began to realize that if I wanted a particular set of LGB-affirmative and antiheterosexist actions and attitudes from heterosexuals, I had best be prepared to do similarly as a White person about racism. My sense of empathy for and coalition with people of color was the key to my early involvement in antiracism work. Relying exclusively on such, however, became problematic. If non-LGB individuals were not engaged as allies on LGB issues, I found it very hard to be engaged on "their" issue of oppression. Their failure to hold what I perceived as their end of the "coalition bargain" (working on heterosexism) had so much emotional impact on me that I found it hard to hold my end of the "bargain" (working on racism and other oppressions).

A race-based perspective emphasizes that racism is not like all other issues of diversity and oppression/privilege. I intellectually understood that there were differences among racism, heterosexism, sexism, and other forms of oppression and would never have made a simple assertion that all oppressions were the same. Consistent with an inclusive perspective and my own coalition mentality, however, I was much more attuned to seeing all issues of oppression as being like all other issues of oppression and sometimes acted accordingly (Carter, 1995; Carter & Qureshi, 1995).

I made, and allowed the making of, comparisons "to racism and racial civil rights in educational and social advocacy efforts on LGB issues" (Croteau, 2001). In this case, I was not using my own gay experience to better understand race and racism; instead, I was appropriating the experiences of people of color to promote gay liberation. I also remember often listening to addresses and training sessions on multicultural issues in various professional contexts and having intense emotional energy invested in whether sexual orientation would be included. I would be relieved and able to focus only if it was included. If not, I felt the hurt of anti-gay oppression and of having that oppression rendered invisible yet again. The hurt was often so great as to leave me unable to focus on the training, and I missed many opportunities for growth on issues related to race and racism. Of course, the irony of my need to assert equal attention to LGB issues was that my own development did not reflect equality across racial and sexual lines. I did not feel anywhere near the same level of ownership and efficacy in dealing with race and racism as I felt in dealing with sexual orientation and heterosexism.

As I have persisted in engagement with antiracism work, I am now slowly getting more in touch at a personal, "felt" level with the collective of experiences of White people in this country: "privileges Whites are assigned, racism Whites are taught, and the necessary struggle (and joy) of the process of becoming anti-racist" (Croteau, 1999, p. 31). I can never really know what racism is like for people of color, but I am beginning to learn that I do know firsthand what racism is like for White people. Doing antiracism work is now becoming *my* issue instead of something I do only in the spirit of coalition with people of color. I now see that racism was the direct cause of my painful intrapersonal and interpersonal struggles illustrated previously. I acutely feel the pain of the separation that racism sometimes causes between me and important colleagues and friends of color. I am becoming aware of how White privilege undermines my own humanity if I am not actively engaged in the struggle against racism. I am now finding a personal stake and, subsequently, a more empowered voice in talking about racism.

With this new racial consciousness, it seems I am now sometimes able to operate from a truly inclusive perspective with both sexual orientation and race being a "felt" part of my everyday experiences. But more recently, I have been coming to understand that even that full sense of an inclusive multicultural perspective is too limiting. I am beginning to think that I can truly understand or appreciate my own racial heritage and identity only if I can also see multicultural issues from a race-based perspective. It is only in working on this book that I have begun working toward a "both/and" approach that incorporates both inclusive and race-based perspectives. In reading in preparation for this chapter, I have really "listened" for the first time to those who promote the race-based perspectives on multicultural issues. I am coming to understand the "superordinate" nature of racism and a White ethnocentric worldview in shaping all my perspectives and experiences, including those specifically related to my race *and* my sexual orientation.

I did have some initial insight into this when I wrote about my experience with racist "eggshell" walking around the counseling staff of color (Croteau, 1999). I saw racism at that time from a purely individualistic viewpoint, as personal psychological or moral failure. Accepting that I had been racist thus was just too threatening. A solely individualistic perspective is "unforgiving" and fails to take into account the collective inheritance or "socially learned reality of racism" (p. 30). In that essay, I also recognized that my first step in seeing beyond an individualistic worldview was linked with my "coming out" experience. I had to recognize that my own self-loathing for being gay was not about my individual psychological or moral failure, but instead about having internalized the collective oppression of LGB people. I had to overcome the blinders of ethnocentric individualism to recognize my own oppression as a gay man. Overcoming those ethnocentric blinders in coming out thus "opened a new, less exclusively individualistic, window by which to understand myself and the world around me" (p. 31). Slowly then, I began to use this more collectivistic and "oppression-sensitive perspective to understand my own experiences a White American dealing with racism" (p. 31). And now I am actually beginning to be able to see just how central individualism is in shaping how I see all kinds of experiences in my everyday personal and professional life, how my White American cultural worldview is a "superordinate" factor in my life.

In fact, in writing this chapter, I have come to a new, more race-based, understanding of my coming-out experience as a gay man. I started my life blind to my position of privilege as a White man. I saw myself solely as an individual, and I did not worry about prejudice or discrimination being directed my way. I never really faced, or ever even considered, any external barriers due to who I was. I had the luxury of feeling that success was largely a matter of taking advantage of the opportunity that was available to me. Of course, I never perceived this as privilege at that time, it just seemed like the way the world was. As I grew into adolescence and my sexual awareness, I came to believe that my potential for success in life was conditional on keeping my sexuality a secret. For me, as a gay White American man, coming out meant giving up a world in which merit determines outcome, in which individual initiative determines social advancement. Although I could not articulate this intellectually as I was coming out, I am convinced that a key obstacle to my doing so was knowing that coming out would mean giving up a life based exclusively in privilege. When I did finally come out, I had to make the choice to prize my own sense of integrity and capacity for love over a life in which oppression would never be more than someone else's distant reality. As I was coming out in the early 1980s, there was an explicit recognition among gay men that coming out meant having to give up the American idea of life behind a white picket fence (house in the suburbs, wife, kids, car, and a dog). The color of the fence takes on new meaning for me with the realization of just how central my heritage of White racial privilege and culture is to all aspects of my life, including being a gay man.

Now at times I am able to feel connected to both my sexual orientation and racial heritages and identities. Now at times I am also able to think and act from a "both/and" perspective, involving inclusive and race-based perspectives. In these times, I find myself stretching to new places that hold much promise in advancing my multicultural journey. One final example illustrates how some of this plays itself out in my current professional life.

In all aspects of my professional life, but especially in professional organization work, I am fortunate to be a part of several working groups that are quite diverse and for which multicultural issues are quite important. Recently, in two of those work groups, I have witnessed two colleagues make statements about race and sexual orientation to which I had strong, emotionally mixed reactions. Both the colleagues who made these comments were people with whom I have a significant connection professionally and/or personally. Both were people of color and heterosexual. They argued in compelling ways for how the group of professionals to which we both belong was failing to attend to issues of race or racism and/or approaching work with White Eurocentric cultural blinders. One colleague talked about how that failure to address racism affected him personally, and both talked about the effect on the work of the group. In illustrating the lack of attention to issues of race and racism, both colleagues made a comparison to sexual orientation issues. One colleague stated that the professionals in the work group were much more comfortable discussing other issues of diversity, such as sexual orientation. The other colleague stated that awareness in the broader professional community surrounding the work group was much greater for issues of sexual orientation than for race.

My reactions to their statements were intense. On one hand, I felt very angry about the part of the comments that seemed to me to minimize the extent and impact of heterosexism. I had to very consciously restrain myself from going on rant and asking my colleagues a long series of angry questions: Who gave you the right to assess the status of sexual orientation issues and antiheterosexism work, and what gives you the authority and expertise to make such an assessment? Do you have any idea how demeaning it is for me to constantly have the morality of my life and my love for my partner of 18 years debated not only in the wider society but also in professional settings such as conference programs, the classroom, and clinical supervision groups? Do you know what it is like to have these anti-LGB beliefs about the immorality or sinfulness of homosexuality tolerated by the majority of professionals around me in the name of freedom of expression or religious tolerance? Do you know what it is like to literally be the "only one"; the only openly LGB person in every employment situation in my career? Do you have any appreciation of the effects of the anti-LGB vandalism and harassing phone calls I have experienced in professional contexts? Do you have any idea how many LGB students or professional colleagues come to me with their stories of oppression and pain within the very professional communities that you falsely described as being so far along on these issues?

Despite all this anger, I very much wanted these groups to embrace the challenge on racism that was offered by my colleagues. I was personally drawn to the prospects of a more genuine focus on racial issues in the work of these groups. I was excited that such a focus could open more personal and professional growth in my own racial identity and awareness, an area of growth that had become increasingly rewarding. I also thought that such a focus would open up the possibility of deeper and more genuine connection with my colleagues of color, and I very much wanted to deepen those connections.

I was emotionally in touch with both my proud gay and White antiracist identities and commitments. In essence, at that moment I was living out of, and feeling intensely, both my race and sexual orientation. In the midst of these intense feelings, I was also keenly aware that I felt torn between acting out of an inclusive perspective versus acting out of a race-based perspective. On one hand, I was pulled toward an inclusive view of social oppression: I knew I could not allow oppression on the basis of sexual orientation to be excluded or trivialized by my colleagues' comments. But on the other hand, from a race-based perspective, I knew how enormously difficult it had been for my work groups to directly discuss racism. We were about to have much-needed and much-avoided discussions of racism, and I did not want what I said about heterosexism to detract from that. In the end, I think a nascent "both/and" consciousness about race-based and inclusive perspectives allowed me to make intentional, balanced, and productive responses in these two situations.

In one case, in the smaller work group, I expressed my anger and aired my assessment of the actual status of LGB issues in our work group. When so challenged, my colleagues were supportive, as I had expected them to be. I was then able to join with my colleagues in fairly quickly returning the discussion to dealing with issues of race and racism. In the other larger work group, I set aside my reactions to LGB issues temporarily, and supported and added to the discussion of the need to attend to race and racism. I then confronted my colleague individually later about his remarks about sexual orientation issues. We had a productive discussion, and now in his advocacy for racism, he is always careful not to make what might be an incomplete, misleading, or potentially harmful assessment of sexual orientation issues. Thus, in both situations, some progress was made on both racism and heterosexism.

Current Perspectives Regarding Adopting a Diunital Approach to Race and Sexual Orientation. I described my shifts in multicultural consciousness from an exclusive focus on sexual orientation toward a more genuine inclusive perspective that centralized race as well as sexual orientation in my life, and finally toward adding a more race-based perspective on how my White privilege and cultural heritage play a superordinate role in my life. Nevertheless, I know that my own sense of gay identity and pride is that place inside of me where I can always go to find my sense of inner strength and centeredness. It is my home in a way that no other identity or place could ever be.

It is sometimes painful to put a race-based perspective on multicultural issues alongside an inclusive perspective. It is painful to see that that attention to LGB issues can and often does function as a diversion so that we White people do not have to deal with racism. It can be painful to accept and acknowledge the superordinate nature of race and racism in the United States, given how profound my own gay experience is in my life. I certainly cannot think that my race is always superordinate to my sexual orientation in the sense of psychological salience, though sometimes it is. I also do not think my race is always superordinate in terms of what is most salient to others. For instance, my being White undoubtedly has greater salience to others in the more anonymous encounters I have in everyday life (e.g., going to the grocery store), but it is often not most salient to others in settings such as work, community involvement, friendship networks, and family, where I live my life openly gay. So as I struggle with this, rather than focusing on race as superordinate in a psychological or social sense, I am currently working toward realizing that race is superordinate for me in a cultural sense. The dominant White Eurocentric worldview upon which social institutions and interpersonal norms are built in this country is my "home" cultural perspective; the worldview that comes quickest and most natural for me is the worldview that is privileged in this society. Furthermore, the sense of White privilege is the socially defined space that I began life with, my first "given" so to speak. In that sense, it is the base out of which I construct my life as a White gay man in a racist and heterosexist world.

As with much of my multicultural journey, I have found this joining of race-based perspectives with inclusive perspectives to sometimes be painful and confusing. Yet for me, it seems to be a most promising avenue for my continued growth in my understanding and awareness about race, sexual orientation, and other forms of diversity and privilege/oppression. With that continued growth, I hope to continue to be amazed at the unfolding richness that my multicultural journey brings to my personal and professional life.

Our Stories as Invitation
and Stimulus for Self-Exploration

In the first section of this article, we reviewed the literature on race-based and inclusive perspectives in multicultural counseling. We described the tensions that can arise among counseling professionals as either a race-based or an inclusive perspective is taken. We proposed exploring a "both/and," or diunital, approach to managing the tensions inherent in these two perspectives. In the second section, we then used this diunital approach as a lens through which to reflect on and describe our experiences in navigating race and sexual orientation. Now, in this third section, we want to assist counseling professionals in employing our stories as stimuli for exploring and reflecting on their own experiences and for charting new directions for their own navigation of race and sexual orientation. We do this by first giving some context for such reflections in the contrasts, commonalities, and limitations in our two stories. Then, we leave the reader with a series of questions to help in their own reflections on navigating race and sexual orientation and on making sense of race-based and/or inclusive perspectives on multicultural issues.

Madonna's story is about an African American heterosexual woman whose journey was first anchored in the clear salience of her experiences of race and racism and who saw multiculturalism from a race-based perspective. She is moving toward greater understanding of sexual orientation issues and to an appreciation and recognition of the useful components of an inclusive perspective on multicultural issues. Jim's story is of a White gay man who began his life immersed in privilege. Coming out as gay was his first experience with personal awareness of oppression; thus, his initial anchor was more centered in a perspective inclusive of sexual orientation and not focused on race. He is in the process of discovering the centrality of White culture and privilege in his life and is beginning to hear and understand the power of race-based perspectives in contributing to his own multicultural understandings and competence. Thus, Madonna seems to be moving from an understanding centered on race and a race-based perspective toward greater understanding of sexual orientation and more appreciation of inclusive perspective on multicultural issues. In contrast, Jim seems to be moving from an understanding centered on sexual orientation and an inclusive perspective toward greater understanding of race and more appreciation of race-based perspectives.

Despite these differences in the directionality of our stories, we seem to share the common struggle to add to the multicultural perspective and issue of oppression that is our "home base." Madonna is a "Black heterosexual woman who has experienced very painful racist episodes," and she is starkly honest about finding it "hard to believe that heterosexism and homophobia could be as painful or difficult to bear as racism." Yet she believes that heterosexism and other forms of nonracial oppression are "too painful and intolerable for words," and she values the importance of striving to understand the intersections of race, ethnicity, gender, sexual orientation, and other cultural group memberships. Jim recognizes that his sense of gay identity and pride is "home" in a way that other aspects of identity may never be. Yet he is recognizing just how pervasive and central his White cultural privilege has been in shaping all aspects of his life, including those connected with being gay.

We also both seem to share a common struggle to be conscious of the tensions that arise when either a race-focused or an inclusive perspective is taken and to let such consciousness guide our actions. Our stories point toward the importance of taking one perspective in ways that are conscious and respectful of the point of view of the other perspective. When a race-based perspective is taken, the challenge becomes how to not devalue heterosexism and other forms of oppression and how to consider the potent ways in which other forms of diversity interact with race in people's lives. For example, in articulating her current perspective, Madonna asserts a more race-based perspective when she gives race and ethnicity a central status as "vital cultural foundations for how people understand." In the face of such a race-focused assertion, however, she moves on quickly to also assert some degree of inclusiveness, saying that "all cultural memberships are important," that "all individuals are multidimensional," and that "intersections of cultural group memberships" shape people's lives.

When taking an inclusive approach, the challenge becomes how to recognize the special centrality of racism in United States culture and how to not allow the focus on heterosexism and other issues of oppression/ privilege to result in the avoidance of racism. For example, Jim described colleagues' comments that presented important challenges to racism but also implied the minimizing of heterosexism. He took definitive action to confront the minimization of heterosexism, to insist on true inclusion. But at the same, he was strategic about the timing and duration of his confrontation; he did not want his insistence that the group recognize the reality of heterosexism to detract from the much-needed focus on race and racism that was taking place.

As we reflected on the commonalities and convergences in our two stories, we became acutely conscious that our stories are very limited in explicating the experiences of counseling professionals in navigating race and sexual orientation. Our stories are bounded by our individual experiences and histories, as well as our sexual and racial social group memberships and identities. Counseling professionals will have many contrasting experiences due to individual differences and personal histories even when they share particular racial and sexual group memberships. For example, both authors grew up in relatively homogenous environments, racially and sexually. Madonna grew up in predominantly African American neighborhoods and schools, and Jim grew up in the largely White suburbs personally isolated from people of color. Neither Jim nor Madonna had close relationships with openly LGB people as they grew up. White LGB and heterosexual African American counseling professionals who grew up with more racial and sexual diversity will undoubtedly have different perspectives and experiences concerning race and sexual orientation.

Counseling professionals who do not share our two particular combinations of racial and sexual identities are even more likely to have divergent experiences and perspectives. We are particularly conscious about potential divergence of experiences among people of color who have a minority sexual orientation. Jim's consciousness about his minority sexual orientation emerged in the context of racial privilege; a person of color's consciousness about his or her minority sexual orientation will emerge instead in the context of racist oppression. Madonna's own racist oppression is her comparative context for understanding someone else's sexual orientation oppression. In contrast to Madonna's experience, a person of color with a minority sexual orientation is experiencing both racial and sexual oppression at a personal level. Emerging perspectives of and about LGB people of color are shedding new light on LGB psychology (e.g., Fukuyama & Ferguson, 2000; Greene, 2000). In similar fashion, we would expect stories from people who face both racial and sexual oppression to be unique and important stimuli for counselor self-reflection about inclusive and race-based perspectives and the navigation of race and sexual orientation in the counseling professions. In fact, many more stories need to be told from counseling professionals who are diverse from us in many different ways to broaden and diversify consideration of the issues we introduce here.

How can counseling professionals make use of our stories, given that the stories are so limited to our own personal and cultural group contexts? Direction can be found in common practices in clinical training and supervision. Counseling professionals are used to hearing about the clinical experiences of colleagues and supervisors and using those experiences to inform clinical practice. In this process of learning from other clinician's experiences, competent counselors do not simply imitate what worked and avoid what did not work. Instead, they use information about clinical experiences of colleagues and supervisors as stimulus material for critical reflection that takes differing client contexts into account. We hope that our stories, however divergent from the experiences of any particular reader, can stimulate critical contextually sensitive reflection in a wide diversity of counseling professionals.

To further invite and enable reflection, we conclude this chapter with a series of reflective questions. We envision these questions being useful for private self-reflection as well as for small-group discussion in the classroom and other training and supervision settings.

1. What are your own experiences of the relative psychological, social, and cultural salience of your racial identity/experiences and your sexual identity/experiences? Reflect on this question from both current perspective and a historical perspective. What sense do you make of any differences in salience?

2. What do you believe about how race and racism compare with other social and cultural group membership and sources of oppression, especially sexual orientation and heterosexism? Do you see race and racism as superordinate in this country in any way? If so, how so? If not, why not? What are your experiences with sexual orientation or other diversity issues diluting attention to race and racism?

3. In what ways do you think of all issues of oppression/privilege (i.e., racism, heterosexism, sexism, ableism, etc.) as sharing similarities and having equal potential salience? What about your beliefs and experiences around how various issues of diversity/oppression intersect with one another?

4. What are your experiences with the tensions between race-based and inclusive perspectives in navigating race and sexual orientation? Think of times when multicultural issues were exclusively focused around race and how you experienced those times. Also think of times when multicultural issues were broadly focused on an array of issues of oppression/privilege, including sexual orientation and how you experienced those times.

5. What are your experiences with race-based versus inclusive tensions when race and issues of oppression/privilege other than sexual orientation are considered (i.e., when race and gender are considered, when race and disability-ability are considered, etc.)?

6. Does a diunital or "both/and" approach in regard to race-based and inclusive perspectives make sense to you in any way? How so? How would your ways of making sense of a "both/and" approach compare and contrast with Madonna's? With Jim's?

7. As you consider the stories presented here and your reflections on the previous questions, identify some areas for growth and some avenues for productive actions in navigating race and sexual orientation in your professional and personal life.

References

Bingham, R. P., Porche-Burke, L., James, S., Sue, D. W., & Vasquez, M. J. T. (2002). Introduction: A report on the National Multicultural Conference and Summit II. *Cultural Diversity and Ethnic Minority Psychology, 8,* 75–87.

Carter, R. T. (1995). *The influence of race and racial identity in psychotherapy: Toward a racially inclusive model.* New York: John Wiley.

Carter, R., & Qureshi, A. (1995). A typology of philosophical assumptions in multicultural counseling and training. In J. G. Ponterotto, J. M. Casas, L. A. Suzuki, & C. M. Alexander (Eds.), *Handbook of multicultural counseling* (pp. 239–262). Thousand Oaks, CA: Sage.

Constantine, M. G. (2001). Addressing racial, ethnic, gender, and social class issues in counselor training and practice. In D. B. Pope-Davis & Hardin L. K. Coleman (Eds.), *The intersection of race, class, and gender in multicultural counseling* (pp. 341–352). Thousand Oaks, CA: Sage.

Constantine, M. G. (2002). The intersection of race, ethnicity, gender, and social class in counseling: Examining selves in cultural contexts. *Journal of Multicultural Counseling and Development, 30,* 210–215.

Croteau, J. M. (1999). One struggle through individualism: Toward an antiracist White racial identity. *Journal of Counseling and Development, 77,* 30–32.

Croteau, J. M. (2001, August). Mississippi Delta reflections: Doing/being queer and White in counseling psychology. In L. A. Douce (Chair), *Fellows' addresses.* Presented at the annual convention of the American Psychological Association, San Francisco.

Croteau, J. M., Talbot, D. M., Lance, T. S., & Evans, N. J. (2002). A qualitative study of the interplay between privilege and oppression. *Journal of Multicultural Counseling and Development, 30,* 239–258.

Fassinger, R. E., & Richie, B. S. (1997). Sex matters: Gender and sexual orientation in training for multicultural counseling competencies. In D. B. Pope-Davis & H. Coleman (Eds.), *Multicultural counseling competencies: Assessment, education, and training, and supervision* (pp. 83–110). Thousand Oaks, CA: Sage.

Fukuyama, M. (1990). Taking a universal approach to multicultural counseling. *Counselor Education & Supervision, 30,* 6–17.

Fukuyama, M. A., & Ferguson, A. D. (2000). Lesbian, gay, and bisexual people of color: Understanding cultural complexity and managing multiple oppressions. In R. Perez, K. DeBord, & K. Bieschke (Eds.), *Handbook of Counseling and Psychotherapy With Lesbian, Gay, and Bisexual Clients* (pp. 81–106). Washington, DC: American Psychological Association.

Garnets, L. D. (2002). Sexual orientations in perspective. *Cultural Diversity and Ethnic Minority Psychology, 8,* 115–129.

Greene, B. (2000). Beyond heterosexism and across the cultural divide: Developing an inclusive lesbian, gay, and bisexual psychology: A look to the future. In B. Greene (Ed.), *Education, research, and practice in lesbian, gay, bisexual, and transgendered psychology* (pp. 1–45). Thousand Oaks, CA: Sage.

Hays, P. A. (2001). *Addressing cultural complexities in practice.* Washington, DC: American Psychological Association.

Helms, J. (2001). Life questions. In J. A. Ponterotto, J. M. Casas, L. A. Suzuki, & C. M. Alexander (Eds.), *Handbook of multicultural counseling* (pp. 22–29). Thousand Oaks, CA: Sage.

Helms, J. E., & Richardson, T. Q. (1997). How "multiculturalism" obscures race and culture as differential aspects of counseling competency. In D. B. Pope-Davis & H. L. K. Coleman (Eds.), *Multicultural counseling competencies: Assessment, education and training and supervision* (pp. 60–79). Thousand Oaks, CA: Sage.

Locke, D. C. (1990). Point/counterpoint: A not so provincial view of multicultural counseling. *Counselor Education & Supervision, 30*(1), 18–25.

Lowe, S. M., & Mascher, J. (2001). The role of sexual orientation in multicultural counseling: Integrating bodies of knowledge. In J. A. Ponterotto, J. M. Casas, L. A. Suzuki, & C. M. Alexander (Eds.), *Handbook of multicultural counseling* (pp. 755–778). Thousand Oaks, CA: Sage.

Monette, P. (1992). *Becoming a man: Half a life story.* San Francisco: HarperCollins.

Pope, M. (1995). The "salad bowl" is big enough for us all: An argument for the inclusion of lesbians and gay men. *Journal of Counseling & Development, 73,* 301–305.

Pope-Davis, D. B., & Coleman, H. L. K. (Eds.). (2001). *The intersection of race, class, and gender in multicultural counseling.* Thousand Oaks, CA: Sage.

Reynolds, A. L. (2001a). Embracing multiculturalism: A journey of self-discovery. In J. A. Ponterotto, J. M. Casas, L. A. Suzuki, & C. M. Alexander (Eds.), *Handbook of multicultural counseling* (pp. 103–112). Thousand Oaks, CA: Sage.

Reynolds, A. L. (2001b). Multidimensional cultural competence: Providing tools for transforming psychology. *The Counseling Psychologist, 29*(6), 833–841.

Reynolds, A. L., & Pope, R. L. (1991). The complexities of diversity: Exploring multiple oppressions. *Journal of Counseling and Development, 70,* 174–180.

Robinson, T. (1993). The intersections of gender, class, race, and culture: On seeing clients whole. *Journal of Multicultural Counseling and Development, 21,* 50–58.

Robinson, T. L. (1999). The intersections of dominant discourses across race, gender, and other identities. *Journal of Counseling & Development, 77,* 73–79.

Robinson, T. L., & Howard-Hamilton M. F. (2000). *The convergence of race, ethnicity, and gender: Multiple identities in counseling.* Upper Saddle River, NJ: Prentice Hall.

Sue, D. W. (2001). Multidimensional facets of cultural competence. *The Counseling Psychologist, 29,* 790–821.

Toporek, R. L., & Gerstein, L. H. (Chairs). (2002, August). *Collaboration among counseling psychologists—Linking diversity, oppression and social justice.* Roundtable conducted at the annual convention of the American Psychological Association, Chicago.

Weber, L. (1998). A conceptual framework for understanding race, class, gender, and sexuality. *Psychology of Women Quarterly, 22,* 13–32.

Section III

Deconstructing, Envisioning, and Making Practical Suggestions

The purpose of the final section of the book is to employ the preceding narrative-oriented chapters to explicitly deconstruct the professional discourse on sexual orientation and to make suggestions for navigating and creating positive change in this discourse. The task of writing these chapters was daunting because the authors wanted to do justice to the compelling work of the preceding chapter authors, who courageously and forthrightly shared their personal experiences. The authors of these last three chapters sought to integrate the narrative material in creative and useful ways that could facilitate insight into the current discourse on sexual orientation, as well as illuminate practical paths toward action in challenging heterosexism and working toward equity.

In this section, the narrative chapters are cited frequently. Sometimes, they are cited simply to let the reader know which chapters illustrate the ideas being discussed. Other times, narrative chapters are cited along with some specific description of the authors' experiences as a way of making the ideas being expressed immediately concrete. The reader should also note that in this final section, the citations to preceding chapters in this book are made in the format of the author's last name followed by the chapter number.

The first of the three chapters in this section of the book, Chapter 22, describes the current state of the discourse regarding sexual orientation in the counseling professions and envisions a discourse of greater equity. The aim here is to understand the current overall social and institutional norms in the profession and to suggest necessary changes to those norms. Chapter 23 focuses on academic and clinical training. The authors of this chapter examine the narrative material in the book for implications in promoting sexual orientation equity in education and training. The final chapter,

Chapter 24, focuses on individual counseling professionals. By examining affect, relationships, and power in the stories in this book, the authors of this chapter draw suggestions for individuals in working toward equity on sexual orientation issues in their professional lives.

22

Toward a Discourse of Sexual Orientation Equity in the Counseling Professions

Kathleen J. Bieschke

The Pennsylvania State University

James M. Croteau

Western Michigan University

Julianne S. Lark

Independent Practice, Kalamazoo, MI

Beverly J. Vandiver

The Pennsylvania State University

While great progress has been made on lesbian, gay, and bisexual (LGB) issues in counseling, there remains much ignorance, neglect, and bias (see Croteau, Lark, & Lance, Ch. 1 of this volume). Scholars have reflected on how to counter such biases and advance LGB-affirmative perspectives in counseling. For instance, several recent authors make recommendations concerning the further development of the LGB scholarly literature or the improvement of LGB professional training efforts (e.g. Bieschke, Eberz, Bard, & Croteau, 1998; Bowman, 2003; Croteau, Bieschke, Phillips, & Lark,

1998; Douce, 1998; Morrow, 1998; Mobley, 1998; Phillips, 2000; Phillips, Ingram, Grant Smith, & Mindes, 2003; Rodolfa & Davis, 2003). While we welcome such discussions and see them as vital in identifying directions in advancing LGB-affirmative perspectives, we think that what has been neglected in such considerations is a collective self-examination of social and institutional norms around sexual orientation in professional counseling communities. Thus, our focus in this chapter is on a critical exploration of the norms within the counseling professions, employing the powerful voices contained in the narratives of the preceding chapters in this book.

Robinson (1999) asserted that there is a "dominant discourse" about sexual orientation and other social and cultural categories in societies such as the United States. Robinson defined "discourse" as the ideas and assumptions in a given social unit that underlie social interchange and individual meaning making. In the counseling professions, as in our broader society, the discourse about sexual orientation includes the ideas and assumptions that establish heterosexuality as dominant (i.e., normative and superior). In this dominant discourse, LGB orientations are excluded or devalued. The aim of this chapter is to employ the preceding narratives to deconstruct the discourse of dominance concerning sexual orientation in the counseling professions and to envision a counterdiscourse that promotes equity.

In writing this chapter, we read the narrative chapters (Chs. 2–19) in this book as well as the two chapters (Chs. 20, 21) containing narrative perspectives on special topics. Our goal was to identify the underlying ideas and assumptions (i.e., the discourse) about sexual orientation in the counseling professions that needed exposure and critique. We did not conceptualize our work as qualitative research, per se, though our process bore some similarities to common qualitative techniques (e.g., data from people who could provide descriptions of sought-after experiences, group consensus procedures for identifying themes, etc.). In contrast to some qualitative methods, however, our aim was not to systematically represent the narrative authors' perspectives or to deduce theory from their perspectives. Rather, the narrative perspectives of informed professionals serve as stimuli for our development of a critical and potent examination of the heterosexist discourse in the counseling professions. To our reading of the narratives and our critical analysis, we brought a good deal of professional experience with LGB, feminist, and multicultural issues, as well our own collective identities as White and African American; heterosexual, lesbian, and gay; and male and female.

After reading the narratives, we recognized that the dominant discourse of heterosexism remains an active force in the counseling professions. In the first section of this chapter, we used the experiences of the narrative authors to identify some ideas and assumptions that underlie the continuing dominance of heterosexism in the counseling professions. We also recognized the unquestionable existence of current ideas and assumptions in the counseling professions that contradict the dominant discourse and affirm LGB orientations. These latter ideas and assumptions can be seen as a "counterdiscourse" that challenges the (heterosexist) dominant discourse (Eliason, 1996). This counterdiscourse is the focus of the second section of the chapter, and we describe how it was operative in the experiences of the narrative chapter authors. We then share our views about how the existing counterdiscourse is oversimplified and therefore rendered less potent in contradicting views of heterosexual dominance in the third section of the chapter. We illustrate our views with examples from the narrative chapters. Embedded in this discussion are suggestions for increasing the complexity, the depth, and, ultimately, the effectiveness of the counterdiscourse of equity.

The Heterosexist Dominant Discourse

All the narrative chapter authors provided ample testimony indicating that the heterosexist dominant discourse is alive and in effect in the counseling professions, resulting in the devaluation and exclusion of those who identify as LGB or LGB affirmative. We describe the heterosexist discourse within three separate headings: overt homonegativity, elusive homonegativity/heterosexism, and role of silence, though we see these three aspects of the discourse as intertwined and mutually reinforcing.

Overt Homonegativity

The dominant discourse is in large measure driven by a well-considered preference for heterosexuality and a denigration of those who identify as LGB. Our narrative authors provided us with persuasive evidence that the homonegativity present in the larger cultures of the United States was also markedly present in their experiences in the counseling professions. In their professional lives, they reported being subject to a wide variety of overt homonegative actions and attitudes, including (a) homophobic jokes, epitaphs, and name-calling; (b) labeling LGB people as deviant and sinful; (c) myriad homophobic and biphobic stereotypings; (d) reaction of social discomfort or ostracism toward LGB people or issues; (e) anti-LGB vandalism; (f) ridicule or criticism of LGB-affirmative notions; (g) discouragement from engaging in, or disclosing, professional activities related to LGB concerns; (h) the questioning of professional competence due to minority sexual orientation; (i) advice to appear less LGB-like; and (j) exclusion from job-related tasks and/or employment. The anonymous narrative authors in the Fukuyama, Miville, and Funderburk chapter (20) related numerous incidents of overt homonegativity. For example, one author told of an internship supervisor joking with a colleague about a gay male client in the restroom: "Do you want to go in there and make a man out of him, or do you want me to do it?" Yet another author related the response she received from a potential counseling employer following her reluctant disclosure that she was partnered to a woman: "Well, I want to know if that's going to be a problem. I mean, we can't have you bringing your sexual orientation into work everyday and flaunting it around. This is a place of business, and there's no room for that kind of display here."

Incidences of overt homonegativity were also numerous in the individually authored narrative chapters. For example, it was customary for the person holding Pope's (Ch. 18) leadership position in one professional organization to attend the meeting of another counseling professional organization. Pope was barred from such attendance; however, because he was perceived as "self-serving" and "ignorant" due to his criticisms of discrimination against lesbian, gay, bisexual, and transgender (LGBT) individuals in the military. Goodman (Ch. 11) witnessed an esteemed colleague attempt to do conversion therapy with a lesbian friend. And Adams (who identifies as an out lesbian) reported being told by three colleagues that "because homosexual acts did not result in procreation, such acts were not normal, and therefore homosexuality was disordered" (Ch. 2). In one job, Wiebold (Ch. 19) was asked whether she knew any of those "dykes, queers, and candy-ass faggots."

Homonegativity in the heterosexist dominant discourse was often expressed in the context of religious views (e.g., Chan, Ch. 6; Chen-Hayes, Ch. 7; Fukuyama et al., Ch. 20; O'Brien, Ch. 14). One anonymous author described the chilling words of a "very religious man" who worked in a hospital for children: "He then went into how queers were fine, going to hell, but fine, but they had no place counseling kids, or being around kids for that matter" (Fukuyama et al., Ch. 20). O'Brien (Ch. 14) described his decision to "just keep my mouth shut about my life" when going into a training environment with "some very conservative Christian influences" where therapists "kept Bibles on display in their office and drew heavily from them in their work." Chen-Hayes (Ch. 7) stated that a "staff member with a conservative religious belief system" actually went through his mailbox and then filed a complaint with the administrator of his department about gay literature that had been in the mailbox. Chan (Ch. 6) movingly elucidates the psychological price of the religious-based homonegative discourse as he recalled how "when I prayed at night, I asked God in tears to take back my life as soon as possible because He must have made a mistake in creating my 'wrong existence.'"

Covert and Elusive Homonegativity and Heterosexism

At times, homonegative or heterosexist ideas and assumptions were somewhat less overt. In such instances, the negative discourse was not overtly expressed but was more covertly present or suspected to be covertly present. For example, Adams (Ch. 2) was never quite sure why she was never asked to speak in the sole class period devoted to counseling LGB individuals even though she was an out lesbian and acknowledged as an expert. Furthermore, after Wiebold (Ch. 19) revealed her sexual orientation to a manager in order to dispel his romantic intentions toward her, she became fearful about the "backlash I would experience from the manager and his longtime friends, my coworkers." These fears were apparently confirmed in her negative exit evaluations when she left the job a few months later. Though the evaluations were not explicitly homonegative, Wiebold saw the negative comments about "coworker 'relationship issues'" as confirming her fears of sexual orientation discrimination.

Often, the homonegativity and heterosexism expressed did not seem to be clear to those perpetuating it. As Douce (Ch. 8) observed, "People participating in the dominant discourse do not see its limits." For example, one of Douce's colleagues assumed that she was not able to work effectively with a wide range of clients and issues because she was feminist and lesbian. O'Brien's (Ch. 14) zealous coworker most likely was unaware of her heterosexism as she repeatedly tried to set him up on a date with a woman. Some people may be "clueless," as Bowman (Ch. 4) described herself at the beginning of her journey as an ally. Furthermore, LGB issues may simply be seen as irrelevant or unimportant, leading to the exclusion of thorough discussions of sexual orientation from graduate coursework (e.g., Adams, Ch. 2; Carrubba, Ch. 5; Goodman, Ch. 11; O'Brien, Ch. 14).

Finally, the heterosexist discourse was also expressed through good intentions gone astray. For example, O'Brien (Ch. 14) reported being counseled to avoid "ghettoizing myself" by identifying with the gay community when applying for clinical experiences. In applying, he was "warned by some people not to be 'too gay,'" to "let people read between the lines by reviewing your activities and interests," and to avoid appearing "too political." In the same vein, Carrubba (Ch. 5) received advice regarding being open about being bisexual in the application process. She reported "caringly" being advised to not disclose that she was bisexual in face of the abundance of biphobic possibilities: Would clinical sites find it "okay to be gay or lesbian" but not bisexual? Would she, as bisexual, be perceived "as 'gay' enough for sites that wanted gay candidates"? Would sites seeking lesbian and gay students "think that I said that I was bisexual to appear gay?" Similarly, Chen-Hayes (Ch. 7) was advised to publish a piece of research focused on LGB issues in "a real journal" rather than an "easy to publish in" LGBT journal. To Chen-Hayes (Ch. 7) the implicit message was clear: "LGBT journals weren't seen as scholarly or important." Though such advice may be well intentioned, sometimes warning of real possibilities for bias in perceptions and selections, this type feedback ultimately denigrates LGB people and experiences. All the authors who reported experiencing this kind of advice seemed to find it "incredibly invalidating" (O'Brien, Ch. 14).

The Role of Silence

Silence played a major role in maintaining the dominant discourse, often leaving the narrative authors confused and unsure in the face of such silence. O'Brien (Ch. 14) expressed the sentiments of many narrative authors: "When I experienced silence [about sexual orientation] on the part of the supervisors or faculty, I remained unsure of how 'safe' it was to come out." In fact, silence left authors having to look hard for cues about their safety in the environment. Fukuyama and her colleagues (Ch. 20) discussed how "the vigilance that is developed to screen for safety" is a constant necessity, especially in the face of silence. One counseling professional described how, in order to protect herself, she "continually analyze[s] . . . interactions with people to determine whether there is any heterosexual bias" (Ch. 20). Carrubba (Ch. 5) described being vigilant about nonverbal information to help make meaning of silence: "I am always looking to see whether people flinch or look uncomfortable when I talk about LGB-related topics." Phillips (Ch. 17) tried to make meaning of the silence that followed her coming out as bisexual and noted that only a few people looked at her. Most cast their eyes down on the floor or looked away. As O'Brien (Ch. 14) noted, "silence in regard to sexual orientation begets the 'null environment' (Betz, 1989). Silence leaves LGB professionals confused, and the safest option is to assume silence means that individuals "agree with the pathological viewpoint of LGB persons." In an environment of silence, Bowman's (Ch. 4) words ring true: "Fear of repercussions often paralyzes."

LGB individuals struggle with enacting the silence themselves, because being silent can be a healthy and protective response for LGB individuals when the discourse is hostile. In addition, silence enacted by LGB and ally individuals is often a refuge from the amount of mental and emotional energy required to handle the discrimination and the internal feelings that result from the dominant discourse. Adams (Ch. 2) stated, "Interrupting any dominant discourse takes a great deal of energy" and that "feeling outraged is particularly exhausting when your numbers are so few." On the other hand, remaining silent can be costly too, as is evident in the narrative of one counseling professional who reported having berated herself "a million times" for not taking a more affirmative stance in an interaction with a homophobic supervisor.

We agree with Fukuyama and her colleagues (Ch. 20) that an LGB professional's choice about being silent about his or her sexual orientation is a "complex issue, taking into consideration variables such as cultural context, multiple oppressions, and identity." In fact, we believe that the choice of individual counseling professionals to be silent regarding their own sexual orientations or LGB-affirmative stance is too often seen in pejorative and ethnocentric ways that fail to take into account the reality of multiple oppressions and differing cultural contexts for sexual orientation and identity. For example, Johnson (Ch. 12) identifies the toll of the long legacy of racist stigma about Black sexuality as a major factor for why he and other African Americans are often rendered "practically voiceless on any matter related to sexuality," including sexual orientation.

Nevertheless, *at the level of the discourse in the profession,* silence about sexual orientation, whether enacted as a weapon of heterosexual dominance or enacted as a way to seek haven from such discourse, ultimately supports the heterosexist dominant discourse. Furthermore, silence as a weapon and silence as a haven can work together to make it almost impossible to disrupt the dominant discourse. One counseling professional (Fukuyama et al., Ch. 20) described a concrete example of this dilemma. When a group member came out in group there was silence (silence as a weapon). The group leader then wanted to address the silence and not give the group "the privilege of avoiding" the topic. This group leader, however, felt obligated to respect the wishes of the group member who had disclosed his or her sexual orientation and did not want additional attention (silence as a haven). The leader was left feeling quite "upset" and stuck as a result of the combined effects of silence as weapon and silence as haven, and thus the heterosexist dominant discourse was left unchallenged.

In conclusion, the heterosexist dominant discourse in the counseling professions continues to thrive and operate at both obvious and elusive levels. While silence can offer a necessary haven for LGB individuals, silence also renders LGB individuals invisible and devalued, keeping the heterosexist dominant discourse firmly in place. There is a strong LGB-affirmative counterdiscourse in place in the counseling field, however, and we briefly describe it in the next section. We then provide suggestions for how to increase its complexity and depth to better challenge the pervasiveness and intricacy of the dominant discourse.

The Counterdiscourse

Along with the examples that illustrated the existence of a heterosexist dominant discourse in the counseling professions, heartening accounts from narrative authors demonstrated the presence of a strong counterdiscourse. Such accounts are perhaps not surprising, given the leadership role the national associations within the counseling professions have assumed in regard to LGB issues. In particular, the Association for Gay, Lesbian, and Bisexual Issues in Counseling (AGLBIC), a division of the American Counseling Association (ACA), was founded in 1975 and has worked tirelessly to educate counselors about issues confronting LGBT clients.

Furthermore, the Society for Counseling Psychology (formerly known as Division 17) has had a Section for LGB Awareness since 1996 and is perceived as a leader within the American Psychological Association (APA) in support of LGB issues.

Several authors noted that the counseling professions are relatively LGB-inclusive and -affirmative places within a heterosexist society. Gallor (Ch. 10) noted that she chose to enter the counseling profession because of its reputation for LGB affirmation and multicultural sensitivity. Adams (Ch. 2) stated, "I feel much more optimistic and less marginalized within the profession of counseling psychology, compared with psychology . . . and compared with the various institutions at which I have worked." Dworkin (Ch. 9) wrote that her university positively recognized her scholarship work on LGB issues in her tenure and promotion process. Pope (Ch. 18) noted that he has received a great deal of support from both individual colleagues and counseling organizations in his journey to becoming an openly gay president of two major national counseling associations.

Many narrative chapter authors (e.g., Adams, Ch. 2; Carrubba, Ch. 5; Chan, Ch. 6; Gallor, Ch. 10; Perez, Ch. 16; Phillips, Ch. 17; Wiebold, Ch. 19) described with gratitude how particular academic and practice settings in counseling were inclusive and affirmative of LGB issues, provided them with openly LGB role models, and challenged them to increase their awareness of LGB issues. Several heterosexual counseling professionals noted that some of their first developmentally significant encounters with LGB people or issues occurred within a professional context (e.g., Bowman, Ch. 4; Goodman, Ch. 11; Perez, Ch. 16). Carrubba (Ch. 5) provided numerous examples of affirmation in her training program. She discussed the importance of having openly LGB people in her department, including the "huge impact" of a close friendship with a fellow gay male student and his partner. Carrubba explained how LGB topics could be broached in her graduate classes and especially how "amazing" it was for her "to have an entire course just on LGB issues." She credited her training program with helping her connect to the larger LGB community and providing her with meaningful opportunities, such as being involved with LGB-affirmative training on campus through speaking on LGB panels in university classes. Other chapter authors also report very positive training experiences. For example, Gallor (Ch. 10) stated she feels "unbelievably fortunate" to have both supportive colleagues as well as an out lesbian faculty adviser who have helped her navigate sexual orientation and multicultural issues.

Chapter authors who are faculty members in training programs also noted the LGB-affirmative counterdiscourse in their programs and the power it has in the lives of students as well as themselves. For example, Wiebold (Ch. 19) described the "amazing experience" of her colleagues inviting her "to attend LGBT cultural events" and recognizing "my partner and our life together." She explained how "this open acknowledgement" helped her find "congruence between my life as a lesbian and as a counseling professional" and stated that her "energy . . . previously invested in passing was now accessible to invest in my contribution to the counseling profession." Similarly, Chan (Ch. 6) noted just how powerful such affirmation could be in the lives of students: "Because of the liberating environment and affirmative experiences within my training program, I . . . [now] openly affirm my identity both inside and outside of the professional circle."

Narrative chapter authors also discussed how they were challenged toward deeper levels of awareness by the LGB-affirmative counterdiscourse in the counseling professions, challenges that often occurred in counseling practice and clinical supervision. As Perez (Ch. 16) focused on LGB issues in his internship, "through thoughtful, challenging, and encouraging supervision and education," he discovered his own biases and homophobia. Berkowitz (Ch. 3) noted that in his first job, he counseled a gay client and thought he was being "very tolerant and understanding of his [the client's] dilemmas and pain, in the neutral and nonjudgmental way I had been taught." Through feedback and supervision, Berkowitz learned "that this young man [the client] had doubts about my support and acceptance of his sexual orientation," and he realized that he had to be "active and clear" about his LGB affirmation. Thus, the presence of a counterdiscourse not only provides a safer and more nurturing climate in which to study and work but also challenges individual counseling professionals toward greater levels of understanding and appreciation of heterosexism and LGB lives.

Without a doubt, training programs, internships, and practice settings are more LGB affirmative than they were before the counterdiscourse emerged in the 1970s. Douce (Ch. 8) illustrated the striking contrast with former times in the counseling professions when, for instance, the only acknowledgement of sexual orientation was done nonverbally or in heavily coded language. Furthermore, it was the norm then for counselors and psychologists to engage in the "unintentionally cruel" practice of trying to change a client's same-sex orientation, as illustrated by Goodman (Ch. 11) in discussing what happened to one of her friends. The counterdiscourse has indeed created a much more affirmative climate for LGB issues in the counseling professions: Most narrative authors reported that the counseling professions have been a relatively good place for them to come out as LGB; to develop as a heterosexual ally; and/or to deepen their understanding and appreciation of LGB concerns.

Making the Counterdiscourse More Effective

Within the counseling professions, LGB and heterosexual ally counseling professionals have made it harder for the assumptions of superiority or exclusivity in regard to heterosexuality to remain in place by engaging in bold self-disclosure and visibility and/or working toward LGB-affirmative practice and scholarship. Certainly, the brave participation of each of the narrative chapter authors in the counterdiscourse, through the personal act of writing their own narratives, serves as a stellar example of the efforts of many counseling professionals over the last 25 years to bring awareness, visibility, and equity for LGB persons. The building of a discourse of sexual orientation equity is indeed already under way. To continue the journey toward equity in the counseling professions, both LGB persons and heterosexual allies need to keep speaking out and continue to engage in the activities that directly disrupt the negative assumptions, silences, and exclusions of the heterosexist dominant discourse. Despite these valiant efforts, however, we recognize that these narratives also illustrate how the current LGB-affirmative counterdiscourse is lacking adequate depth and complexity. Thus, progress toward a discourse of equity around sexual orientation has been limited and continues to be far from fully realized.

Perhaps the most widely agreed upon tenet of the counterdiscourse among most (but not all) counseling professionals is that "it's okay to be gay." Widespread acceptance of such a belief is certainly a step in the right direction but leaves much ground to be covered. Put starkly, the counterdiscourse, as it currently stands in the counseling professions, is far from adequate in challenging heterosexism, due to its shallowness, oversimplification, and lack of inclusivity. To fully counter the sophisticated, complex web of the heterosexual dominance in the discourse, counter-LGB-affirmative notions in the counseling professions must achieve greater complexity and depth. The counterdiscourse must go beyond superficial platitudes and delve into areas that are, without a doubt, more complicated and far riskier. Failure to adequately address the difficult and complicated issues related to sexual orientation and identity will enable the heterosexist dominant discourse to continue its pervasive influence.

We identified four interrelated ways to render the LGB-affirmative counterdiscourse more effective in promoting genuine equity, including (a) integration of advocacy into the definition of affirmation, (b) incorporation of complex and socially constructed views of sexual orientation and identity, (c) positioning sexual orientation within the web of interrelated social and cultural identities and contexts, and (d) engaging in difficult exploration and dialogue. Though presented separately for the sake of clarity, all of these suggestions for facilitating the depth and the complexity of the counterdiscourse interrelate to one another.

Integration of Advocacy Into the Definition of Affirmation

A counterdiscourse with the central tenet that it is "okay to be gay" is not focused on the deeply rooted social and institutional aspects of heterosexism and therefore does little to truly challenge the dominant discourse.

As we discussed earlier in the section describing the heterosexist dominant discourse, silence in the face of social injustice and the absence of social advocacy activities only enhances the heterosexist status quo. Furthermore, as Adams (Ch. 2) asserted, "There is an allure to random acts of inclusion, because without changing the system, these acts can be held up as examples of how equity exists." Thus, well-meant bursts of isolated LGB affirmation can create an illusion of true inclusion and thus serve to maintain the heterosexist dominant discourse in the counseling profession. We believe that affirmative beliefs must be translated into systemic action both at the personal as well as the institutional level.

Believing that being gay is healthy and acceptable but failing to engage in social advocacy helps enact the silence about sexual orientation that is part of the dominant discourse. As Bowman (Ch. 4) stated, "LGB counseling professionals and students need allies to speak out and be true to their consciences, not a 'silent majority' standing behind them in the shadows." "Silence begets the 'null environment,'" which, in turn, excludes LGB individuals and makes them invisible, leaving them at the mercy of continued discriminatory institutional policies (O'Brien, Ch. 14).

Clearly, as counseling professionals, we are called to put our knowledge into practice to further social change (e.g., Conyne, 2000). As Adams (Ch. 2) stated,

> If our professional role includes being a social change agent and we are called to prevention as much as we are to remediative treatment (Romano & Hage, 2000), we should be troubled if the programs with which we are affiliated aren't engaged in some sort of prevention efforts to confront heterosexism.

Both Goodman (Ch. 11) and Perez (Ch. 16) noted that advocacy efforts should be directed at larger social change and at social change within the professions:

> If the counseling profession is to become truly active in addressing the social diseases of heterosexism and homophobia, our profession also needs to turn the mirror on to ourselves, to ask the difficult questions, to examine the ways that heterosexism and homophobia are present in the counseling profession, and to work actively and visibly toward ways to disarm their effects. (Perez, Ch. 16)

To truly counter the dominant discourse, the definition of affirmation must include social advocacy activities. O'Halloran (Ch. 15) pointed out that social advocacy efforts will differ depending on where one is in the process of ally development, and we would extend her statement further to include LGB development as well. Actions may range from using inclusive language (Berkowitz, Ch. 3) to organizing against institutional discrimination

(Adams, Ch. 2) to "crashing through the lavender ceiling" (Pope, Ch. 18) to achieving a critical mass of LGBT students (Carrubba, Ch. 5; Chen-Hayes, Ch. 7; Gallor, Ch. 10). Such activism can "generate a ripple effect of further changes" (Chan, Ch. 6). Otherwise, as Adams (Ch. 2) conveys, heterosexism will thrive through a reciprocal reinforcement of the dominant discourse at the individual and institutional levels.

Incorporation of Complex and Socially Constructed Views of Sexual Orientation and Identity

Currently, the counterdiscourse in the counseling professions supports a bifurcated view of sexual orientation. Carrubba (Ch. 5) referred to this view as "the two-box explanation" (i.e., lesbian/gay vs. heterosexual). Carrubba (Ch. 5), Dworkin (Ch. 9), and Phillips (Ch. 17) all discussed how they have been marginalized as a result of identifying as bisexual. Phillips noted that, at best, the lack of inclusion of bisexual issues in the counseling professions creates a null environment in which biphobic notions can thrive. These three authors illustrated the multitude of biphobic notions that abound in the counseling profession. For example, Carrubba (Ch. 5) reported being confronted with stereotypes about bisexual individuals: "Aren't you attracted to everyone you see, so how do you focus on your life? . . . Do you think you'll eventually decide that you're lesbian (or straight)?" Phillips (Ch. 17) directed our attention to the "disservice" done "to bisexual people (clients, students, colleagues)" when their experiences are assumed to be "the same as those of gay men and lesbian women." Indeed, the extent of ignorance about bisexuality and the no-win situations faced by bisexual counseling professionals are strikingly illustrated by considering one aspect of the plight of the three bisexual-identified narrative chapter authors. Dworkin's (Ch. 9) struggle is to be recognized as a bisexual woman rather than being immediately perceived as lesbian because of her relationship with a woman. Carrubba and Phillips have had to struggle to be seen as legitimately bisexual because of their relationships with men. The sexual identities of these individuals are rendered invisible because the existing counterdiscourse often portrays a simplified picture of sexual orientation as defined by the sex of the romantic or life-partner relationship.

Carrubba (Ch. 5), Dworkin (Ch. 9), and Phillips (Ch. 17) are not the first to suggest that the prevailing model of sexual orientation is a dichotomous one (e.g., Croteau et al., 1998). The counterdiscourse in the counseling professions, however, remains lacking in inclusion of bisexuality in ways that are meaningful and substantial. As Phillips (Ch. 17) stated, "It often seems easier for counseling professionals to add 'bisexual' to the label of 'gay and lesbian' and/or to advocate for inclusion of bisexual issues than . . . to integrate bisexual issues in meaningful and nonstereotypical ways." Douce (Ch. 8) argued that the social constructivist perspective on sexual orientation holds great promise for allowing for more inclusion of a variety of ways in which sexual orientation and gender are constructed in individuals' lives, particularly constructions involving the potential for fluidity in sexual orientation (see Chen-Hayes, Ch. 7; Dworkin, Ch. 9). A social constructivist perspective also allows for understanding two other complexities: transgender experiences and culturally centered notions of sexual orientation.

More complex and socially constructed conceptualizations of sexuality may open the way for the counseling professions to begin to consider transgendered issues. The book editors were unable to identify a counseling professional who identified as transgendered and was willing to write a narrative. This clearly illustrates how transgender issues are largely absent from the LGB-affirmative counterdiscourse in the counseling professions. In our estimation, the counseling professions are just beginning to take steps toward understanding transgendered individuals. Two narrative chapter authors made relevant comments on how little the counseling professionals have paid to transgender issues. Chen-Hayes (Ch. 7) identifies as a gender-variant gay man and "found most students affirming" and that "some faculty colleagues were a bit wary and used a 'control-the-deviance' theme" with him in regard to behavioral manifestations of gender variance (i.e., he was warned not to "drag" in the vicinity of his work environment). Dworkin (Ch. 9) noted that though other members of her faculty are now incorporating attention to LGB issues into their courses, she is the "only faculty member of the counselor education program to discuss transgender issues." Furthermore, she stated that many of her colleagues "do not even know what this term means." The realization that sexual orientation can be nondichotomous and socially constructed may help the professions consider that the gender dichotomy itself is socially constructed. Only when the discourse on sexuality stretches to such considerations will issues and concerns of the transgendered population begin to be addressed in the counseling professions.

A socially constructed view of sexual orientation helps to focus attention on the influence of contextual variables on the construction of sexual identities. Race, ethnicity, and culture are key contextual factors that are often overlooked by the current counterdiscourse of LGB affirmation. In the following section, we turn our attention to strengthening the counterdiscourse through a more conscious incorporation of how culture, race, racism, and other social or cultural realities shape the experience of sexual orientation and heterosexism.

Sexual Orientation Within the Web of Interrelated Social and Cultural Identities and Contexts

A major criticism of current LGB-affirmative perspectives in counseling-related fields is the failure of those perspectives to consider other forms of diversity and oppression. Only oversimplified, exclusive, and inaccurate ideas can emerge from a counterdiscourse that considers sexual orientation in isolation from other social and cultural realities. Such beliefs lack the power to fully contradict the dominant discourse concerning sexual orientation as well as the dominant discourses concerning race, ethnicity, gender, and other forms of diversity. When the narrative authors situate themselves and their experiences within an interrelated web of multiple social identities and cultural contexts, they stand apart from the usual counterdiscourse and speak with a compelling authenticity illustrating the depth and power of an LGB-affirmative counterdiscourse that is centered in multiculturalism.

Race, culture, and other forms of diversity profoundly influence the shaping of individuals' experiences of sexual orientation and heterosexism. Fukuyama and her colleagues' (Ch. 20) commentary discussed how vulnerability due to racism, the relative saliency of sexual verses racial identities, and a collectivistic cultural orientation may shape the experience of sexual orientation, particularly as it relates to coming out to others. For people with White racial privilege who have a primary identity as LGB and an individualistic cultural orientation, decisions about the open disclosure of a minority sexual orientation may have to do with personal integration and health, as well as creating awareness among others in one's life. For people of color for whom both racial identity and sexual identity are salient, decisions about openness may center around the risks of multiple oppressions, the centrality of an identity in a particular context, and the effects of disclosure on family and ethnic community. As Chen-Hayes (Ch. 7) commented, it is culturally inappropriate to assume "that being out is universally good," as is the assumption that being more private is "a restrictive stance in the world, surrounded by unhealthy secrecy" (Fukuyama et al., Ch. 20). Other salient social identities and oppressions can also shape the experience of sexual orientation and its disclosure. For example, at one time in her career, Wiebold (Ch. 19) needed the medical benefits in her counseling job to obtain life-sustaining care related to her disability; therefore, she felt she could not risk being openly lesbian at work because the cost of a potential job loss was just too high.

The effects of race, culture, and other social identities on the experience of sexual orientation extend beyond issues of openness and disclosure. Berkowitz (Ch. 3) discussed learning "to use the opportunities" afforded by his "unearned privilege" as "straight White male" to undermine the social oppression faced by LGB people and others. Similarly, Croteau (Ch. 21) recognized that his struggle to initially accept himself as a gay man was partially associated with White privilege and White cultural assumptions. That is, embracing his stigmatized identity as gay meant experiencing life no longer governed solely by individual meritocracy. Perez's (Ch. 16) journey as a heterosexual ally working on his own heterosexism was profoundly influenced by connecting his developing pride and understanding of racism as a Filipino man to the struggles of LGB people. "I painfully realized then that my biases and homophobia were the same oppressive forces as the racial discrimination and prejudice that I experienced." Bowman (Ch. 4) recognized that at one time in her life, her ability "to be an effective LGB ally was blocked while I came to a better understanding of myself as an African American woman moving in a predominantly Caucasian world." At another point in Bowman's life, her experiences with racism allowed her to be able to relate to LGB colleagues' and students' "feelings of being alone, somehow separate" and their "hypersensitivity . . . never knowing when the next negative experience will materialize."

The counterdiscourse of sexual orientation equity needs to mirror the pervasive way that race, culture, and other social identities influence and interconnect with sexual orientation. For Gallor (Ch. 10), it was impossible to tell her story in a way that separated "my lesbian self from my Hispanic self or my gendered self from my lesbian self." Johnson's (Ch. 12) story about sexual orientation would lose all meaning if it were to be stripped of the historical and cultural context of the stigmatization of African American sexuality. Douce's (Ch. 8) story would be gutted without the interwoven tale of her journey as a feminist in the last three decades. The everyday reality of Wiebold's (Ch. 19) life as a lesbian can be fully understood only with her account of how the relative salience of her professional, disability, and sexual identities can shift from moment to moment, even as she simply walks down the hall at her workplace.

A counterdiscourse that artificially considers sexual orientation in isolation from racial and other cultural contexts is a discourse void of deeper meaning and evocativeness. Pope (Ch. 18) also found it impossible to separate his sexual identity from "my native Cherokee ancestry, my life-long disability, my rural upbringing, and all that constitutes my personal cultural identity." He likened this integration of his identities to the beautiful handmade quilt given to him by fellow tribal members to welcome him into "Elderhood" of the St. Francis River Band of Cherokee. Each panel was fashioned by a different tribal member, and, for Pope, represented how each part of his "cultural identity is distinct yet truly part of a whole that has developed" over the course of his life. Douce (Ch. 8) criticized the most current multicultural counterdiscourse for its focus on the relationship of one specific oppressed group to the majority. She says that the only way for the LGB counterdiscourse to emerge from the margins of the profession is for it to begin to address the reality of multiple identities and cultural contexts. It is time for LGB-affirmative counseling professionals to begin sewing a quilt-like discourse that places sexual orientation in its complex racial and cultural contexts.

While we strongly believe that the counterdiscourse needs to more fully integrate multiple social identities and cultural contexts, such a shift toward complexity and inclusiveness will be painful, giving rise to unexplored conflicts and necessitating difficult exploration and dialogues.

The fourth and final area we have identified for strengthening the counterdiscourse concerns the need for engagement in difficult exploration and dialogue.

Engaging in Difficult Exploration and Dialogue

A counterdiscourse that truly promotes equity must allow for complex, in-depth exploration and discussions of sexual orientation that may be difficult and intense. Failure to do so may result in the creation of a dangerous and disingenuous situation in which superficial levels of awareness and declarations of LGB normality serve as effective cover for deep-rooted heterosexism. We believe that the counterdiscourse on sexual orientation issues must support engagement with difficult issues at both the individual and the interpersonal or communal levels.

The narrative chapter authors' main task was to share experiences that exposed the sexual orientation discourse in the counseling professions. Despite the intended focus on the external discourse, virtually all the authors shared their internal processes in struggling to overcome their own heterosexism and/or develop deeper levels of LGB affirmation. For the heterosexual chapter authors, they often shared their painful discoveries of homophobic and heterosexist behavior and attitudes. For example, Berkowitz (Ch. 3) discussed how he has learned to accept that he is "guilty of engaging in homophobic thoughts and actions even when I may not be aware of them or their effects." Johnson (Ch. 12) asked himself to not stop at the easy acknowledgement of overcoming some aspects of personal homophobia, but, instead, to look at hard current questions:

> Why haven't my understanding and commitment grown more over the past 20 years? Why have I been so reluctant to reflect seriously on issues surrounding lesbian and gay sexuality as a counseling professional? How can I be so committed to racial justice and be so indifferent toward lesbian and gay rights?

Similarly, LGB chapter authors often shared their own, sometimes painful, process of first coming to self-affirmation, developing more affirming ways to incorporate their LGB identities into their lives, and learning to better confront or cope with heterosexism. For example, Douce (Ch. 8) stated, "After a brief period of therapy searching for the source of my perversion, I decided that I was the healthiest person I knew." In concluding his narrative, Chan (Ch. 6) explained,

> Over the years, gradually learning to accept that I live in an imperfect world where discrimination is tied to sexual orientation, I have gained a bit of wisdom about my role in changing the impact of this oppression.

> Instead of allowing helplessness to eat away my self-esteem, I rather choose to use myself to create a more safe and affirming environment for myself and others; that is, taking responsibility myself to transform the heterosexism around me.

In addition to supporting the intense personal exploration discussed by the narrative authors, the counterdiscourse must also promote interpersonal and community engagement with the complex and painful issues that will emerge as the counterdiscourse deepens in the ways we have discussed thus far. As the counterdiscourse on sexual orientation moves toward becoming more multicultural, the difficult interpersonal and communal issues will arise concerning simultaneously dealing with multiple identities and cultural contexts. As Croteau and Constantine (Ch. 21) discussed, the sensitive issues that arise around race and sexual orientation are embodied in the tension between two perspectives that have been identified in the multicultural counseling literature (Carter, 1996, Carter & Qureshi, 1995). On one hand is a multicultural perspective that is race based and envisions race and racism as primary and superordinate to other issues of diversity and oppression. On the other hand is a multicultural perspective that is inclusive and places sexual orientation, race, and other forms of diversity alongside one another for consideration and attention. Croteau and Constantine (Ch. 21) argued that these two divergent perspectives underlie many of the tensions that are felt in the everyday work of counseling professionals concerning race and sexual orientation.

Too often, "an inclusive perspective can, and often does, result in the minimization of the cultural centrality of race and racism in the United States and in the avoidance of racism all together by shifting the focus to other issues of oppression such as heterosexism" (Croteau & Constantine, Ch. 21). In her own narrative about these issues, Constantine, an African American heterosexual woman, described her own struggles with this tension. She is "fairly certain that understanding and experiencing discrimination based on same-sex sexual orientation is not equivalent to understanding and experiencing racial discrimination." She explained what seems to be at the heart of this difficult issue for many counseling professionals of color. She thinks that White counseling professionals will often "broaden the discussion of race and racism" to include heterosexism and other oppressions in reaction to their discomfort with racial issues. Constantine asserted that this defensive reaction often leaves her and other people of color "bereft of having true and honest dialogues about racism" and "feeling frustrated and mistrustful" of those "who avoid engaging with me or other people of color at this level."

Equally problematic are instances when a race-based perspective can, and often does, result in the exclusion or minimizing of heterosexism and other nonracial issues of oppression/privilege, as well as the neglect of the significance of the complex intersections across race, ethnicity, sexual orientation, class, disability, gender, and other social and cultural identities. Feelings about such exclusions are described by several narrative chapter authors in this book. Adams (Ch. 2) reported feeling "outraged" when "multicultural competence does not include competence with LGB individuals" and "counseling organizations' concerns for religious tolerance and not perpetuating racism are greater than its concern for reducing heterosexism." Douce (Ch. 8) thinks that many "experts in multiculturalism limit real oppression to characteristics that are immediately obvious and 'in your face,' excluding sexual orientation." In the face of this exclusion, Douce asserted, "as long as we [LGBT people] can be killed just for who we are and be denied our basic civil rights in the name of God (as defined by the religious Right), then we are oppressed."

Croteau and Constantine (Ch. 21) suggested that one avenue to approaching these tensions is to take what Reynolds calls a "diunital," or "both/and," approach (Reynolds, 2001a, 2001b) to race-based and inclusive perspectives. While we agree that such an approach seems fruitful, here our focus is on the process modeled by Croteau and Constantine (Ch. 21) in embracing these tensions and engaging in honest self-exploration and dialogue concerning the issue. Croteau and Constantine's own narratives can be models for the intense self-scrutiny and risk-filled dialogue that must take place to address this difficult issue. For example, Croteau, a White gay man, shared his painful discovery that his own tension about the exclusion of sexual orientation in more race-based multicultural trainings kept him from engaging with valuable and much-needed opportunities to confront his racism and develop an antiracist White identity. Constantine, as "a Black heterosexual woman . . . has experienced very painful racist episodes." While she finds "it hard to believe that heterosexism and homophobia could be as painful or difficult to bear as racism," she reminds herself that she has "never been told that my membership in the Black racial group was 'immoral' and 'pathological.'" Despite her struggle with comparing racism and heterosexism, she clearly strives to be a strong heterosexual ally, cognizant "that being a member of any oppressed cultural group is sometimes much too painful and intolerable for words." If the LGB-affirmative discourse is to become deeper and more inclusive of multicultural issues, it must begin to embrace this riskier process of exploration and open dialogue about painful and difficult issues such as those that arise from the tension between race-based and inclusive multicultural perspectives.

Another difficult and painful issue—negotiating sexual orientation within the context of religious views that are nonaffirmative—surfaces in many of the narrative chapters (e.g., Adams, Ch. 2; Douce, 8; Fukuyama et al., Ch. 20; Mobley & Pearson, Ch. 13; O'Brien, 14). It is indeed a great challenge to engage with difficult issues when doing so means engaging with views that are explicitly derogatory toward LGB people and lives. The

Mobley and Pearson (Ch. 13) narrative chapter in this book is a personal tale of such painful engagement and provides a model for how such issues can be negotiated interpersonally. Mobley, an African American gay man, and Pearson, an African American heterosexual woman, were bonded in their shared experience as graduate students and as African Americans navigating a predominantly White educational environment. Pearson described having "major dissonance" among her identities as a Christian with non-LGB-affirmative beliefs, as a professional required to be gay affirmative, and as an African American wanting to affirm Mobley, her gay African American colleague. Inevitably, a "cultural impasse" occurred. Because Mobley and Pearson wanted to remain in community with one another, they worked to resolve the impasse. Their resolution required more than countering hetero-sexism. It required "a safe space" where both persons' "hurt" could be shared and heard. At the time of their impasse, Pearson said that Mobley's strong negative initial reaction to her nonaffirmative beliefs felt rejecting as she experienced those beliefs as a "central part" of her. Pearson obviously rose to the challenge and took on the exploration of LGB issues. Mobley too was challenged to check his "unconscious disregard for individuals . . . who may genuinely struggle to accept, affirm, or embrace" LGB issues. He both maintained a strong LGB-affirmative stance and worked to create "a safe space for another [Pearson] to respond genuinely."

We believe that as the LGB-affirmative counterdiscourse gains greater depth in the ways we outlined, a variety of difficult issues will emerge and present challenges to counseling professionals who assert this counter-discourse. Engagement with difficult issues must be the cornerstone for a more effective LGB-affirmative counterdiscourse. Such a commitment may mean engaging with the painful self-exploration of the depth of one's own biases and prejudices. Risky dialogues about the painful realities of racism, even when such dialogue requires temporarily letting go of the press to deal with heterosexism, may be necessary. Courageous assertions of LGB affir-mation may have to be coupled with the intentional creation of safe interper-sonal space for the expression and exploration of genuine heterosexist viewpoints. If the counterdiscourse does not embody the process of engaging with difficult issues, then deeper and more complex growth in the discourse cannot take place. A simplistic and shallow counterdiscourse, however wide-spread it becomes, can be effective only in making heterosexism more covert, where there will continue to be oppression toward "sexual minorities, with-out ever whispering or shouting a single word" (Mobley, Ch. 13).

Conclusion

We have argued that the narratives dramatize that (a) a discourse of heterosexual dominance is alive and well in the counseling professions and leaves a daily trail of fear and oppression in its wake, (b) a coherent counterdiscourse of LGB affirmation in the counseling professions is also clearly present and has served to provide a measure of safety to counseling professionals who identify either as LGB or as allies, and (c) the counterdiscourse can become more effective in promoting equity if it has more depth and complexity in the four ways we discussed.

Writing this chapter was a privilege. We were moved by the courageousness of the authors in telling stories in the face of a dominant discourse that punishes or marginalizes such storytelling. We were struck by the brutal nature of dominant discourse in our field and the lack of personal safety experienced by LGB people or allies. The depth of the material in the narratives challenged us to go further in our thinking about how to promote equity in the counseling professions. We were inspired to increase our own commitments to equity and hope this chapter, as well as the book, contributes to leaving readers equally inspired.

References

Betz, N. (1989). Implications of the null environment hypothesis for women's career development and for counseling psychology. *The Counseling Psychologist, 17,* 136–144.

Bieschke, K. J., Eberz, A. B., Bard, C. C., & Croteau, J. M. (1998). Using social cognitive career theory to create affirmative lesbian, gay, and bisexual research training environments. *The Counseling Psychologist, 26,* 735–753.

Bowman, S. L. (2003). A call to action in lesbian, gay, and bisexual theory building research. *The Counseling Psychologist, 31,* 63–69.

Carter, R. T. (1996). *The influence of race and racial identity in psychotherapy.* New York: John Wiley.

Carter, R., & Qureshi, A. (1995). A typology of philosophical assumptions in multicultural counseling and training. In J. G. Ponterotto, J. M. Casas, L. A. Suzuki, & C. M. Alexander (Eds.), *Handbook of multicultural counseling* (pp. 239–262). Thousand Oaks, CA: Sage.

Conyne, R. K. (2000). Prevention in counseling psychology: At long last, has the time now come? *The Counseling Psychologist, 28,* 838–844.

Croteau, J. M., Bieschke, K. J., Phillips, J. C., & Lark, J. S. (1998). Moving beyond pioneering: Empirical and theoretical perspectives on lesbian, gay, and bisexual affirmative training. *The Counseling Psychologist, 26,* 707–711.

Douce, L. A. (1998). Can a cutting edge last twenty-five years? *The Counseling Psychologist, 26,* 775–783.

Eliason, M. J. (1996). An inclusive model of lesbian identity assumption. *Journal of Gay, Lesbian, and Bisexual Identity, 1,* 3–19.

Mobley, M. (1998). Lesbian, gay, and bisexual issues in counseling psychology training: Acceptance in the millennium. *The Counseling Psychologist, 26,* 784–794.

Morrow, S. (1998). Toward a new paradigm in counseling psychology training and education. *The Counseling Psychologist, 26,* 795–806.

Phillips, J. C. (2000). Training issues and considerations. In R. Perez, K. DeBord, & K. Bieschke (Eds.), *Handbook of counseling and psychotherapy with lesbian, gay, and bisexual clients* (pp. 137–156). Washington, DC: American Psychological Association.

Phillips, J. C., Ingram, K. M., Grant Smith, N., & Mindes, E. (2003). Methodological and content review of lesbian-, gay-, and bisexual-related articles in counseling journals: 1990–1999. *The Counseling Psychologist, 31,* 25–62.

Reynolds, A. L. (2001a). Embracing multiculturalism: A journey of self-discovery. In J. A. Ponterotto, J. M. Casas, L. A. Suzuki, & C. M. Alexander (Eds.), *Handbook of multicultural counseling* (2nd ed., pp. 103–112). Thousand Oaks, CA: Sage.

Reynolds, A. L. (2001b). Multidimensional cultural competence: Providing tools for transforming psychology. *The Counseling Psychologist, 29,* 833–841.

Robinson, T. L. (1999). The intersections of dominant discourses across race, gender, and other identities. *Journal of Counseling and Development, 77,* 73–79.

Rodolfa, E., & Davis, D. (2003). A comment on a haunting number and a challenge for psychology. *The Counseling Psychologist, 31*(1), 78–84.

Romano, J. L., & Hage, S. M. (2000). Prevention and counseling psychology: Revitalizing commitments for the 21st century. *The Counseling Psychologist, 28,* 733–766.

23

Those Who Care, Teach

Toward Sexual Orientation Equity in Academic and Clinical Training

Y. Barry Chung

Georgia State University

Catherine J. Brack

Georgia State University

Evident in the narratives of this book as well as existing research and literature is the continuing heterosexist dominant discourse in the counseling professions that creates inequity for lesbian, gay, and bisexual (LGB) persons (Bieschke, Eberz, Bard, & Croteau, 1998; Bieschke, McClanahan, Tozer, Grzegorek, & Park, 2000; Haldeman, 1994; Phillips & Fischer, 1998; Rudolph, 1988). Drawing from the narratives of this book, Bieschke, Croteau, Lark, and Vandiver (Ch. 22) identified three aspects of the heterosexist dominant discourse: overt homonegativity, covert/elusive heterosexism, and silence. They also discussed the existing LGB-affirmative counterdiscourse indicated by these narratives and offered an agenda for structuring a stronger counterdiscourse. Building on Bieschke and her colleagues' ideas, the current chapter focuses on suggestions for systemic efforts that strengthen the counterdiscourse in academic and clinical training settings, whereas Lidderdale, Lark, and Whitman (Ch. 24) offer suggestions for individual counseling professionals.

We believe that academic and clinical training can play a fundamental role in this counterdiscourse for the following reasons. First, formal academic and clinical training is a prime time to obtain knowledge, attitudes, and skills as a counseling professional. Consequently, this is an important developmental phase for counseling professionals to learn to become sensitive, affirming, and competent with regard to sexual orientation diversity and LGB issues. Provision of LGB-affirmative training during this formal training process can have a major impact on future generations of counseling professionals. Second, academic and clinical training settings can be viewed as microsystems that mirror the counseling professions at large. To counter heterosexism in the larger counseling professions, those involved in academic and clinical training may start with these microsystems. Faculty, staff, and students of all sexual orientations can benefit from a training atmosphere of affirmation and equity that is instrumental to personal and professional growth. Third, successes in LGB-affirmative training and creation of an affirmative training environment will also have an impact on any persons who have interactions with these students, faculty, and staff (e.g., clients, consultees, university community, community at large, colleagues, professional organizations, consumers of scholarly work). Therefore, the counterdiscourse in the microsystems of academic and clinical training settings can have a far-reaching impact in the counseling professions.

Since the late 1970s, literature has emerged that specifically addresses LGB issues in academic and clinical training in the counseling professions (e.g., Buhrke, 1989; Buhrke & Douce, 1991; Croteau, Bieschke, Phillips, & Lark, 1998; Glenn & Russell, 1986; Iasenza, 1989; Norton, 1982; Phillips, 2000; Thompson & Fishburn, 1977). The narratives of this book and Bieschke and her colleagues' synthesis of these narratives in Chapter 22 further serve as rich sources for training implications. The purpose of this chapter is to offer recommendations for addressing the heterosexist dominant discourse in the counseling professions through academic and clinical training. Our goal is not to compile a comprehensive list of all possible suggestions. Rather, we propose a systemic and strategic framework that can be used to create a training environment for a stronger LGB-affirmative counterdiscourse.

It may be helpful to introduce the two authors of this chapter to put our suggestions in context with regard to our perspectives. Barry is an openly gay associate professor of counseling and counseling psychology. Cathy is a heterosexual ally, a university counseling center associate director and coordinator of clinical services, as well as former training director. Grounded in the narratives of this book and our professional experience, we offer a strategic framework for academic and clinical training that counters heterosexism. We first discuss five aspects of academic training: academic courses, recruitment and retention, establishing an LGB-affirmative environment, research and publication, and advocacy and community outreach.

This section is followed by a discussion of clinical training with specific suggestions for supervision. We conclude with our own narratives regarding our experiences with training on LGB issues and hopes for the counseling professions.

Academic Training

Academic Courses

Consistent with a comprehensive approach to multicultural training, we offer three suggestions. First, all multicultural counseling courses should include training on LGB issues. Second, a specialized course or training program should be offered that provides training on LGB counseling. Third, all counseling courses should include some elements of LGB training. We further discuss these three recommendations below.

Multicultural Course. In recent years, multicultural counseling courses have been required in most counseling and counseling psychology programs (Carter & Qureshi, 1995). However, there is no consensus about whether a multicultural counseling course should focus on race and ethnicity or should be inclusive of other dimensions of cultural diversity. For example, Goodman's (Ch. 11) students told her that there seems to be a competition for attention among the different cultural dimensions in multicultural courses, and LGB issues often lose out. Tensions between attention to race versus sexual orientation were further discussed by Croteau and Constantine (Ch. 21). Due to the fact that most training programs do not offer a specialized LGB course beyond the multicultural course, we believe a strategy similar to the diunital approach discussed by Croteau and Constantine is appropriate for structuring multicultural counseling courses. Sue and Sue (2003) provided an example of this approach through the three revisions of their multicultural counseling textbook since its first publication in 1981, moving from an exclusive focus on race and ethnicity to devoting special chapters to other cultural dimensions (sexual orientation, age, gender, and disability), while maintaining a major focus on race and ethnicity. Other current multicultural textbooks have used a similar approach (e.g., Baruth & Manning, 2003). Instructors may also use multiple textbooks to cover race, ethnicity, and other cultural dimensions (e.g., Atkinson, 2004; Atkinson & Hackett, 2004). We encourage instructors to include a dialogue about the tensions between the race-focused and inclusive approaches to help students understand different views of multiculturalism and become sensitive to the possibility of using comfort zones in certain cultural dimensions (e.g., sexual orientation) to avoid difficult self-reflections in other cultural dimensions (e.g., race). Croteau and

Constantine (Ch. 21) provided examples of such self-reflections in their struggle with these tensions. Consistent with the use of a narrative approach, guest speakers for various cultural dimensions can be particularly helpful for stimulating understanding and self-reflections.

Multicultural courses are unique opportunities to address the interaction of various cultural identities. A number of the narrative authors pointed out the importance of understanding multiple cultural identities (Chen-Hayes, Ch. 7; Douce, Ch. 8; Dworkin, Ch. 9; Fukuyama, Miville, & Funderburk, Ch. 20; Gallor, Ch. 10; Goodman, Ch. 11; Johnson, Ch. 12; Mobley & Pearson, Ch. 13; Wiebold, Ch. 19). Douce stated, "The exclusion of LGBT within group differences in multicultural discourse and curriculum feeds the attempts to push what is now marginalized back into invisibility." LGB identities do not exist in isolation to other cultural identities. A challenge for multicultural counseling instructors is to facilitate an awareness of the interrelatedness of multiple identities. Furthermore, experience and knowledge of one form of oppression can be helpful for understanding another form of oppression. For example, Goodman (Ch. 11) discussed how her experience of feeling different growing up as a smart girl and nonobservant Jew in a sexist and Catholic community may have helped her become more accepting of differences in sexual orientation. Perez (Ch. 16) gained a better understanding of his heterosexism when he realized his internalized racism. However, the transference of understanding different forms of oppressions is not necessarily automatic but requires conscious efforts to resolve cultural impasses. Mobley and Pearson's (Ch. 13) narrative depicts the way they resolved their cultural impasse, which involved Black identity, religious beliefs, and sexual identity. Perez suggested engaging in such difficult dialogues to facilitate this process.

Specialized Training on LGB Issues. We encourage the inclusion of a course or training program (e.g., seminar series, workshops) that specifically addresses LGB counseling issues. Chan (Ch. 6) spoke of being empowered by such a course which "offered a safe environment in which students had opportunities to share their own sexual identity development and to examine heterosexist biases and internalized homophobia." Dworkin (Ch. 9) designed and taught an LGB-affirmative therapy course. Readers might refer to several discussions of such courses (e.g., Pearson, 2003; Rudolph, 1989; Whitman, 1995). The American Psychological Association (APA) "Guidelines for Psychotherapy With LGB Clients" (Division 44/Committee on Lesbian, Gay, and Bisexual Concerns Joint Task Force, 2000) can be helpful for structuring such a course. We support the construction of a Web site that collects syllabi and training protocols across the country so that instructors can exchange ideas about LGB training courses. Similar Web sites are available on multicultural courses (e.g., National Council on Family Relations, 2003).

Infusion of LGB Contents in All Courses. A comprehensive approach to training requires the infusion of LGB issues in all course offerings (Phillips & Fischer, 1998; Rooney & Chung, 2001). The value of this approach is supported and emphasized in a number of narratives (Adams, Ch. 2; Carrubba, Ch. 5; Chan, Ch. 6; Dworkin, Ch. 9; O'Halloran, Ch. 15). Adams stated that "random acts of inclusion" are not sufficient to counter historical heterosexism. Dworkin (Ch. 9) believes that when all professors address LGB issues in all courses, it will be difficult for students to avoid such training. Literature is available that provides specific suggestions for infusing LGB issues into counseling courses, such as personality and human development, counseling theories, community counseling, assessment, groups, consultation, couple and family, career counseling, professional issues, practicum and internship, and research (Buhrke, 1989; Buhrke & Douce, 1991; Iasenza, 1989; Norton, 1982). For example, Goodman's (Ch. 11) training program has a "Couple and Family" course rather than a "Marriage and Family" course. Case examples in all courses should include LGB contexts.

One final suggestion, which applies to curricular infusion as well as multicultural and LGB-specific courses, is that special attention needs to be given to bisexual issues beyond nominal inclusion. Carrubba (Ch. 5), Dworkin (Ch. 9), and Phillips (Ch. 17) discussed how bisexual persons are often marginalized and stigmatized by both heterosexual and lesbian/gay communities. Dworkin still has to constantly assert to others that she is bisexual, not lesbian. Some people may not be able to accept a person's bisexual identity if the person is with a same-sex partner (e.g., Dworkin) or a different-sex partner (e.g., Phillips). Bieschke and her colleagues (Ch. 22) further discussed problems associated with the social construction of sexual identity and sexual orientation. Faculty can help students understand the fluid nature of these dimensions and how social construction has arbitrarily defined them by oversimplified categories.

Recruitment and Retention

While universities across the country have begun to establish strategic plans for the recruitment and retention of underrepresented faculty and students, counseling training programs need to ensure that these strategic plans include LGB persons when defining underrepresented groups. Current recruitment and retention efforts focus on racial/ethnic minorities and women, which is very important for a multicultural education. However, to counter a heterosexist dominant discourse, it is also important to recruit and retain LGB faculty, staff, and students. Sexual orientation diversity should be considered an asset to any academic programs. The presence of openly LGB faculty and students can have a profound effect on the whole program, as supported in a number of narratives (Adams, Ch. 2;

Carrubba, Ch. 5; Chen-Hayes, Ch. 7; Dworkin, Ch. 9; Gallor, Ch. 10).
Carrubba felt that a large representation of diverse people, including but
not limited to sexual orientation, brings more awareness and sensitivity
to cultural differences. Gallor spoke of her fortunate experience of being
mentored by an out lesbian faculty advisor. The presence of LGB faculty
and students provides not only support and a community with a safer
climate for LGB persons but also opportunities for heterosexual persons
to gain awareness on LGB issues. Below, we discuss efforts for recruitment
and retention, respectively.

Recruitment. A recruitment statement that explicitly welcomes LGB
faculty, staff, and student applicants can be particularly helpful because
LGB persons often have to worry about potential discrimination and a hostile or unsupportive academic climate. Adams (Ch. 2) emphasized the need
to encourage and inspire LGB people to enter the counseling professions. Chen-Hayes (Ch. 7) discussed his preference for academic programs
located in or close to major cities because of access to the LGB community
and resources. Programs that do not have such geographic advantage will
need to work harder to recruit LGB faculty and students. Provision of information about LGB groups, organizations, and community resources should
be part of the recruitment process. Carrubba (Ch. 5) suggested that training
programs should connect LGB persons with the local LGB community.

Retention. Adams (Ch. 2), Chen-Hayes (Ch. 7), and Dworkin (Ch. 9)
discussed issues pertaining to LGB faculty retention. Concerns over tenure
and promotion might affect a faculty member's decisions, such as whether
to come out, how to behave, whether to conduct LGB research, and how
to address LGB issues in teaching. For example, Chen-Hayes wondered
whether he could dye his hair. Suggestions were made to Dworkin to remove
all LGB scholarly work from her tenure and promotion document. Several
narrative authors mentioned that a "null environment" (Betz, 1989) is inadequate for facilitating an LGB-affirmative atmosphere (Berkowitz, Ch. 3;
Gallor, Ch. 10; O'Brien, Ch. 14; Phillips, Ch. 17). Evaluative bodies (e.g.,
department chair, college dean, promotion and tenure review committee)
need to explicitly communicate to the faculty that discrimination based on
sexual orientation will not be tolerated and that LGB scholarship is valued.
Furthermore, evaluation of faculty performance should take into account the
unique issues facing LGB faculty. For example, LGB journals should be
considered appropriate outlets for publication, especially because mainstream journals might not be fully understanding or as receptive to LGB
articles. When reviewing student evaluations of instructors, one should be
aware that students might give negative feedback about an instructor simply
because of the instructor's LGB orientation or advocacy for LGB issues, as
in the case with Dworkin (Ch. 9). Dworkin's experience further suggests that

LGB faculty members may also experience work overload because of demands related to LGB issues. The whole faculty should share responsibility for work on LGB issues in order to avoid burnout on the part of LGB faculty. Finally, LGB-affirmative faculty, regardless of their sexual orientations, may experience resistance or negative reactions from students and colleagues. Support systems should be provided to help faculty manage these often emotionally draining experiences. For example, program or department chairs should support LGB-affirmative faculty members when they experience negative reactions (e.g., in Ch. 7, Chen-Hayes's department administrator reprimanded the staff member who examined Chen-Hayes's mail containing a gay video catalog). Time may be set aside during faculty meeting or retreat to process any negative experiences and to discuss methods for improving the training program's LGB-affirmative atmosphere.

Similar recommendations apply with regard to the retention of LGB students. There needs to be explicit statements regarding the training program's position on sexual orientation diversity. Such statements could be included in all printed brochures, course syllabi, and the program's Web site. Faculty role models and mentors should be available for students interested in LGB issues. An LGB student group or organization could be formed to provide a community for LGB students and to facilitate LGB awareness in the program. Mechanisms should be provided for students to report experiences with heterosexism in the academic program. Finally, the following suggestions for creating an LGB-affirmative environment can be helpful for retaining LGB students.

Creating an LGB-Affirmative Environment

The heterosexist dominant discourse may go unnoticed even within a seemingly supportive academic environment. The importance of an LGB-affirmative training atmosphere cannot be overstated. Chan (Ch. 6) discussed significant changes in his sexual identity and personal development within an LGB-affirmative training program. Creation of an LGB-affirmative environment requires deliberate efforts in climate assessment, goal setting, strategic planning, implementation, and evaluation. Buhrke and Douce (1991) provided some specific recommendations for creating an LGB-affirmative environment. We discuss below three strategies to establish and maintain this environment: climate assessment, mentoring, and forming an LGB organization.

Climate Assessment. Academic programs should regularly conduct formal and informal climate assessment regarding LGB issues. This assessment could be part of multicultural climate assessments or conducted independently. Faculty retreat, student town hall meetings, or surveys are some appropriate means. These assessments are helpful to find out the perceived adequacy of LGB faculty and student representation, coverage and quality of LGB training, support and mentoring, and issues in equitable treatment for LGB persons. For example, do programs that are good at acknowledging and celebrating personal occasions (e.g., weddings and newborn babies) also acknowledge occasions that are significant to LGB persons (e.g., commitment ceremonies, arrival or death of a pet)? What are students' perceptions about how sexual orientation issues are dealt with by instructors and other students? Carrubba (Ch. 5) posed a number of other questions to consider with regard to a training program's support for LGB persons (e.g., whether it is okay to mention one's same-sex partner in a conversation, to bring a same-sex partner to a departmental social function, or to wear a gay pride freedom ring). An open and inviting climate assessment, conducted publicly or anonymously, might be helpful for tapping into those areas. Based on these assessment results, goals may be set and actions implemented to improve the climate.

Mentoring. A number of the narrative authors mentioned the need for LGB or ally faculty role models and mentors (Adams, Ch. 2; Chen-Hayes, Ch. 7; Gallor, Ch. 10; O'Brien, Ch. 14; Phillips, Ch. 17; Pope, Ch. 18). Students can work through their internalized heterosexism with the assistance of mentors and role models. Faculty can also model the process of learning to deal with heterosexism. For example, the author of Narrative 7 in Chapter 20 (Fukuyama et al.) disclosed to his students his discomfort with the discussion of homosexuality in the previous class meeting, and this disclosure led to a fruitful discussion of his complicity as a teacher in the discourse. Mentoring is particularly important when students are facing internship and job applications, according to Bowman (Ch. 4), Carrubba (Ch. 5), and Chen-Hayes (Ch. 7). Mentors can assist LGB students in the assessment of risk, identity management, preparation of application materials, and interviewing strategies. Although well-intended advice for nondisclosive identity management can be invalidating (as stated by Bieschke et al., Ch. 22, and O'Brien, Ch. 14), it is also irresponsible to allow students to make decisions without considering risks associated with openness. Mentors need to help students evaluate the environment and their options, and to empower students to make decisions according to their own comfort levels. Pope (Ch. 18) also mentioned the need to mentor students and junior professionals to overcome barriers to leadership positions in the counseling professions. Networking locally and nationally can provide a sense of belonging, resources, and mentors outside of the academic program. For example, Chen-Hayes (Ch. 7) found his home quickly in the Association for Gay, Lesbian and Bisexual Issues in Counseling (AGLBIC), and Gallor (Ch. 10) found support in APA Division 44 and in APA Division 17 Sections on the Advancement of Women, LGB Awareness, and Ethnic and Racial Diversity.

In addition to LGB mentors, LGB ally faculty members play an important role in countering heterosexism. Bowman's (Ch. 4) efforts as an ally earned her an "honorary lesbian" button. Dworkin (Ch. 9) spoke of her relief when other faculty members also cover LGB issues in their teaching. O'Halloran (Ch. 15) discussed how becoming an LGB ally may follow a developmental model. Berkowitz (Ch. 3) further contended that being an ally is a life issue, not just a professional one. Allies need to be prepared to face discrimination because of the positions they take and because assumptions may be made about their sexual orientations. For additional recommendations for LGB and ally mentors, readers may refer to Lark and Croteau's (1998) qualitative study about mentoring relationships.

LGB Organization. LGB students often desire a sense of belonging and acceptance in their academic programs. This need is clearly displayed in the first four narratives of Chapter 20 (Fukuyama et al.). An LGB organization or informal group can be particularly helpful for enhancing an LGB-affirmative atmosphere in academic programs in counseling. Chen-Hayes (Ch. 7) founded a graduate student LGBT campus group when he was a doctoral student. An institutional chapter of AGLBIC was recently formed at Georgia State University. Groups like these can welcome participation of LGB faculty and students and their allies. They can be used to provide communities for LGB faculty and students, and to facilitate awareness, knowledge, and skills with regard to LGB issues. Some activities may include social gatherings, national coming-out day, reviewing course syllabi for LGB infusion, and organizing seminars.

Research and Publication

Gallor (Ch. 10) suggested that LGB research is needed in any counseling program in order to convey to students that LGB issues are valued. However, stigma may be associated with conducting LGB research. For example, Dworkin (Ch. 9) was advised to remove her LGB scholarship from her promotion and tenure materials. Chen-Hayes (Ch. 7) was advised to submit his paper to a "real journal" rather than an LGBT journal. Adams (Ch. 2) and Bowman (Ch. 4) also pointed out that students wonder whether engaging in LGB research may adversely affect their careers and whether people may make assumptions about their sexual orientations because of doing LGB research. When submitting LGB articles to mainstream counseling journals, authors may encounter reviewers who are biased against, or uninformed about, LGB issues and research methodology.

Professional organizations such as ACA and APA should implement strategic efforts to educate editors and editorial board members to value LGB scholarship and become more knowledgeable about methodology appropriate for LGB research. Similar training should be done in all counseling training programs. Research grants and awards that specifically support and reward LGB research could be expanded. For example, Adams (Ch. 2) was encouraged by receiving a departmental research award for her senior thesis about lesbians.

Advocacy and Community Outreach

Pedersen (1988) proclaimed that multiculturalism is the fourth force in counseling and psychology (after psychodynamic, behavioral, and humanistic). We suggest that social justice and advocacy could become the fifth force. Fassinger (1998) proposed a scientist-practitioner-advocate model of training for counselors. Both the 2001 National Counseling Psychology Conference and the 2004 ACA Annual Convention designated advocacy as their conference themes. The Counselors for Social Justice, a division of ACA, was recently formed to seek equity and an end to oppression and injustice for all social groups. A number of narrative authors in this book also emphasized the importance of advocacy for LGB issues, social justice, and community outreach (Adams, Ch. 2; Chen-Hayes, Ch. 7; Fukuyama et al., Ch. 20; Goodman, Ch. 11; Perez, Ch. 16; Phillips, Ch. 17). For example, both Adams and Chen-Hayes suggested that counseling programs should take an active role in lobbying for domestic partner benefits at their institutions, as well as to counter any institutional heterosexism. Chen-Hayes also advised that workshops be provided to other academic departments to address how to create an LGB-affirmative climate. Bowman (Ch. 4) pointed out that faculty and staff need to use the power given to their positions to advocate for students who, with less power, tend to be more vulnerable. According to Perez (Ch. 16), research and publication can also be means for advocacy. Continuous efforts are needed to ensure that organizations in the counseling professions are affirmative and welcoming to LGB persons. We hope that advocacy training will soon be infused in all counseling training programs.

Clinical Training

Many of the suggestions made for academic training would apply equally to clinical training. Rather than repeat a similar analysis and set of suggestions for clinical training, we will focus specifically on clinical supervision as a core element of clinical training. Before turning to clinical supervision, however, several broad issues and suggestions concerning clinical training settings and their structures are worth noting.

Attention must be given to the inclusion of trainees and staff members who are diverse in sexual orientations and racial/ethnic identities. In the previous section on academic training, we proposed some recruitment and retention methods that apply equally to clinical training sites. In her narrative, Gallor (Ch. 10) stated that "with very few similar others surrounding me, becoming visible left me and my differences exposed and vulnerable." For LGB trainees, having others who are similar to them can help to reduce their feelings of vulnerability. The presence of openly LGB staff and trainees can also facilitate heterosexual persons' development as allies.

Attention must also be paid to having a staff (trainees, training staff, and support staff) that is not heterosexist; is knowledgeable about multicultural issues, particularly sexual orientation; is willing to learn more about LGB people's experience; and is willing to explore their own attitudes and reactions toward sexual orientation. Training sites need to encourage all trainees to obtain opportunities to work with clients of various sexual orientations in individual, group, workshops, or other outreach programs. Furthermore, it is very important that clinical training sites offer diversity workshops and training seminars that have a specific focus on LGB issues. Such training should include an exploration of attitudes, beliefs, and feelings rather than providing only didactic information (Buhrke & Douce, 1991; Lundberg, 2001). LGB-affirmative training should also be infused into all regular training experiences (e.g., including LGB couples in couples counseling, implications of sexual orientation on career decisions, the differential effects of trauma on LGB persons, and the implications of trainees' sexual orientations on their professional development; Buhrke & Douce, 1991; Halpert & Pfaller, 2001; Thiel, 1996).

Finally, before directly addressing the provision of clinical supervision, we wanted to make a note about the structure and atmosphere concerning clinical supervision at training settings. From the narratives of this book, it is clear that counseling professionals can be heterosexist, whether overtly (Adams, Ch. 2; Chan, Ch. 6; Chen-Hayes, Ch. 7; O'Brien, Ch. 14; Pope, Ch. 18; Wiebold, Ch. 19) or covertly (Adams, Ch. 2; Carrubba, Ch. 5; Goodman, Ch. 11; Wiebold, Ch. 19). Trainees are in a vulnerable position to deal with supervisors who are heterosexist. Chapters 14 (O'Brien) and 20 (Fukuyama et al.) illustrated difficult experiences of supervisees who encountered heterosexist supervisors. Training sites need to make clear that consulting with staff other than one's supervisor is not only acceptable but encouraged. This open environment would allow trainees to consult with staff whom they perceive to be more accepting. It is also important that training staff recognize the limitations of their colleagues in the area of LGB issues (e.g., lack of self-awareness, heterosexism, lack of knowledge) and approach their colleagues to discuss their concerns about the impact of these limitations on trainees and on clients. Training staff should not assume that the trainees would come to them when feeling stuck with their supervisors. If there is a training coordinator or director, that individual should be accessible to trainees and should meet regularly with them individually to provide opportunities to discuss differences concerning sexual orientation.

Supervision is a core element of clinical training and a very important way for trainees to learn to become LGB-affirmative counselors. To be effective in this training process, it is important that supervisors use appropriate training approaches that correspond to the trainee's level of functioning with regard to LGB issues. Stoltenberg and Delworth's (1987) model describes three developmental levels of supervisee functioning with implications for supervision strategies. Bruss, Brack, Brack, Glickhauf-Hughes, & O'Leary (1997) adapted this model to describe three levels of supervisees' development specific to LGB issues. We briefly examine some supervisee developmental issues at each of the three levels and make suggestions for providing supervision concerning those issues. While both LGB and heterosexual supervisees can be in any of the three developmental levels in the model, our discussion focuses mostly on heterosexual supervisees except when noted.

Level 1: Didactic Learning

Trainees at Level 1 generally rely on their personal experiences and worldviews in approaching LGB issues. In working on LGB issues, these trainees tend to be self-focused, may have difficulties empathizing with clients, and are dependent on the supervisor for guidance on LGB issues. Trainees at this level are more likely to be influenced by stereotypes, misconceptions, and biases in their work with LGB clients. To effectively assist trainees to grow, it is important to assess their levels of homophobia, knowledge about sexual orientation, willingness to learn about the LGB experience, and willingness to explore their own attitudes and reactions toward sexual orientation (Bruss et al., 1997). The primary goal of supervision at this level is to educate the trainee on LGB issues through didactic learning. Ideally, before starting supervised counseling experiences, trainees at Level 1 will have been exposed to LGB issues in their academic coursework, including the role of oppression based on sexual orientation, coming out and its impact, and dating and relationships. Supervision can then build on whatever knowledge base the trainee possesses. Supervision groups can include case presentations of work with LGB clients and role-plays of different approaches. Supervisors can share their own experiences working with LGB clients and may role-model appropriate interventions (Iasenza, 1989).

Bruss et al. (1997) discussed two concrete things that supervisors can teach supervisees to do: (a) pay attention to their use of language (e.g., not to assume partners are the opposite sex or that current partners are the same sex as past partners) and (b) create a supportive office environment (e.g., displaying a rainbow sticker or books about LGB issues). Reducing anxiety (e.g., reassuring trainees that biases and lack of knowledge are common at this stage of training) can help trainees to be open to exploring their biases (Bruss et al., 1997). Supervisors should model and encourage open discussion of differences (sexual orientation, race, ethnicity, etc.) to help all trainees to feel more comfortable discussing their own differences and those of their clients, as well as their lack of knowledge about those differences. In his narrative, Perez (Ch. 16) discussed his first master's practicum, where he worked with a lesbian client who was,

> Patient with me through my blundering of interventions, my heterosexist bias, and my cultural assumptions. Supervision during this time was enormously helpful to me, to start to confront my biases and my homophobia and to help me begin to see the ways in which my biases and homophobia could hinder my work and connection with my clients.

If trainees are not knowledgeable about the local LGB community, providing a reading list and a list of resources in the community that specialize in LGB services (hotlines, organizations, and therapists) can educate trainees (Bruss et al., 1997).

Level 2: Encouragement of Trainee Independence

Trainees at Level 2 have gained increasing awareness of LGB issues, although some stereotypical thinking may remain. They may struggle between dependence and autonomy in supervision concerning LGB issues. Supervision at this level can advance from providing support to confronting and challenging, as well as encouraging trainee independence. Instead of providing expertise on LGB issues and being the source of information, supervisors can challenge trainees to learn independently about LGB issues and to examine their own LGB-related beliefs, feelings, attitudes, and behavior (Bruss et al., 1997). To assist trainees to continue to work on their own heterosexism, supervisors can point out behaviors during intake assessment, conceptualization, and therapy that suggest a heterosexist bias, and explore these with the trainee in supervision (Buhrke, 1989). Buhrke and Douce (1991) identified common errors in conceptualization that suggest a heterosexist bias, including inaccurate information and anti-gay attitudes, attributing problems to sexual identity issues without exploring other difficulties, looking at intimate and family issues in heterosexual terms, and overpathologizing LGB clients during the coming-out process.

Supervisors can also challenge trainees to deal with transference and countertransference issues in counseling (Bruss et al., 1997; Buhrke, 1989). One transference issue could be LGB clients' mistrust and anger toward heterosexual counselors because of heterosexism and rejection they have experienced from other people (Buhrke & Douce, 1991). If trainees understand the basis of this mistrust and anger, they can better deal directly with the underlying issues. Another example of countertransference and transference issues could involve sexual attraction (Bruss, et al., 1997; Buhrke, 1989). An example is provided by Perez (Ch. 16) when he discussed his predoctoral internship experience. He stated,

> A pivotal experience for me was addressing my homophobia in supervision when dealing with issues of attraction toward me from one of my gay clients. Through thoughtful, challenging, and encouraging supervision and education, I realized that the stereotypes I held about LGB people were the mirror of the cultural biases and prejudice that had targeted me because of my race.

Level 3: Learning to Use Self as an Instrument

Trainees at Level 3 can understand individual differences among LGB clients and the clients' cultural contexts. These trainees are more confident with their clinical judgments and are able to use supervision effectively. The role of the supervisor at this level is to confront discrepancies, encourage exploration and integration, and facilitate the use of self as an instrument of change. Because these trainees are more aware of their own reactions to clients, they can learn to use these reactions as a tool in their therapy with LGB clients (Bruss et al., 1997). Trainees are usually less defensive at this stage and more open to feedback about strengths and weaknesses in dealing with LGB issues, as well as challenges to their approach.

For heterosexual trainees, one critical task at this level is to examine discrepancies between their self-perceptions of LGB affirmation and the effectiveness of their approaches. Berkowitz (Ch. 3) discussed his experience with a gay client:

> I thought I was very tolerant and understanding of his dilemmas and pain, in the neutral and nonjudgmental way I had been taught. Thus, I was surprised to receive feedback . . . that this young man had doubts about my support and acceptance of his sexual orientation. I was counseled to be more open and clear about my acceptance . . . I realized that my clinical tolerance and neutrality left this client confused about my feelings and triggered his internalized homophobia . . . to be a good therapist and provide a healing environment, I had to be active and clear about my position and commitment to being an ally.

For LGB trainees, it is important to help them explore the impact of their own sexual orientations on their work with LGB clients and not to assume that their sexual orientations make them knowledgeable about all aspects of LGB experience or make them unbiased (Bruss et al., 1997; Buhrke & Douce, 1991).

Conclusion and Closing Narratives

The suggestions in this chapter may seem ambitious, but we believe that systemic efforts such as these are necessary for countering the long-standing heterosexist dominant discourse in the counseling professions. These efforts cannot rely on only a few LGB counseling professionals and allies. Every individual involved in academic and clinical training is needed in this movement. It may also take generations to accomplish the goal of creating an affirmative place for people of all sexual orientations. Therefore, it may be helpful to think about this movement as a journey—a lifelong commitment—and to periodically reflect on where we have come from and where we should be heading. This reflection can be facilitated by listening to other people's stories, which is the very spirit of this book. For this reason, we conclude this chapter with our own narratives. We focus here on our experiences related to academic and clinical training, as well as our hopes for the future. We hope that our stories will inspire your reflections on your own journey toward sexual orientation equity in the counseling professions.

Cathy's Story

After reading the narratives in this book, I realize again how lucky I have been in my training. When I was looking for a doctoral program, my main focus was on convenience. Thus, I did not investigate how open the department was. I got very lucky in my program. Although my program did not include a class in multicultural counseling (this was before APA requirements) and certainly lacked in training on race and ethnicity, we did learn about LGB issues. In my Marriage and Family Counseling class, although the readings focused primarily on heterosexual couples, many of the case examples were of gay couples. In my Human Sexuality class, I learned about research and counseling with LGB and transgender (T) clients (more G and T than L and B). More important, I met and heard the stories of people who had struggled with coming out or with recognizing that their gender identities and their biological genders did not match. In addition, my program was diverse in ethnicity, race, sexual orientation, and religion, with individuals who were openly gay, lesbian, or transgender. My internship also was LGB-friendly. One of my fellow interns was openly lesbian and offered training to the group in working with LGB clients. I was lucky with my current job, too. One of my colleagues, a gay male, told me this was the most open work environment he had ever been in; that says a lot. Again, I was lucky. If I were not toward the straight end of the continuum, I could not have depended on luck. I would have needed to be more cautious with my choices. I hope we can make changes in our training in the counseling professions that make being cautious, and even being lucky, unnecessary.

Barry's Story

I have been a faculty member for over 7 years and have been out to colleagues and students right from the start. My colleagues in the department are accepting and supportive, but my experience with students has varied. I infuse LGB materials into all of my courses and naturally incorporate some personal experiences in my lectures to illustrate ideas, examples that sometimes reveal my sexual orientation. In the beginning years, when our department had a collaborative counseling program with a religious institute, I often encountered students from that institute who would openly voice their negative views and beliefs about homosexuality. After our department terminated that collaborative relationship, such comments became infrequent. However, I don't believe that heterosexism is absent among our students, as I sometimes receive negative student evaluations that have something to do with LGB issues. "Dr. Chung is one-sided in his views on homosexuality." "There is too much coverage on LGB issues." "Dr. Chung seems to have a personal political agenda in his lectures." I had wondered whether students would make those kind of comments about the way I deal with racial/ethnic or gender issues, because I discuss these issues as well and approach them in similar ways. Somehow, I have never received negative comments related to those cultural dimensions. On the other hand, I have also received positive comments, such as, "This is the first course I have taken that provides an in-depth coverage of sexual orientation issues." One time, I ran into a former student in a gay establishment. He told me that having me as an openly out faculty member was instrumental in his coming-out process, especially coming from a fundamentalist religious background. I know that the deconstruction of heterosexism is a battle that I must continue. Although the work is far from done, I know that I am having an impact, large for some and small for others. I also know that this is a battle that cannot be done by myself. I am pleased that more openly LGB faculty members are available and that heterosexual faculty members are becoming allies. I know that when I retire and look back at this journey, I can proudly say, "I was there."

References

Atkinson, D. R. (Ed.). (2004). *Counseling American minorities* (6th ed.). New York: McGraw-Hill.

Atkinson, D. R., & Hackett, G. (Eds.). (2004). *Counseling diverse populations* (3rd ed.). New York: McGraw-Hill.

Baruth, L. G., & Manning, M. L. (2003). *Multicultural counseling and psychotherapy: A lifespan perspective* (3rd ed.). Upper Saddle River, NJ: Pearson Education.

Betz, N. (1989). Implications for the null environment hypothesis for women's career development and for counseling psychology. *The Counseling Psychologist, 17,* 136–144.

Bieschke, K. J., Eberz, A. B., Bard, C. C., & Croteau, J. M. (1998). Using social cognitive theory to create lesbian, gay, and bisexual affirmative research training environments. *The Counseling Psychologist, 26,* 735–753.

Bieschke, K. J., McClanahan, M., Tozer, E., Grzegorek, J. L., & Park, J. (2000). Programmatic research on the treatment of lesbian, gay, and bisexual clients: The past, the present, and the course of the future. In R. M. Perez, K. A. DeBord, & K. J. Bieschke (Eds.), *Handbook of counseling and psychotherapy with lesbian, gay, and bisexual clients* (pp. 309–335). Washington, DC: American Psychological Association.

Bruss, K. V., Brack, C. J., Brack, G., Glickhauf-Hughes, C., & O'Leary, M. (1997). A developmental model for supervising therapist treating gay, lesbian, and bisexual clients. *The Clinical Supervisor, 15,* 61–73.

Buhrke, R. A. (1989). Incorporating lesbian and gay issues into counselor training: A resource guide. *Journal of Counseling and Development, 68,* 77–80.

Buhrke, R. A., & Douce, L. A. (1991). Training issues for counseling psychologists in working with lesbian women and gay men. *The Counseling Psychologist, 19,* 216–234.

Carter, R. T., & Qureshi, A. (1995). A typology of philosophical assumptions in multicultural counseling and training. In J. G. Ponterotto, J. M. Casas, L. A. Suzuki, & C. M. Alexander (Eds.), *Handbook of multicultural counseling* (pp. 239–262). Thousand Oaks, CA: Sage.

Croteau, J. M., Bieschke, K. J., Phillips, J. C., & Lark, J. S. (1998). Moving beyond pioneering: Empirical and theoretical perspectives on lesbian, gay, and bisexual affirmative training. *The Counseling Psychologist, 26,* 707–711.

Division 44/Committee on Lesbian, Gay, and Bisexual Concerns Joint Task Force. (2000). Guidelines for psychotherapy with lesbian, gay, and bisexual clients. *American Psychologist, 55,* 1440–1451.

Fassinger, R. E. (1998, August). *Gender as a contextual factor in career services delivery: A modest proposal.* Paper presented at the American Psychological Association Annual Convention, San Francisco.

Glenn, A. A., & Russell, R. K. (1986). Heterosexual bias among counselor trainees. *Counselor Education and Supervision, 25,* 222–229.

Haldeman, D. C. (1994). The practice and ethics of sexual orientation and conversion therapy. *Journal of Consulting and Clinical Psychology, 62,* 221–227.

Halpert, S. C., & Pfaller, J. (2001). Sexual orientation and supervision: Theory and practice. *Journal of Gay & Lesbian Social Services: Issues in Practice, Policy & Research, 13,* 23–40.

Iasenza, S. (1989). Some challenges of integrating sexual orientations into counselor training and research. *Journal of Counseling and Development, 68,* 73–76.

Lark, J. S., & Croteau, J. M. (1998). Lesbian, gay, and bisexual doctoral students' mentoring relationships with faculty in counseling psychology: A qualitative study. *The Counseling Psychologist, 26,* 754–776.

Lundberg, E. J. (2001). Preparing psychologists to work with gays and lesbians: A survey of practicum and internship training directors (Doctoral dissertation, California School of Professional Psychology, 2000). *Dissertation Abstracts International, 61,* 6141B.

National Council on Family Relations. (2003). *Resource manual for teaching about ethnic minority families and other diversity issues.* Retrieved November 18, 2003, from http://www.asn.csus.edu/em-ncfr/down99/manualintro.htm.

Norton, J. L. (1982). Integrating gay issues into counselor education. *Counselor Education and Supervision, 21,* 208–212.

Pearson, Q. M. (2003). Breaking the silence in the counselor education classroom: A training seminar on counseling sexual minority clients. *Journal of Counseling and Development, 81,* 292–300.

Pedersen, P. B. (1988). *A handbook for developing multicultural awareness.* Alexandria, VA: American Association for Counseling and Development.

Phillips, J. C. (2000). Training issues and considerations. In R. M. Perez, K. A. DeBord, & K. J. Bieschke (Eds.), *Handbook of counseling and psychotherapy with lesbian, gay, and bisexual clients* (pp. 337–358). Washington, DC: American Psychological Association.

228 DECONSTRUCTING, ENVISIONING, AND PRACTICAL SUGGESTIONS

Phillips, J. C., & Fischer, A. R. (1998). Graduate students' training experiences with lesbian, gay, and bisexual issues. *The Counseling Psychologist, 26,* 712–734.

Rooney, S. C., & Chung, Y. B. (2001, March). *Infusing lesbian, gay, and bisexual psychology into academic training programs.* Paper presented at the 4th National Counseling Psychology Conference, Houston, TX.

Rudolph, J. (1988). Counselors' attitudes toward homosexuality: A selective review of the literature. *Journal of Counseling and Development, 67,* 165–168.

Rudolph, J. (1989). Effects of a workshop on mental health practitioners' attitudes toward homosexuality and counseling effectiveness. *Journal of Counseling and Development, 68,* 81–85.

Stoltenberg, C., & Delworth, U. (1987). A study of Hogan's model of counselor development and supervision. *Journal of Counseling Psychology, 30,* 235–244.

Sue, D. W., & Sue, D. (2003). *Counseling the culturally diverse: Theory and practice* (4th ed.). New York: John Wiley.

Thiel, M. J. (1996). Lesbian identity development and career experiences (Doctoral dissertation, Western Michigan University, 1995). *Dissertation Abstracts International, 56,* 4665A.

Thompson, G. H., & Fishburn, W. R. (1977). Attitudes toward homosexuality among graduate counseling students. *Counselor Education and Supervision, 17,* 121–130.

Whitman, J. S. (1995). Providing training about sexual orientation in counselor education. *Counselor Education and Supervision, 35,* 168–176.

24

Drawing From the Collective Wisdom of LGB-Affirmative Counseling Professionals

Reflections on Affect, Relationships, and Power

Melissa A. Lidderdale

Western Michigan University

Julianne S. Lark

Independent Practice, Kalamazoo, Michigan

Joy S. Whitman

DePaul University

Bieschke, Croteau, Lark, and Vandiver's (Ch. 22) discussion of the status of the discourse on sexual orientation in the counseling professions captured the continued complexity and necessity of the work ahead. It is clear that the heterosexist dominant discourse in the counseling professions has begun to be dismantled, but it is also clear that the lesbian-, gay-, and bisexual (LGB)-affirmative counterdiscourse must deepen and expand. This chapter, therefore, will build on Bieschke and her colleagues' discussion of the implications of the narratives for deconstructing the heterosexist dominant discourse by focusing on how individual counseling professionals can conduct their lives in ways that can challenge the discourse. Where Bieschke and her colleagues' task was to identify implications at the discourse level, and Chung and Brack's (Ch. 23) task was to identify implications for academic and training environments, our task in this chapter is to identify the implications for individual professionals.

This book opens with a quotation from Paul Monette (1992), in which he stated that "our stories have died with us long enough. We mean to leave behind some map, some key, for the gay and lesbian people who follow— that they may not drown in the lies, in the hate" (p. 2). Monette suggested that this map for others is created as "we piece together the tale of the tribe." As we turn to the task of writing the final chapter in this book, we see the stories from the narrative authors as well as the commentary in the other chapters as having "pieced together" part of the "tale of the tribe" offering a body of collective wisdom. From this body of wisdom, we will enunciate themes that both validate and guide LGB and heterosexual counseling professionals in addressing sexual orientation.

Before turning to the themes, we would like to honor an important aspect of the feminist and multicultural traditions: the grounding of the authors' voices in the authors' own cultural and professional identities. When we listened to the "tale of the tribe" in the stories in this book, the material we were drawn to was influenced by our identities as three LGB-identified professionals with experience in challenging one or more of the dominant discourses (e.g., race, gender, sexual orientation). We believe it is important to specifically declare these cultural and professional "lenses" for the reader as a means of accountability. We do not write with a disembodied voice of authority, but, instead, as three professionals with specific identities and sets of experiences.

Melissa. I am a 31-year-old, White, able-bodied, lesbian woman from a working-class family with German American heritage. Intentionality and mindfulness are important aspects of my life and work. At the writing of this chapter, I am in my fourth year of my doctoral training and in the process of applying for my predoctoral internship in psychology. I have been mentored by LGB-affirmative professionals during my education; and, in turn, I strive to create affirming spaces and to welcome others into supportive networks.

Julianne. I am a 37-year-old White, lesbian woman, 5 years postdoc from a counseling psychology program. I work in independent practice with my partner, who is also a psychologist. I also participate in LGB scholarship and advocacy activities outside of my primary work setting. As a third-generation LGB professional (mentored by an out gay faculty member, who had been mentored by a lesbian pioneer in counseling psychology), I have benefited a great deal from the work done by the two generations before me.

Joy. I am a 42-year-old, partnered, Jewish, White, feminist lesbian raised in a Jewish, White, middle-class family in New York. As a professional, I am a counselor educator at a large university in the Midwest and maintain a small private practice separate from that work. I currently hold positions of leadership in the counseling profession, and through those positions as well as through my work as a counselor educator, I have served and continue to serve as a mentor for LGB students. I feel quite privileged in many ways and am aware of the privilege to have read and commented on the narratives in this book.

Considering the scope and content of the material in the narratives and our perspectives on that material, we chose to address three themes: (1) validating and transforming affect for empowerment in counseling professionals, (2) relationships as sources of empowerment and support, and (3) power issues in challenging heterosexism and promoting LGB affirmation. These three themes (abbreviated to affect, relationships, and power) were chosen for two reasons. First, as we read the narratives, these themes emerged with frequency and richness in the stories of the authors and reflect the experiences of counseling professionals dealing with heterosexism. Second, the analysis of affect, relationships, and power dynamics have proven to be crucial elements in the feminist deconstruction of the dominant discourse around sexism in the United States since at least the 1960s (Brown, 1994); and we believe that similar analysis of affect, relationships, and power holds potential for energizing the work on the counterdiscourse on sexual orientation.

Validating and Transforming Affect

As observed by Bieschke and her colleagues (Ch. 22), an increased consciousness about the effects of the heterosexist dominant discourse was fundamental for ally and LGB narrative authors. This increased consciousness was often facilitated by personal experiences that involved intense emotional reactions to homonegativity and heterosexism. In this section, we first want to describe and validate the emotional experience of heterosexism felt by so many counseling professionals. Then, we turn to a discussion of how counseling professionals can manage or transform the affect they experience amidst the heterosexist dominant discourse. The model of affect management and transformation that we present is meant to empower individual LGB persons and heterosexual allies as they cope with, and challenge, the heterosexist dominant discourse in their daily lives.

The Emotional Experiences of Counseling Professionals in Response to Heterosexism

The narrative authors experienced many intense and uncomfortable emotions in response to heterosexism. Dismay, anger, shame, fear, exhaustion, and aloneness were some of the intertwined and powerful emotions described in the narratives. Reading the narrative chapters themselves is the most intensive way to increase consciousness about these emotional experiences of heterosexism. In the material below, we simply give an overview of the intensity and variety of the narrative authors' emotional experiences of heterosexism.

Several authors mentioned dismay and shock in witnessing the homonegative or heterosexist actions of colleagues or supervisors (e.g., Bowman, Ch. 4; Fukuyama, Miville, & Funderburk, Ch. 20; Goodman, Ch. 11; O'Brien, Ch. 14). In addition to dismay, several of the authors experienced anger when they encountered situations in which they experienced or witnessed physical or emotional threats. For example, Goodman spoke of the anger she felt when she witnessed the hurt a friend experienced in therapy with a counselor who agreed to help her friend change her sexual orientation (Ch. 11). Dworkin experienced shock and anger at the homonegative attacks from some religious people (Ch. 9). Adams noted the emotionally draining nature of "prolonged outrage" that comes from a constant awareness of heterosexism (Ch. 2).

Several LGB authors reported instances in which they experienced intense anger or rage about heterosexism but often found themselves in situations where it was safer for them to remain silent (Adams, Ch. 2; Fukuyama et al., Ch. 20; O'Brien, Ch. 14; Phillips, Ch. 17). LGB authors wrote about the fear of many harmful repercussions; for instance, negative supervisor or academic evaluations, job discrimination, harassment, and loss of relationships (e.g., Chan, Ch. 6; Fukuyama et al., Ch. 20; Mobley & Pearson, Ch. 13; O'Brien, Ch. 14; Wiebold, Ch. 19). Fear and anxiety about repercussions had a profound impact in silencing the narrative authors. For example, Johnson was silenced in his personal and professional advocacy for LGB people at one time by his fear of having "my own masculinity called into question." Fear often also led to heightened vigilance in order to avoid danger and to survive within a homonegative society (Adams, Ch. 2; Carrubba, Ch. 5; Douce, Ch. 8; Dworkin, Ch. 9; Gallor, Ch. 10; O'Brien, Ch. 14; Phillips, Ch. 17).

Shame and guilt were also expressed or alluded to in the stories of several of the LGB authors (Chan, Ch. 6; Fukuyama et al., Ch. 20; O'Brien, Ch. 14; Phillips, Ch. 17; Pope, Ch. 18). Chan wrote powerfully about praying to die each night when he believed that God "must have made a mistake in creating my 'wrong existence.'" At one time, O'Brien felt morally deficit as a gay man and attempted to deny his "true self." Several of the allies also wrote about their experiences of shame or guilt in realizing their contributions to the heterosexist discourse, the realization of being what Berkowitz (Ch. 3) called an "unintentional perpetrator" (e.g., Bowman, Ch. 4; Goodman, Ch. 11; Perez, Ch. 16). LGB people who did not challenge the heterosexist discourse also experienced guilt. In reflecting on her experience of not challenging a homonegative supervisor, an anonymous author wrote poignantly, "Why didn't I stand up and tell him he was full of it, and yes I was gay" (Fukuyama et al., Ch. 20).

As reflected in the narratives, living as an LGB person in a heterosexist society can also lead to powerful feelings of aloneness. Heterosexism separates the individual from meaningful connections with others in several ways. Some authors wrote about the difficulty in establishing intimacy in their relationships that resulted from having to hide aspects of their true selves. For some authors, this had to do with having to conceal their sexual orientations (Chan, Ch. 6; O'Brien, Ch. 14). For other authors who held multiple oppressed identities, the feeling of aloneness had to do with a struggle to find a sense of belonging with others who could affirm all aspects of their identities; sometimes even finding language to share the complexity of their identities with others was difficult (Chan, Ch. 6; Dworkin, Ch. 9; Gallor, Ch. 10; Mobley & Pearson, Ch. 13; Wiebold, Ch. 19). Aloneness also resulted from the loss of relationships with friends, family, and colleagues due to coming out as LGB (Chan, Ch. 6; Fukuyama et al., Ch. 20; O'Brien, Ch. 14). A sense of aloneness was also described when authors experienced heterosexism within their own religious heritages or communities (Chan, Ch. 6; Dworkin, Ch. 9).

Narrative authors often experienced emotional exhaustion, and several of them used words and phrases such as "tiresome" or "energy drain" (e.g., Adams, Ch. 2; Bowman, Ch. 4; Douce, Ch. 8; Dworkin, Ch. 9; O'Brien, Ch. 14; Phillips, Ch. 17). In fact, emotional exhaustion stemming from the buildup of strong emotional reactions to the heterosexist discourse permeate the narrative stories of LGB and ally authors. Some authors wrote about the energy and time involved in being identified as an expert who is expected to educate others on LGB issues (Adams, Ch. 2; Carrubba, Ch. 5; Chen-Hayes, Ch. 7; Dworkin, Ch. 9; Phillips, Ch. 17). Other authors described the emotional toll that is taken by a constant experience of heightened vigilance (Douce, Ch. 8; Fukuyama et al., Ch. 20; O'Brien, Ch. 14). The energy needed to deflect the ongoing confrontation with heterosexism and homonegativity often leaves a person with very little vigor to devote toward challenging the heterosexist discourse.

Validating and transforming the emotions summarized above were crucial in being able to act intentionally to challenge the dominant discourse. The process of increasing consciousness and intentionality in the face of such intense emotions begins with individual self-reflection and results in actions, such as relationship building, community building, and advocacy. The following is our set of process suggestions designed to facilitate consciousness-raising about emotional responses to heterosexism that will empower individuals to challenge the dominant discourse.

Process Suggestions for Transforming Affect to Empowerment

Our process suggestions for transforming affect are based in the rationale that discomforting emotional states, such as those described previously, are usually powerful signals that conscious attention and action are needed. As Neimeyer and Raskin stated (2000), "One's emotional self-organizing processes are primary and powerful in one's life efforts" (p. 50). Several of the narratives and other chapters (e.g., Croteau & Constantine, Ch. 21; Mobley & Pearson, Ch. 13; Pope, Ch. 18) alluded to the importance of managing these intense emotions in order to effectively act to counter the heterosexist discourse. Our intent in this section is to make process suggestions that will facilitate consciousness-raising, self-discovery, and social activism. Through use of these process suggestions, we hope that individuals can increase the complexity and depth of understanding of their own emotional reactions in ways that foster intentionality in challenging the heterosexist dominant discourse.

The suggestions for transforming affect for empowerment are grounded in the narrative and discussion chapters of this book as well as in the literature on combating various forms of oppression (see D'Andrea & Daniels, 1999; Funderburk & Fukuyama, 2001; Hanna, Bemak, & Chung, 1999). The process is presented as a series of suggestions that are both interrelated and function independently. These proposed suggestions provide individuals with a process to increase emotional regulation and expand options for acting in response to intense emotional states; that is, a process for empowerment:

1. Reflect on your own patterns of emotional reactions to heterosexism to increase consciousness of your own emotional life.

2. Use your capacity to tolerate emotional discomfort to allow time and energy for developing the best action response.

3. Choose your coping strategies intentionally to be more effective in challenging the heterosexist discourse.

4. Deepen your interactions and dialogue with others to increase the breadth and complexity of your understanding of issues of diversity.

Suggestion 1: Reflect on Your Own Emotional Reactions. Increased aware-ness and knowledge about one's typical affective reactions (e.g., shame, fear, anger) to the heterosexist discourse is the beginning of the process toward transforming affect in ways that are empowering. Both ally and LGB authors wrote about the importance of self-reflection and understand-ing their reactions to heterosexism and homonegativity (e.g., Goodman, Ch. 11; O'Halloran, Ch. 15; Pope, Ch. 18). Narrative authors in this text suggested that being open to and aware of their feelings was motivation for deeper self-reflection and action. For example, Pope (Ch. 18) wrote about his deeper reflection on his true personal and cultural identities that involved a process "first, to recognize the feelings, acknowledge them honestly and directly, and then decide what to do with them."

An important part of understanding the power of emotional reactions is to reflect deeply on the origins of these reactions. Individuals should identify and examine their early messages about sexual orientation. This suggestion is similar to the process of assigning self-reflective journal writings that are used in multicultural or diversity courses and also similar to suggestions from social constructionist theory for increasing awareness of the effects of social oppression (Neimeyer, 1998). The relationship among heterosexist assumptions, emotional responses, and actions based on those responses should be examined within the individual's life. We encourage individuals to participate in this level of self-reflection with compassion and honesty, which can facilitate the acknowledgement of even the most difficult emotional reactions and their sources. This increased consciousness can validate and increase understanding of the individual's emotional experience, thus allowing for more conscious and intentional responses to difficult situations involving homonegativity or heterosexism.

Suggestion 2: Use Your Capacity to Tolerate Emotional Discomfort. The second suggestion is for individuals to use the ability to tolerate discomfort arising from emotional reactions. The ability to tolerate emotional discomfort allows people to hold a strong emotional reaction without responding immediately with an automatic coping strategy. Several LGB authors wrote about the process of tolerating discomfort in order to chose how best to respond to difficult situations involving heterosexism. For example, Mobley described holding his anger in order to listen to Pearson in their intense dialogue around sexual orientation and religious beliefs (Ch. 13). The personal story written by Croteau also illustrated tolerating emotional discomfort by his not responding immediately to his anger at a heterosexist comment, but instead pausing and waiting for a more effective time to challenge the heterosexist discourse (Croteau & Constantine, Ch. 21). By increasing awareness (Suggestion 1) and tolerating emotional discomfort (Suggestion 2), an individual is no longer bound to automatic responses to heterosexism and can be more intentional in coping and responding to heterosexism (see Suggestion 3 below).

Suggestion 3: Choose Your Coping Strategies Intentionally. To successfully cope internally and externally with the emotional discomfort due to the heterosexist discourse, individuals must become aware of the coping strategies available to them and then evaluate and choose the most effective strategy given the context. Coping strategies can be viewed as more or less effective in countering the heterosexist discourse. The following discussion includes examples from the narratives and critically explores a broad range of coping strategies (rationalization, denial, avoidance, aggression, and engagement) for their effectiveness in countering heterosexism.

Coping strategies, such as rationalization and denial, are common ways to deal with emotional reactions to oppression by diminishing the awareness of pain. The use of these coping strategies might protect the internal experience of the individual but maintains the dominant discourse through the distortion of reality. Both Adams (Ch. 2) and Bowman (Ch. 4) wrote about how the privilege of power for people in the majority can allow them to deaden their internal awareness of the pain inflicted on others. Another example of this involved a training supervisor dismissing a student's experience of outright homonegativity by explaining that the training program "didn't want to lose [a paid practicum site] over an issue like this" (Fukuyama et al., Ch. 20). This training supervisor dismissed the student's painful experience with homonegativity and failed to challenge the heterosexist discourse, in part by rationalizing that the paid practicum site was worth more to the training program.

Denial as a coping strategy can minimize or eliminate the existence of oppression from conscious awareness. Goodman (Ch. 11) wrote about the denial in her earlier belief that "if I was not interested in you as a romantic or sexual partner, what did I care about your orientation?" Denial can also function as a protective coping strategy for LGB individuals to help shield against exhaustion as we "choose our battles." Adams (Ch. 2) revealed that "writing this narrative has been uncomfortable at times because I am forced to examine my marginalized existence more closely. Specifically, I am more aware of how much I have minimized the myriad ways in which the heterosexist discourse is enforced." Similar to Adams's experience, reading the narratives in this book broke through our own denial of the many painful heterosexist and homonegative experiences that are routine in our own lives.

Avoidance as a coping strategy in response to fear results in individuals disengaging from the process of attempting to create change or assert a counterdiscourse. Johnson illustrated this point when articulating his reflection of how fear of losing his acceptance from others kept him from challenging the dominant discourse (Ch. 12). The experience of being silent can be seen as a form of coping with fear through avoidance (e.g., Fukuyama et al., Ch. 20; O'Brien, Ch. 14). Clearly, there will be times when avoidance and disengagement are the most functional self-protective strategies available. We propose, however, that an individual might closely assess the situation for actual threat and levels of safety. This evaluation empowers the individual to intentionally choose to self-protect as needed and to take risks to challenge the heterosexist discourse when possible.

Aggression in response to anger is another coping strategy that is not usually effective in the long run for challenging the heterosexist discourse. Aggression can create situations in which countering the discourse is not effective due to the increased emotional intensity and reactivity that occur in these situations. Aggressive attacks tend to place people on the defensive and to interfere with their ability to remain open and able to hear the other's experience of oppression. Anger, however, can be expressed in nonaggressive ways and can lead to social activism and deeper dialogues around the heterosexist discourse (Chen-Hayes, Ch. 7; Douce, Ch. 8; Pope, Ch. 18). The experience of anger can also lead to deeper dialogues by being interpreted as a signal for an individual to more fully participate in the dialogue through assertiveness combined with empathic listening.

While rationalization, denial, avoidance, and aggression can sometimes facilitate comfort and survival, these coping strategies do not promote social change or counter the dominant discourse. Engagement with uncomfortable emotions and uncomfortable oppressive situations can promote LGB-affirmative change, as well as deepen one's own and others' understanding of oppression and liberation. Courage is needed to manage intense emotions and to approach heterosexist experiences in novel ways that do not allow for the reality of oppression to be altered or avoided. For example, a narrative author in Ch. 20 wrote about her intentional decision to voice her anger to challenge the blatant heterosexism she experienced in a job interview and to walk out of that interview proudly (Fukuyama et al., Ch. 20). This is an example of responding to a challenging situation in a way that is more emotionally and cognitively engaged. Several other narratives illustrated how individuals approached difficult interactions more fully engaged and how these more intentional interactions seemed to result in deeper understanding within and between people.

Suggestion 4: Deepen Your Interactions and Dialogue With Others. Open dialogues and interactions with other people who are willing to challenge the dominant discourse can increase cognitive and affective complexity about diversity (see D'Andrea & Daniels, 1999). Through such dialogues and interactions, an individual experiences here-and-now emotional reactions that allow for the individual to manage affect and to develop confidence in an expanded repertoire of coping strategies. Empathic listening is an example of a strategy for managing affect that blends emotional and cognitive understanding. Openness to the stories of others can lead to empathy and action directed toward changing the discourse. Several ally narratives illustrated the increased depth of understanding that occurred during open dialogues with LGB people. Heterosexual allies O'Halloran (Ch. 15) and Perez (Ch. 16) wrote about the power of being open and listening to others and how this contributed to their dedication toward countering the heterosexist dominant discourse. Similarly, Goodman (Ch. 11) described her witnessing of the struggle and strength of LGB people and how such witnessing "resonates" with her emotionally, tying her empathy for the LGB experience to her experience as a Jewish woman. LGB people can likewise benefit from open dialogues about sexual orientation (e.g., Chan,

Ch. 6; Mobley & Pearson, Ch. 13). Engaging in open dialogues about sexual orientation and heterosexism involves risk for allies and LGB people alike. Such dialogues require making oneself vulnerable to experiencing heterosexism or to being challenged about one's own heterosexism. The risk of discomfort or pain from such dialogues is countered by the benefit they can have in changing the dominant discourse and increasing a sense of connection, understanding, and purpose between people (Berkowitz, Ch. 3; Funderburk & Fukuyama, 2001; Hanna et al., 1999).

In the narrative by Mobley and Pearson (Ch. 13), a process of working through difficult dialogues was modeled. The more complex the differences in identity statuses between people engaged in these dialogues, the more critical it is to listen carefully both to one's own internal reactions and to the reactions of the others. This was especially clear from some of the narratives and chapters describing the intersections of race and sexual orientation (Adams, Ch. 2; Bowman, Ch. 4; Croteau & Constantine, Ch. 21; Fukuyama et al., Ch. 20; Gallor, Ch. 10; Johnson, Ch. 12). Croteau and Constantine illustrated the difficulty and tension that arises between listening to the pain of others who might implicate oneself as an oppressor and listening to one's own pain from being wounded by oppression. To hold that tension and continue in dialogue requires one to validate the pain felt by all without trying to diminish its intensity through equating experiences and/or competing over whose pain was more hurtful. Remaining engaged in difficult and deep interactions with others also requires honesty in examining power/privilege and a willingness to lose the security found in more privileged statuses. As difficult and challenging as open dialogues about sexual orientation and diversity can be, the result can be an increase in connection with others through deeper understanding and a shared commitment to changing the dominant discourse on sexual orientation and other issues of oppression.

We hope that the four process suggestions for managing and transforming difficult emotions can help to empower individuals in challenging the dominant discourse and in developing a strong discourse of sexual orientation equity. Counseling professionals have been trained to be self-reflective, to be aware of our emotional reactions to others, to intentionally choose action that facilitates change, and to deeply understand the stories of others through empathic listening. These skills and characteristics prepare individuals within the counseling professions to manage and transform (Fukuyama et al., Ch. 20; O'Brien, Ch. 14) affect in ways that will empower them to facilitate social change.

Relationships as Sources of Empowerment and Support

The stories of the narrative authors were often situated in a matrix of interpersonal relationships, including those with mentors, faculty, peers, colleagues, significant others, family, and community. While at times, relationships with people who were not LGB affirmative were obstacles to narrative authors in challenging the heterosexist discourse, the focus of this discussion is on relationships that served as sources of empowerment and support for narrative authors. We reflect on four functions of relationships that support (and in their absence, obstruct) efforts to challenge the heterosexist dominant discourse. Relationships functioned to (a) role-model ways to manage identity as an LGB-affirmative professional, (b) encourage the integration of multiple aspects of identity, (c) provide practical advice and emotional support, and (d) catalyze development toward greater LGB affirmation.

Relationships That Role-Model Ways to Manage Identity as an LGB-Affirmative Professional

One of the aspects of relationships identified in the narratives was the role-modeling of various ways to manage identity as an LGB-affirmative professional. *Identity management* refers to the decisions around where, when, and how a person chooses to be open about his or her identity as LGB or as a heterosexual who is LGB affirmative (an ally). We highlight stories in which professionals were role-modeling "outness" as well as stories in which professionals were role-modeling other, less disclosive identity management strategies.

The narrative examples emphasized the powerful affirmation that comes from relating to other professionals who are visibly out, "being" themselves as LGB individuals or as heterosexual allies. Role models seemed especially valuable to the narrative authors when they embodied some particular combination of identities that was similar in important ways to the author's own. Carrubba (Ch. 5) described the importance of seeing how other LGB psychologists managed their identities during her internship. Phillips (Ch. 17) noted the value of "role models of women whose sexuality was more fluid and who identified as lesbian and bisexual" during her graduate training. In contrast, Douce (Ch. 8) noted the limitations of relationships with her early professional role models who could not speak openly about sexual orientation due to the lack of safety around sexual orientation issues in the 1970s, when professionals could well lose their jobs if they were even suspected of being LGB. Therefore, conversations with mentors took place using what Douce described as "code," and Douce and others were "denied the explicit wisdom" that their role models and mentors would have been able to provide under safer circumstances.

In addition to emphasizing the importance that the narrative authors placed on relating with out role models, the narrative authors also pointed toward the need for relationships with professionals who modeled how to be an LGB-affirmative professional while using identity management strategies other than being out. As stories such as those in the chapter by Fukuyama and her colleagues (Ch. 20) illustrated, it can be very important to know when or where not to be open about one's LGB affirmation. Such an identity management position might arise out of a lack of safety in a given environment, a person's cultural construction of identities, or a particular configuration of identities that a person might be attempting to integrate without loss of significant relationships or cultural ties. Fukuyama and her colleagues (Ch. 20) made note of the "pressures or expectations that professionals use their personal lives as a way to fight oppression. Nowhere is this seen more poignantly today than in choices surrounding to live in or outside of the closet." LGB professionals need relationships with role models who will support them in whatever identity management strategies they choose, without the kind of pressure that Fukuyama and her colleagues describe. The politics of this question may be best understood with some review of the history of LGB identity theory.

Traditionally, models of LGB identity development (Cass, 1979; Chapman & Brannock, 1987; Coleman, 1982; Dempsey, 1994) have equated level of outness with level of development (McCarn & Fassinger, 1996, Smith, 1997). As a result, there has been much more emphasis on the type of identity management that focuses on how to come out, stay out, and be out at all times and in all places. McCarn and Fassinger (1996) proposed one of the first models of sexual minority identity formation that did not "assume disclosure behaviors as evidence of developmental advancement" and stated that they believed that "disclosure is so profoundly affected by environmental oppression that to use it as an index of identity development directly forces an individual to take responsibility for her own victimization" (p. 524). In his narrative, Chen-Hayes (Ch. 7) echoed a similar theme as he observes that "well-meaning activists have incorrectly assumed that being out is universally good, but this is a cultural bias." He offered his own example of working with LGB persons of color on his campus and encouraging them to go at their own pace and honor their multiple identities in the process of deciding when and to whom to come out as LGB.

While role-modeling can occur in relationships that involve mutual interaction, it can also take place when there is no direct interaction. Wiebold's story (Ch. 19) of how she managed her identity in one of her jobs by not disclosing her sexual orientation seemed to be a good example of assessing for one's own safety in the environment and the risk that could be created for others (in that situation, her clients) by making one's sexual orientation known in a hostile environment. She may use her story to provide role-modeling in direct interaction with her students or colleagues. Having her story in this book, however, may also make her a role model for readers she will never meet. In LGB history, there has been a tradition of this kind of "relating" to authors or publicly visible figures as role models for managing an LGB identity in the world. As did the narrative authors in this book, we encourage counseling professionals to role-model by telling their stories of identity management in interpersonal as well as more public forums.

It should also be noted that although the concept of identity management is primarily associated with persons of minority sexual orientation, modeling regarding management of openness about one's LGB-affirmative stance is also critical for heterosexual allies. Earlier in his career, Johnson (Ch. 12) questioned his own "failure to challenge heterosexist and homophobic talk" (an expression of being "out" as an ally) and concludes his decision to not be openly challenging had something to do with protecting his "shaky position in the club of 'real men.'" His story shows how allies are faced with potential losses when making decisions about when and where to be "out" as LGB affirmative. Later in his narrative, Johnson shared his current commitment to now join other African Americans in confronting homophobia and heterosexism. He stated that he does not want to be "robbed of the brotherhood and strength of Black gay men because I am afraid of being called gay myself." Johnson's narrative modeled how one heterosexual ally struggled with openly expressing LGB affirmation and then became openly LGB affirmative over time. Heterosexual allies need role models who illustrate a range of options and struggles in expressing an ally stance.

Relationships That Encourage the Integration of Multiple Aspects of Identity

One of the important characteristics of supportive relationships identified by the narrative authors was that the relationships encouraged and supported authors in integrating multiple aspects of their identities. The narrative authors noted that finding relationships that did not require them to divide or split their identities could be very difficult. In environments where there are a limited number of LGB-affirming professionals (smaller towns, conservatively religious regions) it may be difficult to find LGB-affirmative professional colleagues who are also supportive and knowledgeable about other aspects of one's identity. For example, a lesbian woman of color moving to a more rural location with a small LGB-affirmative community may find support for being lesbian in one place or support for being a woman of color in another, but no community of people who are supportive of both of these identities. This lack of relationships that allow and encourage the integration of multiple aspects of identity can be quite difficult, especially when identities are experienced as impossible to separate. Gallor (Ch. 10) noted yearning for that space where she can be the "whole 'me,'" as it is impossible to separate her identities as a woman, a lesbian, and a Hispanic person with Spanish, Cuban, and Middle Eastern heritage. Similarly, Pope (Ch. 18), stated that it is impossible to "fully separate my native Cherokee ancestry, my lifelong disability, my rural upbringing, and all that constitutes my personal cultural identity," including being gay.

Several of the stories from narrative authors illustrated the negative impact of relationships that did require some portion of their identities to be left out. Dworkin (Ch. 9) described the difficulty in finding any single community where she felt supported as a feminist, a lesbian, and a Jew. This became even more complex when she came out as bisexual and as a member of the Secular Humanist Jewish Movement, identities that caused her to be even further marginalized within her LGB and Jewish communities. Carrubba (Ch. 5) described how the affirmation that she received within the LGB community for her identity as a bisexual woman partnered with another woman became less enthusiastic when she was a bisexual woman partnered with a man. Chen-Hayes (Ch. 7) described his experience as a student finding LGB affirmation in a national professional organization but also seeing that organization's limitation being that its affirmation came from a predominantly middle-class perspective. LGB persons and allies who had connections to people who supported their racial, ethnic, and/or gender identities sometimes found that those same people were not affirmative of their minority sexual orientations or identities as allies. In the early part of the Mobley and Pearson narrative (Ch. 13), Mobley found Pearson to be a source of support as she too was also going through experiences of being an African American in a predominantly White environment. Mobley, however, expressed deep hurt when he realized that Pearson was not (at that point) affirming of his sexual orientation. These examples all show how people can end up feeling marginalized when they receive affirmation in their relationships for some aspects of their identities to the exclusion of others.

As described above, relationships that demanded that narrative authors act as if their identities could be separated were experienced as painful. Such demands for separation of identities can also be politically treacherous in the network of relationships that constitute a given work or training environment. When there is a spirit of competition for limited resources in fighting oppression, groups of people are pitted against another in struggling for attention to their own issues of oppression. LGB persons and heterosexual allies may be faced with difficult dilemmas in these competitions. For example, does a lesbian student align with other women in her training environment to combat sexism or with other LGB men and women in the training environment to combat heterosexism? Trying to maintain relationships with colleagues who place value on single aspects of identity can place pressure on the individual to "choose" among identities. Am I a woman, a person with a disability, or a lesbian first? Do I prioritize being a heterosexual ally or a person of color? As illustrated in the stories above, no matter how rich and affirming the support for one aspect of identity, if it is to the exclusion of another aspect, the result can be painful and discouraging for the individual. We believe that professionals who want to work toward a more effective counterdiscourse must find supportive relationships that are inclusive of multiple aspects of their identities and must be committed to providing such inclusivity to others.

Relationships That Provide Practical
Advice and Emotional Support

Narrative authors described the work of being engaged in challenging the heterosexist dominant discourse and building the counterdiscourse as challenging, lonely, emotionally exhausting, and physically draining. They also identified that this kind of work as ever present, not accomplished in a single conversation or over a limited amount of time. Moreover, as LGB issues receive more considerations, there is sometimes a great demand upon the few LGB or LGB-affirmative professionals in a given environment. At one time, Dworkin (Ch. 9) felt like "the token representative of all gay men and lesbians," and, added to an already busy faculty job, she was continuously "called upon to join university and local community committees, give presentations and workshops, and help students with papers on lesbian/gay issues." Faced with this emotionally challenging long-term and time-consuming struggle to change heterosexism, narrative authors reported a particular appreciation for relationships that provided emotional support and practical advice. As Pope (Ch. 18) so eloquently stated, "Few ever do this alone."

Relationships can provide much-needed access to very practical and strategic advice. Bowman (Ch. 4) listed the functions of her mentoring relationships with LGB students to include advice about initial coming out; coaching on decisions around identity management; and strategic planning around where to publish, where to go on internship, and how to job-search. She was also very clear that heterosexual allies need as much mentoring on such topics as do LGB students. As a heterosexual ally, Pearson (Ch. 13) indicated that in the midst of the cultural impasse with Mobley, she consulted someone whom she knew had already dealt with this type of conflict. Several narrative authors illustrated how the need for practical advice continues throughout one's professional career. Dworkin (Ch. 9) noted that she weathered the crisis of colleagues suggesting she remove LGB items from her retention, tenure, and promotion file by consulting an openly lesbian faculty member. Gallor (Ch. 10) shared that she consulted mentors regarding how to approach writing the narrative for this book. Amidst the pain of dealing with a heterosexist incident in a national professional organization, Pope (Ch. 18) knew he needed to "think first and then act," so he called supportive colleagues to talk through his possible responses.

The stress of dealing with heterosexism and working and/or living in LGB-hostile environments was the general reason narrative authors cited for needing emotional support in their relationships. Graduate students sometimes acutely feel the need for such support. As a student, Chan (Ch. 6) identified his LGB-affirmative professor in Hong Kong as "crucial" to his development of a positive identity as a gay man in an otherwise hostile environment. O'Brien's (Ch. 14) out gay supervisor was able to provide "the support and validation for my clinical work that I craved" given the prevalence of nonaffirming people in his clinical training environments at that time. From the perspective of a faculty mentor, Bowman (Ch. 4) talked about the value of mentoring relationships for students who are experiencing an environment that does not feel welcoming. She indicated that for persons of minority identity living in a majority culture, such relationships can make the difference between them "finishing" the program (with some implication of more health and satisfaction) and "surviving" (with the implication of just barely subsisting). As these examples illustrate, emotional support from other people is particularly important for students given their vulnerability in the power structures of the institution, but the need for emotional support continues for professionals postgraduation. Following the incident of anti-LGB bias in his professional organization work, Pope (Ch. 18) noted how a colleague unexpectedly "apologized honestly and directly for the [anti-LGB] attack on me." Pope noted the kindness and caring in that response and was very appreciative of the support. Chen Hayes (Ch. 7) noted the response of his faculty colleague as "outstanding" when she told him that "if anything [something heterosexist] like that ever occurred, she would want to know and would 'raise hell.'"

Relationships That Catalyze Development

Counseling literature aimed at reducing homophobia has long recognized that affirmative attitudes in heterosexual people are related to them having direct contact with LGB people, to give issues of sexual orientation a "face," so to speak (Herek & Glunt, 1993). The underlying principle is that people are less likely to hold prejudices and negative stereotypes of a group when they have related to one of its members as a human being. As the catalytic person in the interaction, Dworkin (Ch. 9) noted how "My very being forces others, including the counseling students, to deconstruct the power and privilege that come with being male, White, heterosexual, and Christian." The narratives written by heterosexual allies often mentioned relationships that gave them those initial "faces" to go with LGB issues, such as Johnson (Ch. 12) sharing an apartment in graduate school with two gay male students in the program. In the stories of heterosexual allies, there was the quality of having been touched by the interaction with another person in ways that were not only cognitively but also emotionally informative. Goodman's (Ch. 11) story of her eyes misting, and choking up with emotion as she saw same-sex couples openly walking hand in hand, clearly addresses the kind of emotional learning that occurs when one is able to see the human reality. Relating to a real person with a face and a story impacts emotions and can have catalytic power to change deeply held beliefs.

Narratives from both LGB persons and heterosexual allies identified relationships as vital sources of honest feedback regarding the ways they were participating in the counterdiscourse. Berkowitz (Ch. 3) noted that "we can create friendships, therapy, and learning environments where others can give us feedback about our unconscious prejudices, where personal discomfort can be used as a growth edge." He welcomed this feedback as an "important part of my journey." O'Halloran (Ch. 15) described having LGB-affirmative faculty colleagues who increased her awareness and frequently "pushed" her to examine her "fears, biases, and teaching methods." Pope (Ch. 18) noted that he has mentors and colleagues who have told him both how great he is as well as providing constructive feedback "on an as-needed and regular basis." His mildly sarcastic tone about the frequency of constructive feedback reflects the reality that although everyone needs honest constructive feedback, it is not as pleasant as receiving encouragement and admiration. It is valuable, therefore, to have relationships that can provide safe spaces for the processing of difficult feedback when necessary. Both the Mobley and Pearson (Ch. 13) and the Croteau and Constantine (Ch. 21) chapters present model dialogues that illustrate this point. Mobley and Pearson valued their connection as African American students in the same doctoral program, a bond that also gave them a context in which to address their cultural impasse regarding sexual orientation. Croteau and Constantine engaged in a difficult dialogue within their chapter about the sensitive issues that arise in considering sexual orientation as well as race in multicultural counseling. Their safe space for this dialogue was undoubtedly related to their shared history of working together in the Society of Counseling Psychology.

Power Issues in Challenging Heterosexism and Promoting LGB Affirmation

A third theme present throughout the narratives has to do with power related to professional status and heterosexual privilege. In discussing professional status and heterosexual privilege below, we focus on understanding the power issues that impact an individual's effectiveness in navigating heterosexism and promoting LGB affirmation in the counseling professions.

Power Issues Related to Professional Status

Status within the counseling profession in degree of professional experience has rank and value. Narrative authors described how the power associated with their own and others' professional statuses influenced decisions on whether and how to challenge the heterosexist dominant discourse. In most situations described in the narratives, higher levels of professional status afforded greater freedom to participate in the LGB-affirmative counterdiscourse. In contrast, graduate students and new professionals often felt they had to be very cautious due to the potential repercussions of challenging the dominant discourse from a position of lower professional status.

Graduate student narrative authors illustrated the difficulty in acting to challenge the dominant discourse when afraid of negative consequences in their graduate training and, ultimately, in their careers. O'Brien (Ch. 14) poignantly illustrated the painful dilemma many graduate students face:

> Academic and clinical supervisors had power over me (legitimate, expert, reward, coercive), and I was often not sure of their positions on lesbian/gay issues. My ultimate goal of getting through my doctoral program was most important, and I protected myself from homophobia that could derail my aspirations.

Thus, O'Brien had to struggle with when, and if, to come out to supervisors and others of greater professional status. One of the anonymous narratives in Fukuyama and her colleagues' chapter (Ch. 20) felt silenced by the heterosexist comments of a clinical supervisor:

> I was a first-semester practicum student with no prior experience. I didn't know about ethics or anything else for that matter. All I knew was that my "career" was sunk before it was started. I was going to get screwed by this guy because I was gay. I didn't tell anyone [about the supervisor's heterosexist comment] for a long time.

The narrative authors with lower professional status often felt silenced and disempowered because of the power inequity that left them particularly vulnerable to heterosexist repercussions for their being openly LGB or acting in LGB-affirmative ways.

The two models of difficult dialogues about oppression in this book, Mobley and Pearson (Ch. 13) and Croteau and Constantine (Ch. 21), took place between peers of relatively equal power. Both Mobley and Pearson risked being hurt and losing an important relationship if their dialogue had not gone well, but neither one of them had the power to evaluate the other negatively or assign the other a failing grade. Croteau and Constantine are colleagues who work at different institutions and hold no particular power in the reward structure of one another's job or career. In contrast, when cultural impasses or conflicts occur between professionals of unequal power, such as students and faculty or supervisees and supervisors, such impasses can carry potential danger to one's training or job. In his narrative, O'Brien (Ch. 14) expressed caution specifically about cultural impasses that occur between heterosexual persons in roles of greater power (faculty, supervisors, etc.) and LGB persons in positions of lesser power (students, supervisees, etc.). As happened with O'Brien,

LGB supervisees may not be in a position to address cultural impasses or challenge heterosexist supervisor behavior. Any such assertion or challenge could be taken out against the supervisee in evaluation.

Heterosexual faculty and supervisors will undoubtedly learn about LGB issues from interacting with LGB students and supervisees; however, they should not be the primary source of the supervisor's education about sexual orientation. In the worst of situations, a student or supervisee could feel very unsafe if the senior professional who holds power over him or her is angry or defensive when confronted about ignorance or bias on LGB issues. Even in the best of situations, when the senior professional is open and grateful for the opportunity to learn, there is the risk of problems from role reversal. A student or supervisee may begin to feel obligated to be knowledgeable and resourceful around LGB issues. In addition, once in the role of educator in the area of LGB issues, students or supervisees may find it more difficult to be in the role of learner in their more general training, making it difficult to admit to inexperience, making mistakes, or lack of confidence.

New professionals are in a position of vulnerability due to a power differential between themselves and potential employers when they are applying and interviewing for jobs. When applying for his first postdoctoral position, Chen-Hayes (Ch. 7) stated, "I interviewed out-of-the-closet on paper; my vita contained LGBT presentations, affiliations, and scholarship interests, but I did not divulge LGBT specifics in the spoken interviews." His in-between position of divulging some, but not all, information speaks to the dance in which many new professionals seeking jobs must engage. The dance often involves offering enough information to assess the climate toward LGB issues in a professional environment yet remaining private enough to protect oneself if the environment is hostile.

Some authors decided to take risks to challenge the dominant discourse even when they were in positions of relatively low professional status such as that of student or job applicant. The anonymous author of Narrative 5 (Fukuyama et al., Ch. 20) related her experience following a heterosexist comment that was made when she was interviewing for a job. She stated,

> I had reached a turning point—either I could nod my head, get through the rest of the interview and get the hell out of there and never go back, or I could take the risk and speak my mind. For one of the first times in my life, I chose the harder option.

From this example, it is clear that power differences in professional status are not the sole determinants of when to risk challenging the dominant discourse. In fact, it has frequently been the case that graduate students and new professionals have taken leadership in creating LGB-affirmative space in professional organizations, academic departments, and counseling agencies. Differences in professional status, however, do create situations of power and vulnerability that need to be considered in interactions around sexual orientation.

Persons with greater professional status or power may have more freedom to choose how and where to challenge the heterosexist dominant discourse. For example, authors such as Dworkin (Ch. 9), Douce (Ch. 8), Pope (Ch. 18), Goodman (Ch. 11), and Croteau and Constantine (Ch. 21) are more senior professionals who hold leadership positions in national professional organizations, serve as mentors, and engage in research and scholarship. All are using their achieved professional statuses to build the LGB-affirmative counterdiscourse. Their narratives reveal, however, that along with greater power comes greater responsibility in using that power. Pope (Ch. 18) described his process of consultation before responding to a homonegative incident that occurred in the context of his leadership of a professional organization. The response he chose would hold great power because of his leadership role in the organization, and he took great care in choosing that response. Douce (Ch. 8) described her intentional extension of welcome to LGB persons who approach her at American Psychological Association gatherings. She does this with the recognition that while she is expressing welcome as an individual, she is also expressing welcome as a highly visible leader who models being an out lesbian. The higher status and power of senior professionals may afford them some reduced degree of vulnerability compared with graduate students, but their status also brings an increased level of responsibility related to the weight and public visibility of their actions.

Although risks and responsibilities exist at all levels of professional status and power, there are generally greater risks for persons with less power and greater responsibilities for persons with more power. Given the power differentials associated with professional status, it is crucial to validate that power matters in planning and implementing actions that challenge heterosexism and contribute to LGB affirmation. By highlighting issues of professional status and power in the narrative chapters, we hope that counseling professionals at all levels of professional status will be better able to recognize the power associated with their own professional status, as well as the risks and responsibilities of that power. We hope that such recognition will enable counseling professionals to maximize their own and others' safety and effectiveness in challenging the heterosexist discourse and creating a stronger LGB-affirmative discourse.

Power Issues Related to Heterosexual Privilege

Funderburk and Fukuyama (2001) asserted that "one may respond to social inequities by asking 'how can I use my power and privilege to better the situation for someone who does not have it?'" (pp. 14–15). Many of the heterosexual allies in the narratives were aware that their privilege as heterosexuals places them in a position of relative power in confronting heterosexism. Berkowitz (Ch. 3) became aware that he "had a voice as a straight White male" that would be heard when the voices of oppressed people were ignored. O'Halloran (Ch. 15) stated, "I have considered how my privileged status as a White heterosexual female impacts LGB persons." For those allies, this awareness came with a sense of responsibility "to be active in my alliance with LGB individuals" (O'Halloran, Ch. 15), to undermine the "unearned privilege" (Berkowitz, Ch. 3), and to "verbalize concerns that LGB and other oppressed students do not believe that they could safely express" (Bowman, Ch. 4).

For individuals whose unearned privilege situates them in powerful positions within the discourse, awareness of that privilege is vital. The stories from allies in this book provide excellent models for the examination of heterosexual privilege. McIntosh (1990) encouraged White individuals to unpack the privilege of their race to more complexly understand how that privilege benefits and harms them. We suggest that heterosexual allies unpack the privilege of their sexual orientation to understand how that privilege benefits them, harms them, and keeps them from being effective allies. Glauser (1999), in her discussion on racism and its effects on individuals, asked the question "How has racism affected my life?" (p. 64). We encourage heterosexual allies to ask themselves: How does my being heterosexual affect my life and my work as an ally?

Conclusion

Affect, relationships, and power are examined in this chapter because they are central themes in the stories of the narrative authors about their experiences with the discourse on sexual orientation in the counseling professions. We hope that this chapter will help individual counseling professionals (a) to transform the affect associated with dealing with heterosexism into effective engagement in countering the heterosexist dominant discourse, (b) to find and develop relationships that support and nurture them in their LGB-affirmative work, and (c) to become more conscious of power and how to use it effectively and responsibly in their work related to sexual orientation. Consciousness about and attention to affect, relationships, and power are key in counseling professionals working toward a complex and vibrant LGB-affirmative discourse.

In our experience, the themes of affect, relationships, and power have been discussed in the oral tradition of LGB-affirmative counseling professionals at professional conferences, in student/faculty advising appointments, in clinical supervision, and in the conversations between colleagues. In fact, the stories and commentary throughout the book will be familiar to those who have engaged in this "oral tradition" of sharing the collective wisdom of LGB-affirmative counseling professionals through word of mouth. With this book, however, the oral tradition has become written. We hope that collective wisdom of the tribe, now inscribed in the widely accessible form of this book, will nurture, inform, and inspire generations of counseling professionals in the work of transforming the discourse in the counseling professionals from dominance to equity.

References

Brown, L. (1994). *Subversive dialogues: Theory in feminist therapy.* New York: Basic Books.

Cass, V. C. (1979). Homosexual identity formation: A theoretical model. *Journal of Homosexuality, 4,* 219–235.

Chapman, B. E., & Brannock, J. C. (1987). Proposed model of lesbian identity development: An empirical examination. *Journal of Homosexuality, 14,* 69–80.

Coleman, E. (1982). Developmental stages of the coming out process. In J. Gonsiorek (Ed.), *Homosexuality and psychotherapy: A practitioner's handbook of affirmative models* (pp. 31–44). New York: Haworth Press.

D'Andrea, M., & Daniels, J. (1999). Exploring the psychology of White racism through naturalistic inquiry. *Journal of Counseling and Development, 77,* 93–101.

Dempsey, C. L. (1994). Health and social issues of gay, lesbian, and bisexual adolescents. *Families in Society, 75,* 160–167.

Funderburk, J. R., & Fukuyama, M. A. (2001). Feminism, multiculturalism, and spirituality: Convergent and divergent forces in psychotherapy. In E. Kaschak (Ed.), *The invisible alliance: Psyche and spirit in feminist therapy* (pp. 1–18). New York: Haworth Press.

Glauser, A. S. (1999). Legacies of racism. *Journal of Counseling and Development, 77,* 62–67.

Hanna, F. J., Bemak, F., & Chung, R. C. (1999). Toward a new paradigm for multicultural counseling. Journal of *Counseling and Development, 77,* 125–134.

Herek, G. M., & Glunt, E. K. (1993). Interpersonal contact and antigay prejudice: Results from a national survey. *Journal of Sex Research, 30,* 239–244.

McCarn, S. R., & Fassinger, R. E. (1996). Revisioning sexual minority identity formation: A new model of lesbian identity and its implications. *Counseling Psychologist, 24,* 508–534.

McIntosh, P. (1990). White privilege: Unpacking the invisible backpack. *Independent School, 49,* 31–36.

Monette, P. (1992). *Becoming a man: Half a life story.* San Francisco: Harper.

Neimeyer, R. A. (1998). Social constructionism in the counseling context. *Counseling Psychology Quarterly, 11,* 135–149.

Neimeyer, R. A., & Raskin, J. D. (2000). *Constructions of disorder: Meaning-making frameworks for psychotherapy.* Washington, DC: American Psychological Association.

Smith, A. (1997). Cultural diversity and the coming our process: Implications for clinical practice. In B. Greene (Ed.), *Ethnic and cultural diversity among lesbians and gay men* (pp. 279–300). Thousand Oaks, CA: Sage.

Index

About the Editors

James M. Croteau is a Professor in the Department of Counselor Education and Counseling Psychology at Western Michigan University. He received his doctoral and master's degrees from Southern Illinois University. Jim is a fellow of Division 17 of the American Psychological Association (APA). His practice, scholarship, and professional training specialties include lesbian, gay, and bisexual (LGB) issues and issues of race and racism in White Americans. He coteaches a graduate course on LGB issues in counseling and development. He has organized and/or edited two special journal issues and published more than 30 journal articles and book chapters. Jim has served on editorial boards for the *Journal of Counseling and Development,* the *Journal of Vocational Behavior,* and *The Counseling Psychologist.* In 2003, he received the Outstanding Achievement Award from APA's Committee on Lesbian, Gay, and Bisexual Concerns.

Julianne S. Lark holds a PhD in Counseling Psychology from Western Michigan University and has 10 years of experience as a clinician. She is currently in independent practice and engages in clinical and advocacy work as an out lesbian. Julianne coteaches a graduate course on LGB issues in counseling and development. She has coauthored nine journal articles and has served as an ad hoc reviewer for *The Counseling Psychologist.*

Melissa A. Lidderdale has a master's degree in Community Counseling from the University of Akron and is currently a doctoral student at Western Michigan University. Her areas of special interest/experience include counseling LGB clients, intersections of multiple oppressed identities, client perception of counseling outcome, and counselor supervision and education. She has worked in college and/or university counseling centers and has cotaught courses on LGB concerns for counseling and psychology graduate students. Melissa is a Trustee on the Executive Board of the Association for Gay, Lesbian, and Bisexual Issues in Counseling (a Division of the American Counseling Association, ACA) and has given 15 presentations at national, regional, and state professional conferences. She has authored one publication on training practitioners to work with LGB clients.

Y. Barry Chung, PhD, is an Associate Professor in the Department of Counseling and Psychological Services at Georgia State University. He received his doctoral and master's degrees from the University of Illinois. His specialties include career development and counseling, multicultural issues, and lesbian, gay, and bisexual studies. He has edited one book and published more than 30 journal articles and book chapters. He has served on the editorial boards of *The Counseling Psychologist, The Career Development Quarterly, Asian Journal of Counseling,* and *Journal of Multicultural Counseling and Development.*

About the Contributors

Eve M. Adams is an Assistant Professor and Director of Training for the Counseling Psychology PhD Program at New Mexico State University. She received her doctorate in Counseling Psychology in 1988 from The Ohio State University. She was a psychologist at the University of Akron's Counseling and Testing Center. Eve serves on the editorial board for the *Journal of Counseling Psychology* and has served on the *Journal of Counseling and Development* editorial board. Her research interests are multicultural identity development, gender role beliefs, sexual orientation, and career development. Her teaching interests are supervision, counseling skills, assessment and career counseling.

Alan D. Berkowitz is an independent consultant who helps colleges, universities, public health agencies, and communities design programs that foster health and social justice. He is well-known for scholarship and innovative programs addressing issues of substance abuse, sexual assault, gender, social norms, and diversity and is the recipient of five national awards for his work in these areas. Alan is the editor and founder of *The Report on Social Norms*.

Katheen J. Bieschke is currently an Associate Professor at Pennsylvania State University in the Department of Counselor Education, Counseling Psychology, and Rehabilitation Services. She received her degree in counseling psychology from Michigan State University in 1991. In addition to working with gay, lesbian, and bisexual individuals in both a college counseling and private practice setting, Dr. Bieschke has written about and conducted research pertaining to the delivery of affirmative counseling and psychotherapy to gay, lesbian, and bisexual clients.

Dr. Sharon L. Bowman is a professor and in her eighth year as Chair of the Department of Counseling Psychology and Guidance Services at Ball State University, in Muncie, Indiana. She also has a small private practice. She earned her doctorate in counseling psychology at Southern Illinois University at Carbondale in 1989. Her research interests center around multi-culturalism, including gender, race and ethnicity, LGB and cross-cultural issues, and vocational development.

Catherine J. Brack, PhD, is an Associate Professor, Associate Director and former Training Director at Georgia State University Counseling Center. Dr. Brack received her PhD in Counseling Psychology from Indiana University in 1989 and came to the Counseling Center in 1990. Her research and clinical interests include feminist, systems, and cognitive therapy; psychological trauma; and supervision.

Maria D. Carrubba, PhD, is currently a Counselor and Coordinator of Substance Abuse Services at the Student Counseling Service for Miami University. Maria has an MA in Substance Abuse Counseling from the University of Iowa and a PhD in Counseling Psychology from the University of Missouri–Columbia. Her specialty area is diversity issues, especially LGBT concerns and issues. Maria was one of the two Diversity Scholars for the 2003 ACCTA Conference and presented a program on "Exploring Issues of Multiple Identity." She also serves on Community Advocacy Alliance, which is the Diversity Training Committee for Miami University.

Kin-Ming Chan was born in Hong Kong. After obtaining his MSW in Hong Kong, he worked in mental health agencies as a social worker for 10 years. He then came to the United States to pursue his doctorate in counseling psychology at Western Michigan University and is still currently working toward his doctorate.

Stuart F. Chen-Hayes, PhD, is an Associate Professor in the Counselor Education/School and Family Counseling program at Lehman College of the City University of New York, in the Bronx. He has published articles on LGBT issues in various journals, has had chapters on LGBT issues published in multiple books, and is a prolific presenter on LGBT issues in counseling and counselor education. His research also includes transforming the school counseling profession, and he is a consultant with the Education Trust's National Center for Transforming School Counseling. He is past president of Counselors for Social Justice, a division of the American Counseling Association. He and his partner's successful journey in creating a multiracial family via surrogacy were featured in the March-April 2004 issue of Gay Parent Magazine.

Madonna G. Constantine is Professor of Psychology and Education and Chair of the Department of Counseling and Clinical Psychology at

Teachers College, Columbia University. She received her PhD in Counseling Psychology from the University of Memphis. Dr. Constantine has more than 80 publications related to her research and professional interests. She currently serves as Senior Editor of the *Journal of Multicultural Counseling and Development* and Associate Editor of *Cultural Diversity and Ethnic Minority Psychology* and the *Journal of Black Psychology*. Her research and professional interests include the mental health of persons of African descent; multicultural competence issues in counseling, training, and supervision; and career development of people of color and psychologists in training.

Louise A. Douce is currently the Director of the Counseling and Consultation Service at The Ohio State University. This multidisciplinary agency serves the full range of counseling and mental health needs of the OSU student body. Dr. Douce is a specialist in college student mental health and has been counseling college students for the past 25 years. She received her graduate degree in counseling psychology from the University of Minnesota in 1977 and has been nationally active in the education and training issues for psychologists, social workers, psychiatrists, and counselors. She has published and presented in the areas of career development for women, multicultural competency with a special focus on LGB issues, supervision and training, and women's issues. She is the immediate past president of the Society of Counseling Psychology, Division 17 of APA and has served in several roles in that Division.

Dr. Sari H. Dworkin is a full Professor of Counselor Education at California State University, Fresno. She is a licensed psychologist and marriage and family therapist. Her area of expertise is LGB client issues. Dr. Dworkin has done extensive writing in this area. LGB clients make up the majority of her part-time therapy practice. In addition, Dr. Dworkin is active at the national levels of APA and ACA. She is a former president of Division 44 of the APA, The Society for the Psychological Study of Lesbian, Gay, and Bisexual Issues.

Mary A. Fukuyama received her PhD from Washington State University and has worked at the University of Florida Counseling Center for the past 22 years as a counseling psychologist, supervisor, and trainer. She is a clinical professor and teaches courses on spirituality and multicultural counseling for the Department of Counselor Education and the Counseling Psychology Program. She coauthored with Todd Sevig a book titled *Integrating Spirituality into Multicultural Counseling,* by Sage Publications. She was recently recognized as a Fellow by Division 17 (Counseling Psychology) of APA. Her practice specialties include working with university students from a developmental perspective, multicultural counseling, and training. She is an active member of the University of Florida's Center for Spirituality and Health, and her current research interests include conducting a qualitative study on "multicultural expressions" of spirituality.

Dr. Jamie R. Funderburk is a Clinical Associate Professor and Licensed Psychologist at the University of Florida Counseling Center. She also holds an appointment as a clinical faculty member of the Counseling Psychology Program at the University of Florida. Dr. Funderburk provides clinical services, outreach, and consultation to University of Florida students, staff, and faculty and provides clinical supervision to graduate students in counseling. She received her PhD from the Counseling Psychology Program in 1987. Dr. Funderburk's research and publications are in the areas of suicide prevention, sexual and interpersonal violence awareness and trauma recovery, and the intersection of feminist and multicultural theories in counseling psychology. Her current research examines moderating influences on the impact of life experiences of both cultural and gender oppression on the well-being of college women seeking counseling.

Susanna M. Gallor is a doctoral student in the Counseling Psychology Program at the University of Maryland, College Park. She is a student affiliate in APA, the Society of Counseling Psychology, the Society for the Psychological Study of Lesbian, Gay, and Bisexual Issues, and the Society for the Psychological Study of Ethnic Minority Issues. Her research interests include lesbian and gay identity and coming-out issues, social support and well-being, multiple minority status issues, and multicultural training and competence.

Jane Goodman, PhD, is Professor of Counseling and Director of The Adult Career Counseling Center at Oakland University in Rochester, Michigan. She has been active in professional associations for more than 25 years. She is a past president of the ACA, currently serves as an ACA Foundation Trustee, and is treasurer-designate of ACA. Her published works include books, guides, monographs, book chapters, and journal articles, primarily in the arena of career development and adult transitions.

Dr. Phillip D. Johnson is an Assistant Professor of Counseling Psychology at Western Michigan University. He has a PhD in Counseling Psychology and a master's degree in Deafness Rehabilitation, and his professional experience is varied. He has worked in the fields of vocational rehabilitation, juvenile justice, and mental health, and for almost two decades he has worked in higher education. He has designed, developed, and directed academic achievement programs for Black and Latino college students and held positions such as Assistant Dean, Staff Psychologist, and Adjunct Assistant Professor at New York University. Dr. Johnson is interested in the topics of oppression and psychodynamically oriented psychotherapy. He is also interested in the psychological experience of African Americans as well as the humanistic and racial themes in psychology.

Teresa S. Lance has a master's degree in Counseling from Central Michigan University and is currently a doctoral student in Counseling Psychology at Western Michigan University. She has co-taught a graduate course on LGB issues in counseling and development. She has worked at college/university counseling centers, where she has been able to further her growth in addressing LGBT issues in clinical work as well as in training and outreach provision.

Marie L. Miville, PhD, is an Associate Professor of Psychology and Education at Teachers College, Columbia University. She is also the Program Coordinator and Director of Training of Counseling Psychology programs at Teachers College. She received her doctorate in counseling psychology from the University of Maryland at College Park. Her doctoral research involved exploring the interrelations of collective identity (gender, cultural) and personal identity among Latinos and Latinas. Dr. Miville also developed the Miville-Guzman Universality-Diversity Scale (M-GUDS), which measures attitudes of awareness and acceptance of how people are both similar to and different from each other. Her current research focuses on resiliency factors affecting identity development among LGBT youth.

Michael Mobley is currently an Assistant Professor at the University of Missouri–Columbia in the Department of Educational, School, and Counseling Psychology. He received his PhD in Counseling Psychology from The Pennsylvania State University in 1998. His areas of interests include perfectionism, racial and ethnic and gay, lesbian, and bisexual identity development, multicultural counseling competencies and training, and application of self-empowerment theory among African American adolescents. Since 1999, he has served as project director/principal investigator of the GEAR UP MU REACH Project, a 5-year, $2.1 million U.S. Department of Education grant.

John M. O'Brien, PhD, is in full-time private practice in Portland, Maine, specializing in the treatment of substance abuse, grief, and lesbian/gay issues. He teaches courses in psychology and addiction part-time at the University of Maine at Augusta. In addition, he is the current Chair of the Section for LGB Awareness for the Society of Counseling Psychology (Division 17) of APA.

Theresa M. O'Halloran, EdD, LPC, CACIII, is an Associate Professor in the Counselor Education Program at Adams State College, Alamosa, Colorado. Since 1997, she has been a counselor educator, training MA- and PhD-level counseling students, and since 1989, a counselor specializing in trauma and addictions treatment for adolescents and adults. Dr. O'Halloran performs research and publication in areas of counselor training methods, career development, and secondary traumatic stress.

Stacey M. Pearson, PhD, is a psychologist and Assistant Director of Psychology Training at the University of Michigan's Counseling and Psychological Services. Currently she serves as the Chair of the Commission for Counseling and Psychological Services (CCAPS) of the American College Personnel Association. She is also Clinical Director of a non-profit counseling center, Turning Point Counseling Services. Dr. Pearson's major research interests are African American women in treatment and multicultural counseling and training.

Ruperto M. Perez, PhD, is Assistant Director for Clinical Services/ Clinical Assistant Professor at the University of Florida Counseling Center. Prior to the University of Florida, he served as Counseling Services Coordinator and Internship Training Director at the Counseling and Testing Center at The University of Georgia from 1993–2002. Dr. Perez is a Fellow (Division 17, Counseling Psychology) of APA, past Division 17 Vice President for Diversity and Public Interest, and current Special Interest Groups Coordinator for Division 17. He is also a member of the APA Board for the Advancement of Psychology in the Public Interest. In addition, Dr. Perez is a current member of ACPA Commission for Counseling and Psychological Services (CCAPS) and has served as Directorate Body member, Commission Chair, and CCAPS liaison to APA Division 17. He is coeditor of the *Handbook of Counseling and Psychotherapy With Lesbian, Gay, and Bisexual Clients,* published by APA.

Julia C. Phillips is the Associate Director of Training at the Counseling, Testing, and Career Center at The University of Akron (UA). She is also an ad hoc faculty member in the Department of Psychology at UA. She received her PhD in Counseling Psychology from The Ohio State University in 1992 and worked at the University Counseling Center at Texas Tech until 1994, when she returned home to northeast Ohio. Her professional interests lie in the areas of training and diversity issues.

Mark Pope, EdD, is currently an Associate Professor of Counseling and Family Therapy at the University of Missouri–St. Louis. He has written extensively on sexual minority issues in general and multicultural career counseling as well as the history of counseling. Dr. Pope is past president of the ACA and National Career Development Association (NCDA). He is a Fellow of NCDA, Society of Counseling Psychology, and APA. He was the recipient of the Robert Swan Lifetime Achievement Award for Career Development as well as the ACA's highest civil rights award, the Kitty Cole Human Rights Award. He also received the California Association for Counseling and Development's Human Rights Award and the Human Rights Award from the American Counseling Association of Missouri. Dr. Pope is also nationally certified as a Master Career Counselor and Master Addictions Counselor.

Beverly J. Vandiver is an Associate Professor of Counseling Psychology at The Pennsylvania State University. The focus of her research is on racial identity, notably in Black racial identity and the development of the Cross Racial Identity Scale (Vandiver et al., 2000), and other cultural identities such as gender.

Joy S. Whitman, PhD, is Associate Professor at DePaul University in the Human Services and Counseling Program. She is a board trustee in the Association for Gay, Lesbian, and Bisexual Issues in Counseling, a division of APA, and a member of the Ethics Committee for ACA. Her research and professional foci center on LGB issues in counseling and the training of counselors working with LGB clients and students, lesbian and bisexual identity management, and mentoring LGB graduate students. She received her doctorate in Counseling Psychology from West Virginia University.

Jennipher Wiebold, PhD, CRC, is an Assistant Professor and a Rehabilitation Counseling/Teaching Program Co-Coordinator at Western Michigan University in the Departments of Blindness and Low Vision Studies and Counselor Education and Counseling Psychology. Dr. Wiebold received her PhD in Rehabilitation Psychology from the University of Wisconsin-Madison. She is a rehabilitation counselor educator specialized in blindness and low vision. Dr. Wiebold's research interests include immersion strategies in rehabilitation counseling curricula, employment issues experienced by persons with blindness or low vision, and quality of life issues among older adults with sensory impairments. She is currently serving on the Board of Directors at the Disability Resource Center.